HARVARD ECONOMIC STUDIES

Volume 154

The studies in this series are published under the direction of the Department of Economics of Harvard University. The department does not assume responsibility for the views expressed.

Negotiating the Law
of the Sea

James K. Sebenius

HARVARD UNIVERSITY PRESS
Cambridge, Massachusetts, and London, England   1984

Copyright ©1984 by the President and Fellows of Harvard College
All rights reserved
Printed in the United States of America
10 9 8 7 6 5 4 3 2 1

This book is printed on acid-free paper, and its binding materials have been chosen for strength and durability.

Library of Congress Cataloging in Publication Data

Sebenius, James K., 1953–
    Negotiating the Law of the Sea.

  (Harvard economic studies; v. 154)
  Bibliography: p.
  Includes index.
    1. United Nations Conference on the Law of the Sea (3rd: 1973–1982: New York, N.Y., etc.)   2. Maritime law.   3. Maritime law—United States.   I. Title.   II. Series
JX4411.S425 1984   341.4′5   83-20163
ISBN 0-674-60686-8 (alk. paper)

Acknowledgments

Trying to acknowledge the contributions of the people who have made this effort possible, worthwhile, and enjoyable is a humbling task. At the same time, it gives me the pleasure of thanking those who encouraged my participation in the Law of the Sea negotiations, those who guided my academic preparation, those who shared these times with me as friends and colleagues, and those from all these groups who pushed me toward a synthesis of analysis and experience.

I am indebted to many participants in the Third United Nations Conference on the Law of the Sea. In particular, I would like to thank George Aldrich, Lance Antrim, William Brewer, Jens Evensen, members of the United States delegation, and the NG2 team for rewarding associations in conference and out of conference. It has been an extreme privilege and pleasure to work with Tommy Koh. By example and through the opportunities and advice he has offered, Elliot Richardson has influenced me greatly; for these and for his other generosities, he has my abiding respect and gratitude.

I have been fortunate in having an extraordinary group of academic advisers, colleagues, and friends. To Ronald Howard, A. Michael Spence, and Richard Zeckhauser go my thanks for particular insights and encouragement. To Richard G. Darman, J. D. Nyhart, and Robert W. White I express my appreciation. I am happy to record a special debt to John Lintner, whose recent death made me see even more clearly how rare were his qualities of intellect and warm support. As will be no surprise to those who know him, Howard Raiffa was a prince of a thesis adviser and, in innumerable ways since, has had a central impact on my development. David Lax has helped to shape this study from its inception in the RIAS offices to its completion at the Kennedy School.

ACKNOWLEDGMENTS

As a friend and collaborator, he has my thanks. For discussions, help, and support in many ways, I owe much to Evelyn Brodkin, Deborah Dupire, Ann Hollick, Carol Jones, Lee Kimball, Peter Merrill, and William Ury.

Particular parts of this study bear the special mark of others with whom I have the pleasure to work. I had extensive discussions with Mati L. Pal on the subjects of Section 1.3. I am grateful to Raymond Vernon for his editorial prowess and, in particular, to the *Journal of Policy Analysis and Management* for permission to use in Chapter 3 a section of my article "The Computer as Mediator: Law of the Sea and Beyond," *Journal of Policy Analysis and Management* 1, no. 1 (1981):77–95 (copyright 1981 by the Association for Public Policy Analysis and Management; used by permission of John Wiley and Sons). I thank the Institute for Contemporary Studies along with my LOS colleague and coauthor, Lance Antrim, for permission to use part of our essay "Incentives for Ocean Mining under the Convention" from *Law of the Sea: U.S. Policy Dilemma*, ed. Bernard H. Oxman, David D. Caron, and Charles O. Buderi (San Francisco: ICS Press, 1983), as a portion of Section 4.5.2.1. Students from Raiffa's Competitive Decision Making course will recognize in Chapter 5 a version of his admonition to "exploit differences." Working with Herman Leonard on a related paper was a pleasure that has greatly sharpened my understanding of those ideas. The imprint of his mind and pen are on several of the better paragraphs in Sections 5.0 and 5.1. Mary O'Keefe prodded us to recognize that even identical people can gain from trade when nonconvexities are present. I thank my coauthor Peter Stan and the *Bell Journal of Economics* for permission to use in Section 5.2.5 a modified version of our joint article "Risk Spreading Properties of Common Tax and Contract Instruments," *Bell Journal of Economics* 13, no. 2 (1982):555–560 (copyright 1982 by the American Telephone and Telegraph Company). Similar appreciation goes to John Geanakoplos and the *Journal of the American Statistical Association* for permission to use in Section 5.2.6 some work that likewise began as part of this study and evolved into a coauthored article, "Don't Bet on It: Contingent Agreements with Asymmetric Information," *Journal of the American Statistical Association* 78, no. 382 (1983):424–426. Finally, I thank the editors of *International Organization* for their help in developing the content and expression of Chapter 6 from its original form and for their kind permission to use a version of the resulting article, "Negotiation Arithmetic: Adding and Subtracting Issues and Parties," *International Organization* 37, no. 2 (1983):281–316.

ACKNOWLEDGMENTS

I appreciate the efforts of Holly Grano, who typed many of the equations; of Joanna Callenbach and Marsha Slomowitz, who prepared the figures; and of Tom Peters, who helped with word processing. Thomas Weeks deserves particular thanks for his work on the index. Duncan Bauer's typing expertise, good cheer, and indefatigable presence at the computer center made each stage of this effort vastly easier and more pleasant than otherwise would have been possible.

I gratefully acknowledge the support of NSF Grant SER76-17502 to the RIAS program at Harvard, where I was a Fellow, and a generous grant that was awarded on the basis of the Doctoral Dissertation Competition of the Division of Research at the Harvard Business School.

Finally, I thank the members of my sometimes skeptical but always loving and supportive family. To them, and in particular to the memory of my grandmother, Martha Prescott Kimble, I dedicate this work.

Contents

Introduction 1

PART ONE

Agreement in the Small, Disagreement in the Large: Financial Arrangements and the Law of the Sea Conference

1 Background: Of Nodules, Navies, and Negotiation 7

Setting the Stage 7
Whence the Law of the Sea Conference? 11
Conference Organization and Procedures 12
Financial Arrangements in the Seabed Regime of the LOS Treaty 13
Summary 23

2 Course of the Financial Negotiations 24

Themes in the Chronology 24
The 1977 New York Session 24
The 1978 Geneva Session 26
The 1978 New York Session 30
The 1979 Geneva Session 34
The 1979 New York Session and Beyond 37
Appendix 1: The Detailed Financial Arrangements Proposals 40
Appendix 2: Description of the MIT Model 45

3 Elements of Agreement 49

Diverse Factors in Agreement 49
Use of an Outside Model 50
Agreement as the Result of Differences 55
Combining Issues 61
Summary 69

4 Disagreement in the Large: Explanation and Evaluation   71
A Framework for Negotiation Analysis   71
Evolution of the U.S. Negotiating Strategy   74
The Shape of the Final LOS Treaty   78
The Central Trade: Navigation and Nodules   80
What Happened? Explaining the Reagan Decision   81
Evaluating the Decision to Reject the Treaty.   84
Summary and Conclusions   106

PART TWO
Agreement in Negotiation: General Propositions

5 Differences and Joint Gains   113
Beyond Common Ground for Negotiation   113
Elements of a Differences Orientation   117
More Formal Difference Analysis   144

6 Negotiation Arithmetic: Adding and Subtracting Issues and Parties   182
A Common Point of Departure   182
Adding and Subtracting Issues   184
Adding and Subtracting Parties   207
Summary and Conclusions   214

Notes   219
Bibliography   234
Index   245

Negotiating the Law of the Sea

Where order in variety we see
And where, though things differ, all agree.

—Alexander Pope
  "Windsor Forest"

An ancient philosopher once said that friendship between men is nothing but a commerce in which each seeks his own interest. The same is even truer of the liaisons and treaties which bind one sovereign to another, for there is no durable treaty which is not founded on reciprocal advantage, and indeed a treaty which does not satisfy this condition is no treaty at all, and is apt to contain the seeds of its own dissolution. Thus, the great secret of negotiation is to bring out prominently the common advantage to both sides and to link these advantages that they may appear equally balanced to both parties. For this purpose when negotiations are on foot between two sovereigns, one the greater and the other the less, the more powerful of those two should make the first advance, and even undertake a large outlay of money to bring about the union of interests with his lesser neighbor . . . The secret of negotiations is to harmonize the interests of the parties concerned.

—François de Callières
  On the Manner of Negotiating with Princes

Introduction

This book is built around an interpretive account of a negotiation in which I took an active part. Drawing on my experience with the Law of the Sea (LOS) conference, I first offer the financial aspects of these deliberations as a case that suggests some propositions about crafting agreement in complex bargaining. Then, through a negotiation-analytic lens, I probe the larger U.S. strategy from its early steps to the 1982 rejection of the treaty. Finally, in a more formal style, I try to generalize some of these ideas. Beyond LOS chronicle and analysis, however, my real quest is for systematic insights into the means for shaping good negotiated agreements.

The extended LOS example is not written from the standpoint of a neutral observer; at the outset I should declare my involvement. My association with the LOS conference began in the summer of 1977, after a year as a Stanford Fellow, assigned to the administrator of the National Oceanic and Atmospheric Administration. I then joined the U.S. Law of the Sea delegation, led by Ambassador Elliot L. Richardson. Shortly after entering the Business Economics program at Harvard the next fall, I began to work with a project at the Massachusetts Institute of Technology that sought to model a deep ocean mining system. Over the next three years, I continued with the U.S. delegation and attended most of the negotiating sessions. I soon started to serve in an informal staff capacity to Ambassador T. T. B. Koh of Singapore, who chaired the LOS Negotiating Group on Financial Arrangements. The group's deliberations constitute a particular focus of this book. From this triple vantage point—that of U.S. delegation member, that of Negotiating Group staff, and that of liaison between the MIT modeling effort and these other two bodies—I had the opportunity to

1

participate in the negotiation and to relate it to the more theoretical approach I was absorbing in Cambridge. The result was my doctoral dissertation, woven from the twin strands of academic reflection and LOS experience. Although analytic and editorial generations separate this study from its ancestor, I have tried to transmit these same strands.

The task confronting the Third United Nations Conference on the Law of the Sea in 1974 was no less than the design of the legal regime to govern more than 70 percent of the earth's surface. The negotiators had to hammer out rules on subjects as contentious as navigational freedoms, territorial bounds, fishing rights, offshore hydrocarbons, marine pollution, and a potentially vast mineral resource in the deep ocean, so-called manganese nodules, unanimously declared to be the "common heritage of mankind." By 1978 the negotiators had reached agreement on more than 90 percent of the draft treaty articles. Seven critical sets of issues became the negotiating focus of the conference. Among these hard-core questions, upon whose resolution the fate of the treaty was expected to turn, were the financial aspects of a sort of mega-mineral contract between "mankind" and future seabed miners. A linked issue concerned the funding of a new international entity that would mine directly on behalf of the international community.

Two years of complex bargaining finally overcame the impasse on these "financial arrangements." Not only was an agreement worked out, but, remarkably, the delegates from more than 150 countries produced a text on the financial terms of contracts that in many ways is more sophisticated than most existing bilaterally negotiated mineral contracts on land. I was intrigued by the substance of this innovative outcome, by the novel procedure for reaching it, by the personalities involved, by the puzzle of how a U.S.-built analytic model could play a prominent role in these politicized deliberations, and by myriad other aspects of the agreement. The controversial U.S. decision not to sign the treaty two years later prompted me to review the origins of the conference and to evaluate the overall U.S. negotiating strategy.

It would be an understatement to say that my participation in this intense process suggested promising directions for the formal analysis of complex bargaining situations. At the same time, an emerging cluster of ideas, informally referred to as "negotiation analysis," with its origins in decision analysis, game theory, and the economics of industrial organization, proved useful to my day-to-day work in the negotiations. The mutual conditioning of academic analysis and conference participation should be evident in the emphases I have chosen.

Part I contains my interpretation of the financial portion of the LOS negotiations. Its background, parties, and issues constitute Chapter 1.

Chapter 2 is a chronology of the financial negotiations from their emergence as a central issue through their resolution. Chapter 3 draws together some of the major factors behind the negotiated agreement. These ideas, although then in much rougher form, were among those that helped to guide my actions at the conference. From agreement "in the small" on financial questions, Chapter 4 seeks to explain and evaluate the U.S. disagreement "in the large" with the entire treaty.

Part II extends and generalizes some of these factors beyond their initial LOS setting. Chapter 5 examines the proposition that negotiated agreements often consist of dovetailed differences among the participants. It investigates potentially useful differences in such areas as values and probabilistic beliefs, as well as attitudes toward risk and time. Emphasis is on the identification of what might be called structural aspects of potential agreements. The analysis deals very little with the means, either procedural or interpersonal, of realizing these potential bargains. The discussion commences with a nontechnical introduction to the main ideas of a "differences" orientation; it concludes by developing the theoretical underpinnings of much of the previous analysis. Mathematically framed results are presented on randomization and betting on the basis of different probabilities, competitive revelation of probabilities, risk sharing, indirect transfer of asymmetrically held information, risk properties of taxation instruments, and methods of blending differences in time preference. These ideas may have broader economic application than just to the study of negotiations. All the discussions requiring more than elementary algebraic or graphic reasoning are segregated in Section 5.2.

Chapter 6 is an investigation of the proposition that the parties and issues themselves, rather than being "givens," are often important choice variables in negotiation. This chapter argues that moves to manipulate issues or parties can be considered useful classes of tactics for negotiation analysis. Simple techniques can relate some of their means, ends, and outcomes to one another. I examine numerous effects of such moves on the zone of possible agreement and the process of reaching it.

I intend Parts I and II to be strongly complementary, but they may be read independently. Within Part I those readers interested in the particulars of the financial negotiations may wish to concentrate on Chapters 1 and 2 and to pass quickly over Chapter 3. Those more interested in general aspects of reaching agreement in multilateral negotiations might skim Chapters 1 and 2, which are largely narrative, and most profitably focus their attention on the propositions of Chapter 3. Chapter 4 deals much more with the broad *substance* of U.S.

Law of the Sea policy, explained and evaluated, however, in simple terms congenial to analysts of negotiation. The two chapters (5 and 6) of Part II are concerned with general aspects of negotiation. They may be read independently of each other, and, for those less interested in LOS matters, Part II may be read without reference to Part I.

The chapters of this study are implicitly connected by their focus on negotiation and by the examples from the LOS conference that are scattered throughout. In order to make each major section self-contained, however, I have not hesitated to repeat explanations or examples if they seemed relevant in more than one place.

PART ONE

Agreement in the Small, Disagreement in the Large: Financial Arrangements and the Law of the Sea Conference

1 Background: Of Nodules, Navies, and Negotiation

1.0 Setting the Stage

Coal-like lumps of metallic ore called manganese nodules carpet much of the deep ocean floor. Although the H.M.S. *Challenger* discovered these curious objects more than a century ago, discussions about them for a long time remained as muted as the 5,000-meter depths of the abyssal plains where they lie. By the early 1970s, however, the regime for possible nodule exploitation had emerged as the subject of intense national and international negotiation.

The nodules contain commercially and strategically promising quantities of copper, cobalt, nickel, and manganese. It is difficult to comprehend the physical extent of the resource; its apparent amount dwarfs known land reserves.[1] Several industrial nations depend on a few, possibly unstable, land sources for these critical minerals. In the mid-1960s a number of mining consortia began spending large sums to develop the sophisticated technology necessary to lift the nodules and to transport them to land for processing.

Because the richest and most abundant nodule grounds lie outside the limits of any nation's jurisdiction, the question of nodule "ownership" grew in step with their emerging commercial potential. In July 1966 President Lyndon Johnson warned, "Under no circumstances, we believe, must we ever allow the prospects of a rich harvest of mineral wealth to create a new form of colonial competition among the maritime nations. We must be careful to avoid a race to grab and hold the lands under the high seas. We must ensure that the deep seas and the ocean bottom are, and remain, the legacy of all human beings."[2] Dr. Arvid Pardo, then the Maltese delegate to the United Nations, cleverly echoed this locution in a famous 1967 speech. He proposed that the seabed beyond the limits of national jurisdictions be declared the "common heritage of mankind" and that nodule exploitation be undertaken on behalf of the international community.[3] In 1970, without opposition, the United Nations General Assembly adopted this "common heritage" principle and proposed the creation of an international regime for the seabed that would ensure "equitable sharing by States in the benefits derived therefrom."[4]

Meanwhile, an enormous increase in the use of the oceans for commercial and military transport, fishing, energy production, and scientific research repeatedly led to frictions and conflicts that emphasized the inadequacies of the existing international laws of the sea. To address this situation, the General Assembly convened the Third United Nations Conference on the Law of the Sea (LOS) in 1973. As an integral part of their agenda, the participants in these mammoth negotiations faced the task of giving substance to the "common heritage" principle.

By 1978 these negotiations—the largest, the longest running, and, according to Henry Kissinger, one of the "most important international negotiations which has ever taken place"—had reached agreement on some 90 percent of the contentious issues.[5] Delegates expected the fate of the proposed treaty to hang on the resolution of seven issues that they had designated as critical and assigned to special negotiating groups. Prominent among these intractable questions was the system of financial payments to the international community (fees, royalties, and profit shares) required of future miners in respect of the "common heritage" principle. A linked issue was the means for financing the first operation of an international seabed mining entity. Together, these two questions comprised the "financial arrangements" for seabed mining. A major portion of Part I of this book describes and analyzes their resolution.

Conference delegates and observers all agreed that accord would be extremely difficult; this was reflected in the designation of the financial arrangements issues as being among the "hard-core" seven. Yet, despite the doubts often expressed in conventional wisdom, two years of intense bargaining finally overcame the impasse on these financial terms in 1979.[6] In fact, during the summer of 1980 the tired negotiators hammered out what they felt to be a nearly final agreement on the *entire* LOS treaty.

The chief American delegate, Elliot L. Richardson, then judged it to be "all but certain" that the treaty would be ready for signature in 1981.[7] Although prospects seemed bright for a while, the proposed convention soon ran afoul of the new American administration. Following a sudden and serious "review" and a few relatively inconclusive negotiating sessions, the draft treaty came up for a vote of the LOS conference membership. One hundred thirty nations, including France and Japan, endorsed it; the United States joined Venezuela, Turkey, and Israel in casting negative votes. When the final treaty was opened for signature in December 1982, one hundred seventeen nations signed, including France, the Netherlands, a number of other western European nations, the Soviet Union and Eastern bloc, China, Canada, and Australia, along with most African, Asian, and Latin American countries. Japan added its signature shortly thereafter, and more adherents seemed likely.[8]

Although the American stance does not doom the treaty, it considerably clouds the future of this extended effort at international lawmaking. For now at least, the result must be counted as a disagreement "in the large." Yet the unexpected agreement "in the small" on financial aspects of the treaty yields general insights when closely scrutinized. (Incidentally, extensive American objections and proposed amendments to the draft text virtually left the financial compromises alone.[9] Nor did the delegations from developing countries exert much pressure for changes in these articles. In fact, Ambassador T. T. B. Koh of Singapore, who chaired the intense financial negotiations, was subsequently elected to the presidency of the entire LOS conference, in part as a result of his skillful work in producing a widely acceptable financial text.)

Apart from broad implications for bargaining accords, several factors make the financial negotiations themselves a worthy subject. These deliberations were carried out by a large group—conference membership included more than 150 countries—with divergent interests and ideologies. Moreover, uncertainty and technical complexity obscured the financial questions, presenting formidable problems of efficient resource exploitation and equitable distribution of benefits. One reason for studying the LOS financial arrangements, therefore, is that its parties and issues share characteristics with many other negotiations.

The issues, the negotiating procedures, and the content of the solution may be directly relevant to at least two particular classes of important bargains. The negotiated regime for the seabed could exert a precedential pull on efforts to construct global policies toward other, at least arguably "common" resources. These might include categories as diverse as the resources of Antarctica, outer space, the moon, and the electromagnetic and satellite orbital spectra. Moreover, interpreting the LOS financial arrangements as a sort of "mega-mineral contract" between "mankind" and seabed miners suggests its relevance to the continuing series of mineral concessions negotiated among Third World countries and transnational mining companies.

The compromise on financial arrangements was particularly marked by sophistication in its risk-sharing mechanisms. One might have expected that economic agreements resulting from a highly political forum of lawyers and diplomats would be fairly crude. The risk-sharing aspects of these provisions, however, negotiated among the more than 150 delegates, exhibit features that are more advanced than those of almost any bilaterally negotiated mineral concession now in existence. The causes of this phenomenon are worth ferreting out.

Chapter 1 sketches just enough background of the LOS conference to make the financial "subnegotiations" comprehensible. As a prelude to Chapter 2's account of the negotiating sessions concerning the financial arrangements, a discussion of certain economic and technical underpinnings of the major disputed items shortens considerably the time necessary to detail the uneven path to compromise.

A variety of factors briefly compete for attention as the narrative unfolds, including the formal and informal procedures employed for education and persuasion, the use of a "single negotiating text" prepared by the chairman, and the dynamics of offers and counteroffers, as well as the extraordinary mediation efforts by certain delegates. Chapter 3 highlights three topics, however, as especially relevant to the process of reaching agreement in these multilateral negotiations. The first concerns the use of a seabed mining engineering-cost model that was developed at the Massachusetts Institute of Technology, the puzzle of its high credibility in such a sharply politicized environment, and its implications for the uses of outside technical information in complex, multilateral negotiations. Second, the proposition evolves that *differences* among conference participants — in values as well as in attitudes toward risk and time — allowed the financial negotiations to be concluded successfully. To the extent that agreements consist of such dovetailed differences, bargainers or mediators should actively seek them out, supplementing the traditional quest for "common ground." Third, the financial arrangements demonstrate how the artful combination of issues can produce a "zone of agreement" where the same issues, if considered separately, might not admit a settlement. Implications of this analysis extend to agenda creation, "bottom-line" formulation, and the order in which issues are settled.

Chapter 4 expands the subject from small to large and from the promise of accord to the reality of discord. By elaborating and extending the propositions developed in connection with the financial issues, this section offers an analytic account of why the Reagan administration decided against the treaty. After an evaluation of the elements of the American rationale, Part I concludes with general lessons for negotiation analysis and the fruitful pursuit of one's interests through agreement (or disagreement) in negotiation.

1.1 Whence the Law of the Sea Conference?

Widespread agreement on the need for an international negotiation to clarify and revise the law of the sea resulted in part from the combination of at least three related factors: the vastly increased intensity of ocean uses, an accelerating trend toward conflicting ocean claims, and the inadequacy of existing international law to handle these problems.

By virtually any measure, use of the oceans has dramatically increased in recent years. Between 1950 and 1975, for instance, seaborne commerce more than quadrupled; the world's fish catch climbed 16 million tons to 69 million tons; and the apparent fraction of world oil and gas reserves located in the seas reached 40 percent.[10] An array of new uses became potentially important: these ranged from manganese nodule mining to exploitation of other ocean minerals (metalliferous muds, diamonds, tin) and to generation of energy by tides, salinity, and temperature differences.

Conflicting claims by states burgeoned during this period, and fears of more such assertions increased. As John Temple Swing noted, "The speed and frequency with which nations asserted unilateral claims into ocean space were almost dazzling . . . During that period [1967–1973] no less than 81 states asserted over 230 new jurisdictional claims of varying degree of importance. Some, like Iceland's move to a 50-mile exclusive fishing zone (precipitating the first of the now famous "Cod Wars"), Brazil's assertion of a 200-mile territorial sea, and Canada's establishment of a 100-mile pollution control zone, precipitated immediate controversies with other states, whose conflicting uses were thereby jeopardized."[11]

Many nations expressed apprehension during the 1960s that the seabed would house nuclear weapons or underwater military installations, and even that competition for strategically located underwater mountains might materialize.[12] Increasing claims by coastal states to resources (mainly fish) and extended territorial jurisdiction served as especially potent stimuli to a new effort at revising the law of the sea. United States and Soviet navies, in particular, along with those of other maritime powers, saw a paramount interest in unimpeded freedoms of the high seas, including passage under, through, and over straits. These military organizations threw their weight strongly behind diplomatic efforts that promised a halt to troublesome restrictions on mobility without the high costs of constant forcible challenges. Of course, coastal states wanted general recognition for their seaward claims, whose status would remain tenuous as long as the major maritime nations refused recognition. This situation, together with reduced international freedom of marine scientific research and global problems such as overfishing, oil spills, discharges, dumping, and marine mammal depletion, warned of growing future disputes.[13]

Peaceful means of handling these disputes had at their core the seventeenth-century legal theories of Hugo Grotius, namely, that freedom of the high seas should prevail beyond a three-mile "territorial" zone (the distance a cannon could then shoot). The United Nations turned its attention to the oceans in the 1950s, as part of its attempt to develop international law generally. The First United Nations Conference on the Law of the Sea in 1958 produced conventions on four classes of maritime activity.[14] These conventions, however, had some glaring omissions: there was no agreement on uniform territorial sea limits or fishing zone limits; the continental shelf (under which most offshore oil appears to lie) had an elastic definition; the texts did not even mention manganese nodules; and pollution control requirements were ambiguous. The U.N. convened a second LOS conference in 1960, but it failed to alter this state of affairs. Widespread acceptance of the 1958 conventions was problematic since fewer than a third of the member states of the world community ultimately ratified them, and many newly independent states further questioned the legitimacy of these accords. These states contended that, since they did not participate in the centuries of legal development that were codified in Geneva, they should not be bound by the results.[15]

Financial arrangements for seabed mining, then, formed part of a seabed regime negotiated in the Third United Nations Conference on the Law of the Sea. Beyond the lure of giving substance to the "common heritage" concept, the conference began its 1973 negotiations in response to a dynamic situation of intensifying ocean use and conflict. Unless action were taken, these disputes threatened to overwhelm the fragile international legal structure set up to resolve them peacefully.

1.2 Conference Organization and Procedures

The conference organized itself into three committees, each with a set of issues for negotiation. Committee I was charged with formulating a regime for the deep seabed; that is, who may exploit seabed resources and under what conditions. Committee II had a mandate to deal with virtually all traditional subjects of maritime law: territorial seas, straits, islands, archipelagoes, the high seas, an economic zone to include living and nonliving resources within 200 miles of coastlines, the continental shelf, and access to the sea, especially by landlocked nations. Committee III dealt with pollution, scientific research, and the transfer of marine technology. A vital but separate group negotiated methods of compulsory dispute settlement.[16] For the most part, these committees carried on separate, parallel negotiations.

The conference adopted rules of procedure virtually requiring that all efforts at reaching consensus be exhausted before votes could be taken. On matters of substance, the rules required a two-thirds vote of those present and voting, provided the two-thirds majority included at least a simple majority of states participating in that session of the conference.[17] Of course, this requirement gave blocking power to any coalition equal to one-third of conference membership. The most significant such group became the "land-locked and geographically disadvantaged countries."[18]

Negotiations proceeded on the basis of "single negotiating texts" that the committee chairmen could modify on the basis of the discussions. Conference organizers intended these texts to provide a basis for negotiation without formally binding any delegation to their provisions. Delegates at early sessions of the conference devoted themselves to working out starting versions of these texts. (Normally a specialized group, such as the International Law Commission, would have worked for some time prior to a conference on a basic negotiating document.) By 1978 the conference stiffened the standard for a chairman's revisions of the text. The new rules required such modifications or revisions of the text to emerge from negotiations themselves, to enjoy widespread support, and to offer "a substantially improved prospect of a consensus."[19]

1.3 Financial Arrangements in the Seabed Regime of the LOS Treaty

1.3.1 The Context of Future Seabed Mining: A "Parallel" System

The negotiations on the financial arrangements formed part of the debate on an overall seabed regime. An outline of the main features of this regime serves as a useful starting point.

Developed countries that saw themselves as potential seabed miners preferred a broad-based international seabed mining framework to one composed of only a few mining nations. These countries strongly supported an International Seabed Authority that would act essentially as a claims registry, more or less passively facilitating the orderly development of mining. Miners might share some revenue from seabed operations with the world community out of respect for the "common heritage" principle.

At the outset of the LOS negotiations, many Third World representatives wanted an international body to be the sole exploiter of seabed resources. Since this idea was in opposition to the claims registry concept espoused by most of the developed world, early negotiations on the subject soon became deadlocked.[20] In the LOS forum, however, negotiation over the conditions for seabed mining was tightly linked to renegotiation of the legal regimes governing a spectrum of other ocean uses, many of which were judged to be crucial by developed maritime nations. Through those connected issues, the numerous coastal developing states in particular could exercise bargaining leverage on the resolution of seabed questions. If one accepts the view that, for the United States, defense interests in preserving navigational freedoms were the strongest motivation in its thinking toward the elements of the LOS package, the case can be made that significant compromises on its preferred seabed positions were inevitable.[21] Other maritime nations may have had similar priorities. Given that most delegates saw early mining by Eastern bloc countries as unlikely, and that almost all developed countries saw improvement in relations with Third World countries as desirable, movement away from original claims registry positions was understandable.

Without mining capability of their own, and conscious that the developed countries were unlikely to agree to a monopoly seabed authority, developing countries also moved from their polar position. By 1976 conference participants began to coalesce behind a split-the-difference compromise which became known as the "parallel" system. On one "side" of the system, private and state organizations could mine, while on the other side an international mining entity—the "Enterprise"—would be established to mine directly on behalf of the international community. For this compromise to have meaning, the Enterprise needed assurances that it could in fact undertake seabed mining. Among other things, it needed access to mining areas, technology, personnel, and finances.

Many delegates worried that the prime "mine sites"—the 40,000 to 60,000-square-kilometer areas necessary to support individual mining operations for their expected twenty- to twenty-five-year lives—would be snapped up early by miners from the developed countries with technological leads. This would leave the Enterprise with lower-quality

BACKGROUND: OF NODULES, NAVIES, AND NEGOTIATION

operations. The solution to this dilemma involved an ingenious method similar to the "I cut, you choose" method of fairly dividing a piece of cake. States or companies making application to the International Seabed Authority to mine on the "private" side would be required to submit two prospected sites. The Authority would reserve or "bank" one of them for later Enterprise operations, and the applicant would mine the other. Provisions also dealt in some detail with technology transfer and training of personnel. Delegates vigorously debated the composition, voting procedures, and powers of the Authority, as well as a temporary system of production controls intended to protect land-based producers of seabed minerals.[22]

Negotiators focused sustained, intense attention on two financial aspects of seabed mining — the so-called financial arrangements — that constituted major ingredients of the parallel system. The first of these issues was the scheme of required payments to the Authority by miners operating on their side of the parallel system. The Authority would decide how much of the funds to distribute directly to member countries and how much to reinvest in Enterprise mining operations. The second financial issue concerned the sources of the funds required to ensure that the Enterprise had an initial mining operation.

As noted earlier, delegates designated the financial arrangements negotiations in 1978 as one of seven "hard-core" issues that stood in the way of the success of the conference. These seven subjects were assigned to special "Negotiating Groups" (NGs), which in day-to-day negotiations largely supplanted the earlier, three-committee structure. The mandate of Negotiating Group 2 (NG2) included the financial arrangements. Singapore's Ambassador to the United Nations, Tommy T. B. Koh, chaired this group.[23]

The treaty, then, specifies that seabed mining must occur in the framework of a "parallel" system. Compromise resulted from negotiation between developed countries that advocated a claims registry system for private nodule exploitation and developing countries that favored mining solely under the auspices of an international organization. Although technology, mine sites, and the governance of the Seabed Authority are critical ingredients of this system, Chapters 2 and 3 focus on the two financial issues: the financial terms of contracts for miners operating in the private side of the parallel system, and the funding of the first Enterprise operation on the other side. (Naturally, there were a host of important but subsidiary issues such as accounting definitions and procedures, terms and repayment schedules for loans, convertibility of currency, and the like. For the most part, the following discussion ignores the resolution of such questions.)

1.3.2 Parties and Their Seabed Interests

The seabed negotiations in general and the financial discussions in particular were truly multilateral in character, with several identifiable, sometimes overlapping, groups of participants. Broadly relevant political divisions included developed and developing countries ("North/South"), Eastern bloc and Western nations ("East/West"), as well as nations that produce or export the minerals that will come from the seabed and those countries that consume or import them ("producer/consumer"). Among and within these groups, interests both conflicted and coincided.

Developed countries with companies likely to mine the seabed promoted nodule exploitation to gain secure access to the minerals and to derive economic benefits (lower prices, higher quantities, tax revenues, employment, and marine technological development). In terms of its 1976 consumption, for example, the United States imported 100 percent of its manganese (critical to and without effective substitutes in steelmaking) and cobalt (used in powerful magnets, aviation alloys, and electronics); 91 percent of its nickel (stainless and high-performance steels); and 24 percent of its copper (wire and electrical). These imports were valued at more than $1.4 billion.[24] This figure, however, does not adequately convey the perceived financial stakes in the debate. The majority of cobalt and manganese imports, for example, originate in a small number of countries that are possibly subject to severe political disturbance.[25]

An ambitious 1979 attempt to quantify the benefits to the United States in 1990 present value terms assumed four mining operations. (Depending on market conditions, of course, there could be from zero up to a probable maximum of a dozen or more projects at the upper limit of the proposed production controls.) Considering profits to U.S. firms, increased consumer surplus from lower prices, reduced likelihood and severity of supply disruptions and cartelization, reduced risk of depletion of reserves, and increased military security, the total benefits of these projects tentatively amounted to $2.5 to 8.5 billion.[26] With potential gains of this magnitude in mind, importers from developed countries and potential miners sought to avoid any possible deterrent effects of the financial arrangements provisions on seabed mining decisions.

Developing countries (the "South") found attractive the possibly large revenue shares from seabed mining as well as the autonomy such money could offer a new Seabed Authority. Through their primary organization, the Group of 77 (G-77), the developing countries generally advocated an exploitation system that would give them both shares of revenue and a degree of direct control over mining operations (in practice, through the Enterprise). They linked seabed mining with North-South relations generally, with demands for a New International Economic Order (NIEO),[27] and with control aspirations analogous to those expressed toward mineral development on land in the General Assembly Resolution on Permanent Sovereignty over Natural Resources.[28] As Bernard Oxman pointed out: "The stated object is 'control.' This emphasis on abstraction hides three underlying objectives of far broader scope: First, greater 'control' of international organizations by developing countries; second, greater 'control' of raw material markets by producers; and third, greater 'control' of national resource development projects by the state. The deep seabeds issue is seen as 'precedent.' "[29] In the financial arrangements negotiations, these preferences translated into a great concern with ensuring that the Enterprise get a secure start and into a desire for substantial revenues from private miners of nodules. Members of the G-77 exhibited significant interest in these precedential aspects of the LOS negotiations for other NIEO issues as well as with the specific effects of the proposed treaty provisions.

Eastern bloc countries, many of whom have substantial land sources of seabed minerals, would likely mine the seabed later than Western companies; thus they acted in a somewhat generous manner with the financial conditions, possibly in order to gain favor with some developing countries. At the same time, they did not wish to be saddled with onerous terms in the future.[30]

Land-based producers of the minerals to come from ocean mining, both current and potential, developed and developing, had an interest in ensuring that seabed mining not occur at all. If the financial arrangements proved too burdensome, however, the overall LOS treaty would not likely go into effect, and, it was feared, mining would go forward unilaterally. In such a case, land-based producers would not enjoy whatever protection the treaty's production controls could provide.

These groupings afford only a rough sense of the interests involved. Within each, a spectrum of viewpoints could be discerned: typically, members might range from radical to conservative; from primarily concerned with seabed exploitation to generally interested in world order; from a pure importer, to a mixed case, to an exporter of the minerals; and along many other scales.

Motivations that were quite apart from national interests of the involved parties prompted other individuals and groups to play important roles in the financial negotiations. The chairman of NG-2 and his staff, a Norwegian minister, and external groups including Quaker and Methodist organizations all developed stakes in the success of the conference and were instrumental in bringing about the financial compromises. Subsequent chapters highlight aspects of their strong influences.

1.3.3 Why Negotiate the Specifics of the Financial Terms of Contracts?

Uncertainty shrouds the costs and revenues of seabed mining. The investment costs constitute a first major area of uncertainty. Developed countries have generally assumed that seabed mining would prove to be technologically feasible. Since the Industrial Revolution, however, cost overrun and delay have been the frequent legacies of large, high-technology projects proposed to operate in hostile environments. Operating costs provide a second unknown, varying primarily with the future prices of energy, chemical reagents, and labor. Finally, world metal markets and their notorious cycles cause substantial revenue uncertainties for ocean miners. For example, from 1972 to 1975 copper prices almost tripled before falling back to their original levels.

Groups that have attempted to model the economic and engineering aspects of seabed operations have directly confronted the cost variability of ocean mining. Whether one looks at a 1974 U.N. study that used capital costs for a single mining-transportation-processing operation of less than $300 million, or the 1978 MIT study that suggested baseline costs of $560 million, or a 1979 German report that placed capital needs at nearly $1 billion, uncertainty looms as a key element in the evaluation.[31]

Negotiation of the fiscal terms to get the Enterprise under way might seem to be a relatively straightforward matter of technical design and hard political compromise. Specifying the details of what, in effect, will be a mineral contract between those who harvest the seabed and the rest of "mankind" may seem premature, however, since the industry is not yet born and its economic profile is such a matter of conjecture. Many conference participants emphasized this point early in the negotiations. A variety of political factors combined, however, to require the negotiation of specific numerical provisions. These factors, briefly examined here, effectively ruled out the option of deferring the particulars of the financial regime until more was known.

Much of the industrialized world placed considerable stock in the assurance of access to seabed resources. The type and magnitude of the financial obligations obviously constituted an important parameter of the access provisions. Developed countries strongly opposed signing a treaty that contained a "blank check" on financial arrangements, especially given aspects of the parallel system that they regarded as unpleasant compromises. These countries feared as well that the bargaining power in a future negotiation between their seabed miners and the Authority would sharply tilt in favor of the Authority with its monopoly power over mine site allocation and its own operating capability.

If deferred, negotiations on the specific contractual terms of seabed mining would be conducted in an uncertain multilateral forum. At that time, few if any participants in such negotiations would have an overwhelming or single-minded interest in seeing mining go ahead, especially since there would then be no actual mining operations. Apart from countries that for ideological reasons might oppose any state or private mining, land-based producers of seabed metals might well try to block ocean mining, perhaps through onerous financial requirements. A foretaste of such a conflict between present land miners and future ocean miners was contained in the bitter and protracted debate at the conference over the system to limit seabed production to some increment of nickel market growth in order to protect land-based producers such as Canada and several developing countries. Potential seabed mining countries felt quite uncertain about the degree of protection that the Seabed Authority's voting procedures would afford their economic interests against such a possible antimining coalition. As a result of these factors, developed countries by and large preferred the certainty of precise financial terms in the convention to those that might arise from a deferred negotiation, especially one in which the other issues of interest to nonmining participants had been previously settled.

Many developing countries, moreover, wanted to secure precise and favorable terms for the financing of the Enterprise. Perhaps they felt apprehension, as well, that future Authority-company negotiations would yield unfavorable outcomes. These factors led to widespread agreement among delegates on the need to specify the financial terms of contracts. The practical difficulties of setting precise terms, given highly uncertain economic conditions, thereby became central to the debate.

1.3.4 *Relevant Trends in Mineral Agreement Negotiations*

Before reviewing a chronology of the conference sessions, it is useful to examine trends in Third World mineral development to illustrate some of the issues underlying the negotiations on seabed financial terms and funding of the Enterprise. The financial terms of contracts essentially involved a determination of how each party—the miner and the Authority—would share in the risks and rewards of an operation. Beyond the immediate distributive aspects of negotiations on Enterprise finance—who pays how much—lay the question of the commercial viability of this international creation, and thus the extent to which it would reflect international control over the resources. Mineral development agreements provided the most tangible precedents for the financial payment and control aspects of seabed exploitation. Because such agreements were frequently in the background of the debates, some of their characteristics merit examination.

Numerous scholars have detailed the evolution of mineral development agreements between Third World countries and transnational firms.[32] There is no point in repeating their analyses here, but it is useful to synthesize from them a few major relevant trends. Among these developments is a shift of some financial risk away from firms and onto governments, with a corresponding rise in the proportional tax bite expected from profitable projects. An associated trend is toward periodic contract renegotiation, generally at the will of the host government. Finally, there is a long-standing tendency, often expressed in the nonfinancial terms of contracts, for countries to try to assert real sovereignty and control over their natural resources. Influences from each of these ideas made themselves felt in the seabed negotiations.

The most obvious shift in the financial terms of mineral development agreements involves a move away from taxation instruments that impose relatively high risk upon the miner in favor of schemes that shift some of the risk to the government. In this way the host may expect to collect proportionately more revenue than would be possible in higher-risk systems. The increasing reliance by governments on income taxes rather than on royalties is a prime manifestation of this phenomenon. As Gillis, Wells, and Bucovetsky wrote: "In spite of their [administrative] advantages, royalties had clearly given way to income taxes as the principal source of revenue for hydrocarbons and for metallic minerals by the early 1960s. In agreement after agreement, the fiscal rules were changed and almost all new agreements placed much heavier reliance upon the income tax for revenue. The shift was almost universal."[33]

Against the advantage of administrative simplicity, royalties pose widely recognized disadvantages for both miners and governments. Royalties vary with revenues and do not take capital or operating cost behavior into account. As a result, miners see a danger that with unexpected cost increases or during depressed periods in unstable metal markets, royalties might easily erase or negate profit margins.

BACKGROUND: OF NODULES, NAVIES, AND NEGOTIATION

Coming "off the top" (before costs are deducted), royalties are often perceived as magnifying the financial risk of an operation.

Governments typically have two problems with royalties. First, efficient resource exploitation generally requires that the choice of ore grade and the timing and amount of production be such that the cost (including a user cost) of producing the last unit of mineral just equals its price. Since royalties effectively reduce the price the miner receives per unit without affecting its extraction cost, they can induce changes in operating decisions that are "rational" for the miner but may be wasteful from the government's point of view. Royalties may cause "high grading" of deposits, reduced production levels, and premature shutdown of operations with consequent revenue loss.

Royalties also do not necessarily capture excess economic returns very well for host governments. Profits may increase as a result of declining costs with stable revenues, in which case the governmental take remains constant. In new industries (such as seabed mining) that are potentially subject to "learning" or "experience" curve effects, this characteristic may become important. If revenues increase dramatically relative to costs, a fixed-percentage royalty will obtain a proportion of the increase, but a much higher levy would be possible. Along with the increasing sophistication of taxing authorities worldwide, which makes collection of profits taxes more certain than before, the twin features of inefficiency inducement and inadequacy in capturing economic rents underlie the shift away from reliance on royalties in mineral contracts.

Profits taxes have taken some fairly complicated forms in recent agreements. These levies can be progressive with the absolute amount of profit, the accounting rate of return on assets, or other measures of economic performance. If the investment risk of a project is associated with the chance that the project will perform poorly by a particular criterion of economic success (net income, payback, discounted cash flow, and so forth), then miners and host countries alike should prefer the profit-sharing method that is tied most closely to that criterion. In practice, long-term mining investments are usually evaluated on the basis of a discounted cash flow or internal rate of return method.[34]

Periodic renegotiation of the terms of mineral contracts is common. The rationale is usually economic: the host country perceives that current financial or other terms are too favorable to the foreign investor. Once the mine is constructed, bargaining power shifts to the host. With the large, fixed investment in place, the "walk-away" threat of the firm correspondingly declines. Renegotiation of a contract thus may be seen as a forceful assertion of control by the state. Renegotiation can also be used as a crude tool for redressing problems that arise from undue rigidity in the original contractual terms. If a financial structure itself cannot capture a "fair" share of "excess" returns in unforeseen circumstances (or if the financial burdens are simply too heavy for the miner), a mandated change in the contractual terms presents itself as an obvious solution.

Although this course of action is common, and even expected, it is not costless, particularly when the renegotiation is against the will of one of the parties. To the extent that contractual terms nominally bind but are in fact treated by miners as only indicative, a "risk premium" against the likelihood of forced contract changes will be implicit in the higher rate of return required for an affirmative investment decision by a firm considering a mineral development project. (Of course, more favorable terms may add to perceptions of unfairness, perhaps hastening forced contract changes.) Renegotiation fear is thought to be partly responsible for the reported shift in mining company investments in developing countries from about 60 percent of the total a few years ago to about 15 percent more recently.[35] Spokesmen for developed countries have typically reacted to this statistic much as did former U.S. Secretary of State Henry Kissinger when he proposed an International Resources Bank: "Nationalization and forced changes in the terms of concessions in some developing countries have clouded the general climate for resource investment in the developing world . . . As a result, commercially viable projects have been postponed, cancelled, or relocated . . . If present trends continue, serious misallocations of capital, management, and technology are inevitable."[36]

Because the financial terms of seabed contracts will be contained in a multilateral treaty whose provisions will be extremely hard to alter, the possibility of renegotiation as a means of dealing with unsatisfactory provisions is much more limited than in a bilateral company-country negotiation.[37] Perhaps, as well, the developed countries' experiences with renegotiation led them to insist upon unchangeable specificity in the text. These influences all put pressure on the LOS financial negotiators to come up with a means other than renegotiation for dealing with the inherent uncertainties of the ventures.

Sustained assertion by developing countries of real "control" over their natural resources constitutes a third related trend, which was first given voice in the 1962 General Assembly Resolution on Permanent Sovereignty over Natural Resources. Developing countries have subsequently expressed this desire, with mixed success, in a variety of departures from the traditional mineral concessions. These variations include outright nationalization, acquisition of majority equity positions in local subsidiaries, or experiments involving what seem to be more acceptable relationships with multinational firms in the form of joint ventures, service contracts, production-sharing agreements, and technical assistance agreements. Behind these last methods, in particular, lies a view of the contractual relation with a transnational company as an unpleasant technological and financial necessity that should be supplanted as soon as feasible by direct national exploitation. The desire of certain delegates for a functioning Enterprise embodied this trend.

1.4 Summary

The financial negotiations in the LOS conference provide the context for inquiry into the process of reaching agreement in negotiations. Increasing worldwide ocean conflict coupled with an inadequate legal structure led to the call for a wholesale reconsideration of the law of the sea. As a "new" resource, agreed to be the "common heritage of mankind," manganese nodules were included in this negotiation along with many other issues. An unprecedented number of countries participated, with a remarkable divergence of ideologies and concrete interests. The parties made compromises from preferred positions on some issues, partly as a result of leverage from other interests. The seabed regime that emerged from this complicated process was known as a "parallel" system.

The negotiators faced difficult tasks since uncertainty characterized seabed economics and the possibility of renegotiation was not a mutually acceptable escape valve. Most delegates eventually found the inclusion of precise figures in the treaty to be politically necessary. Recent trends in mineral development agreements concerning risk sharing, renegotiation, and actual control over the resources shaped the talks on the financial terms of contracts and the financing of the Enterprise.

2 Course of the Financial Negotiations

2.0 Themes in the Chronology

Six negotiating sessions took place in the New York and Geneva facilities of the United Nations over the 1977–1980 period. This chapter traces their evolution from several perspectives, focusing variously on organization and procedures, substantive issues, individuals, national proposals, and negotiating texts, as well as on the understanding that gradually developed about the underlying technical and economic characteristics of seabed mining.

2.1 The 1977 New York Session

Detailed debate on the financial arrangements did not begin until the 1977 New York session, when the main elements of the "parallel system" compromise were in place. Delegates at that session inherited a very tentative financial document which contained neither a definite payment structure nor specific numbers.[1] These first detailed discussions, however, yielded few tangible results.

Near the start of the session, the chairman of Committee I set up a small working group. Discussions proceeded for the most part at a low political level. The rapporteur's resulting text was released without clear philosophy, payment figures, or official status.[2]

The participants reached no general agreement on the likely economics of seabed mining. Available studies were highly aggregated, were typically based on industry sources, and exhibited highly variable results.[3] Many members of the Group of 77 (G-77) took it as an article of faith that mining would be profitable, so profitable in fact that "front-end" payments from private miners could fund the initial Enterprise operations and subsequent revenue shares could be an engine of Third World economic development. Representatives from developed countries expected more modest economic results. Neither group, however, held these profit expectations strongly enough that a contingent agreement could have been reached — even had there been the political skill available to fashion one.

Two financial proposals were offered in Committee I. They were formulated by two countries that were ideological opposites at the conference, the United States and India. If anything, these proposals served to define the extreme limits of a bargaining range. They reflected wide differences in expectations about seabed economics as well as divergent perceptions of the relationships among financial arrangements issues. (The specifics of these and subsequent proposals are detailed in Appendix 1 to this chapter. The effects of different proposals on the economic return of a single mining project are discussed in Section 3.1.2 and plotted in Figure 3.1.)

These two financial proposals reflected divergent philosophies on every dimension. The United States proposed no front-end fees; India suggested a $60 million payment. India proposed a 20 percent *ad valorem* royalty (percentage of gross revenues) plus an effective $15 million yearly charge (five dollars per ton of nodules mined for a 3,000,000-ton-per-year operation); the United States did not propose either kind of payment. The United States suggested a profit-sharing system that was progressive with the accounting rate of return on assets, with rates from 15 percent on low-return projects to a 50 percent marginal rate on high-return projects; India's profit share was set at 60 percent, once 200 percent of the investment costs were recouped. These specific figures are not important in themselves, but they do indicate the great distance that existed between the two parties near the outset of negotiations.

India argued, moreover, that revenue shares ought to be levied on the basis of the *entire* mining, transportation, and processing operations, even when these activities took place on land. The United States held that only that part of the operation in the international area should share its revenues. The latter view required an accounting definition of the seabed portion of the system. Companies expected their early seabed operations, at least, to be vertically integrated from nodule collection through the processing stage. The first market price would likely apply to the processed metals; hence the nodules would be assigned an arbitrary transfer price. It would be necessary, therefore, to specify a method to "attribute" an appropriate part of the entire operation's revenue or profit to the mining sector. If there were a competitive market for raw nodules, of course, such a procedure would not be necessary; the nodule price and mining sector costs could then be used directly to determine mining profits. Given the expected early absence of such a market, however, the United States proposed that 20 percent of the profits of a vertically integrated project be "imputed," "deemed," or "attributed" to the mining sector. This percentage represented an estimate of the likely proportion of the entire capital investment that the mining sector would constitute. In subsequent negotiating sessions, delegates focused much attention on this figure, known as the "attributable net proceeds" or ANP.

Essentially as a gesture to states that do not use explicit price systems, do not recognize the concept of profits, or are simply unwilling or unable to furnish accounting data, the United States also proposed an all-royalty system. Such parallel proposals were seen as necessary inclusions in the text. They generally inspired little discussion in the conference, and such discussion as there was came perfunctorily from Eastern bloc countries. The United States also suggested that the Enterprise should be loan-financed, but with up to 10 percent of its monetary requirements to be furnished by grants from member states. The Indian proposal was silent on this question, as was conference debate generally. The issue was simply immature.

2.2 The 1978 Geneva Session

In the 1978 Geneva session, conference members designated the "financial arrangements" as one of seven critical remaining subjects. They formed a special negotiating group (NG2) to deal with financial questions and named as its chairman the Permanent Representative of Singapore to the United Nations, Ambassador Tommy Koh. Koh brought some unusual credentials to NG2: educated at Singapore, Harvard, and Cambridge, he had been the youngest ambassador ever appointed to the United Nations; he had been the dean of the University of Singapore's Law School in his early thirties; he had been active in the LOS Asian group; and he had been instrumental in the successful negotiations on the crucial straits articles of the draft convention. His appointment significantly raised the political level of the financial discussions, which were widely attended and simultaneously translated into the six official U.N. languages.

The large number of delegates attending the NG2 plenary discussions made progress difficult. Partly in response to this, Koh early on established an open group of "financial experts" to operate in tandem with the larger NG2 meetings. This smaller group produced much creative work that delegates subsequently debated in the larger forum.

COURSE OF THE FINANCIAL NEGOTIATIONS

Shortly before the Geneva session, a group at MIT had published a cost model of a seabed operation.[4] It is hard to overestimate the effect of this model on the deliberations of NG2 in Geneva and in subsequent sessions. In his report, Koh stated: "In the group of financial experts we were immediately confronted with the need to agree on a set of assumptions. Without an agreed framework of assumptions it would not have been possible for us to carry on with our deliberations. We agreed that the best study to date was that undertaken by MIT, entitled, 'A Cost Model of Ocean Mining and Associated Regulatory Issues.'"[5] Such references to the study and repeated use of its "baseline" case assumptions abound in the remainder of Koh's report, reflecting their role in NG2 deliberations. It is worth trying to fathom some of the reasons for the use and acceptance of the MIT study in the generally skeptical and political environment of the conference.

In 1976 a team led by J. D. Nyhart (Professor in the Sloan School and the Department of Ocean Engineering at MIT) initiated a request for funding from the Sea Grant program, a maritime educational arm of the U.S. Department of Commerce. The group wanted to develop a computer model that could compare the performance of a hypothetical deep ocean mining system under various conditions. Nyhart's group received support without any direct connection to the LOS negotiations.

The model itself was framed in such a way as to be innocent of ideological questions. One of its sections worked out the engineering aspects of nodule recovery and processing; these physical results fed into a financial analysis routine. The MIT group developed cost figures on research and development; on prospecting and exploration; on capital investment in mining, transportation, and processing; and on operating costs, including energy, labor, materials, and indirect charges. The team expended a great deal of research effort in deriving and documenting independent estimates of the more than 150 principal parameter values or sets of values for the model's "baseline case." There was, of course, a great deal of uncertainty attached to many of these values. Sensitivity analyses — that is, observing the effect of changing one or more variables while holding the rest constant at their baseline values — constituted a major part of the study. Of course, users could provide their own input assumptions for the model. The report stressed uncertainty, but its methodology was deterministic; a given set of inputs produced a single answer rather than a probable range.

The model had been the subject of two critical review conferences at which academics, technical representatives of all the major mining consortia, and assorted government scientists had offered detailed suggestions on its structure, equations, and parameter values. In the several months between review sessions, the model's creators completely reworked it. The technical report itself made no reference to questions of ideology in the ultimate structuring of the seabed mining industry, and, in fact, made scant reference to the LOS conference. The model had clearly not been designed originally for the international use to which it was being put: for example, the U.S. tax system was built directly into the economic routine, and there was little discussion of the financial provisions in an eventual LOS treaty. These characteristics, perhaps a bit paradoxically, tended to reinforce perceptions of the model's independence.

The baseline profitability results of the study projected about an 18 percent internal rate of return to an enterprise after domestic (U.S.) taxes or, equivalently, a zero net present value at an 18 percent real discount rate. These findings contradicted persistent claims by developed countries that their miners would be unable to pay even minimal proposed fees and royalties. At the same time, this comparatively modest profit prospect dashed the hopes of many developing countries who had felt that seabed mining would be a bonanza, capable of generating untold amounts of revenue for the world community. Because the model's early results fully pleased no delegation, it seemed to gain in general credibility.

Koh was charged with the responsibility of producing a text that would enjoy a substantially improved prospect of consensus in the overall conference. Once the inherited text had been clarified and restructured, he needed numbers and percentages for the various fees, royalties, and profit shares. To get such figures, he pressed participating countries to advance proposals. As a technique of seeking compromise, this had mixed results. Since the countries wanted their positions reflected in the text, and since Koh selected what went into it, there was some tendency for delegations to push their proposals toward the chairman's perceived zone of "fairness." Of course, a request like Koh's to specify national positions tends to focus attention on those positions and may serve to define an adversary process. Nations can easily become committed to their stances and may then require strong political reasons to move from them.

It is interesting analytically to note the similarities between a chairman-controlled single negotiating text procedure and so-called final-offer arbitration. In the latter technique, the parties to a dispute each offers a proposal to an arbitrator, who must choose one of them without alteration. This method supposedly creates an incentive to make "reasonable" proposals, rather than the "extreme" ones that often come about when disputants expect the arbitrator merely to split the difference. Of course, the financial negotiations were a dynamic process with no clear ending, and Koh was not restricted to choosing one proposal in its entirety. Some delegates felt, however, that the more reasonable a proposal was, the more likely that Koh would take it into account in revising the text.

Koh's request produced a series of positions that moved somewhat closer to a central range than the one bounded by the previous proposals from the United States and India. The European Economic Community (EEC), Japan, and the United States came forth with new suggestions on one side, while India reduced its suggested royalty and dropped the idea of an annual charge. The Soviet Union offered a flat royalty on the revenues of the overall operation. (Appendix 1 provides the details.) Proposals on the portion of the overall operation to be subject to international sharing, the ANP, ranged from 20 percent (the United States, EEC, Japan) to 100 percent (India), with numbers from 38 percent to 80 percent informally mentioned by various developing countries.[6] These proposals were still quite far apart in their payment magnitudes, their relative emphasis on the mix of fixed and variable charges, and the ANP figure.

At this point Minister Jens Evensen of Norway proposed a financial scheme detailing the obligations of the prospective miners and of member countries to the Enterprise. Evensen had a great deal of personal prestige, was from a developed country that enjoyed a relatively good reputation in much of the Third World, and was widely respected as the architect of major compromises at the conference. In particular, he had presided over the prickly negotiations that established the basic outlines of the parallel system. Evensen interjected himself into the financial debate in a dramatic way. Although he had not participated in the earlier deliberations of the group of experts, Evensen had seen the impasse and offered what can be described as a split-the-difference compromise. Rejecting an up-front bonus or annual fees as too burdensome, he put forward a scheme with royalty and profit-sharing rates that were much higher than those suggested by developed countries but considerably lower than those in India's proposal. Evensen's ANP figure was 50 percent, midway between the 20 percent figure of the other industrialized countries and the high figure of 80 percent from the non-Indian, developing countries. Evensen also offered a roughly equivalent, royalty-only alternative. As had been his style in other parts of the LOS conference, Evensen then stood back to take the rhetorical heat and listen to the inevitable denunciation from all sides. His more central proposal, however, became a focal point for delegates' attention.

Koh did not feel in Geneva that he could offer a set of figures for financial terms of contracts that would heighten the prospects of consensus. He did, however, suggest that one-third of the requirements for the first Enterprise operation take the form of interest-free loans. Up to this point in the negotiations, only the original U.S. proposal had simultaneously included provisions on financial terms of contracts and Enterprise finance.

2.3 The 1978 New York Session

Negotiating Group 2 met twelve times during the New York session. The gulf between developed and developing countries persisted on the mode and level of required payments, as well as on the portion of an integrated operation that was liable to sharing, the ANP. The preferences of developing countries for relatively high, fixed payments sharply contrasted with the insistence by potential mining countries on more moderate, contingent charges.

Despite commonality introduced by the MIT model, many members of delegations from developing countries assumed that mining would be very profitable. Moreover, they saw payments from miners as financing the initial operations of the Enterprise. Since the successful launching of the Enterprise was seen as a crucial goal, delegates wanted to be quite certain of sufficient funds for this purpose. This combination of goals and beliefs about mining led to a G-77 position that high fixed payments were affordable by the private miners and necessary for the Enterprise. The United States, the European community, and Japan opposed such a system as imposing too high a level of risk on this as yet unborn industry. Eastern bloc countries, apparently less for pragmatic than for ideological reasons, opposed fixed charges as unjustified. As members of "mankind," they argued that a fixed "entry fee" should not be charged for access to their "common heritage."

The concept of an ANP less than 100 percent was widely accepted in Geneva, and negotiations centered on whether appropriate principles could be found for its determination. Developed countries argued for a figure of 20 percent, based on the capital investment in the international area as a proportion of the capital investment in overall integrated operation. Others advocated a labor analogy as relevant, while many countries insisted that the nodules had an intrinsic, *in situ* value that should be reflected in the ANP. The ideological difficulties prompted frequent speculation that only an arbitrary political ANP specification was feasible.

Although the ANP figure had an obvious economic implication — the ANP percentage multiplied by the tax rate equals the effective tax rate on the integrated operation — the choice of ANP rate also had legal and political implications. Many legally trained delegates argued at length about the connection between the ANP figure and the extent of the International Seabed Authority's general and taxing jurisdiction vis-à-vis the states where processing plants were to be located. Frequently, questions of economic ideology, jurisdiction, and legal status overshadowed considerations of the actual economic effect of the ANP choice.

Early in the session an important seminar was held under Quaker and Methodist auspices, away from the United Nations. Koh actively encouraged the seminar sponsors and buttonholed many delegates about attending. This seminar was held on neutral ground that seemed generally remote from the ideological issues that were latent in the seabed mining negotiations. The two sponsoring groups were generally interested in promoting world peace and had taken an early interest in Law of the Sea questions. They had lobbied in favor of treaty provisions, had held numerous off-the-record educational seminars and lunches for delegates since the 1974 sessions, and had published a much-read conference newspaper ("Neptune") that disseminated environmental, technological, and economic information.

Delegates of all political persuasions packed the politically timely and visibly Koh-supported "MIT seminar," which featured the principal members of the MIT team. Over the course of the day they explained the model and discussed factors affecting future seabed profitability. Listeners vigorously questioned many of the model's assumptions, in particular its baseline values. The team's usual response to queries and challenges was to explain the source of the relevant assumption and to demonstrate the model's sensitivity to the factor in question. This technique highlighted the underlying technical and economic uncertainty, but it also seemed to enhance the credibility of the effort.

Criticism of the model came from various quarters, but the criticisms were typically couched in technical, not ideological, terms. For example, EEC members had produced a competing set of estimates — the "European Base Case" — that was considerably less optimistic than the MIT study. In addition, the fact that there was now an independent source of information given credence by national governments had obviously annoyed some industry representatives. Whatever the motivations, the attacks at the seminar by developed country representatives, whether government or industry, had fairly straightforward technical responses and seemed to strengthen the confidence of many G-77 delegates in the model's usefulness.

The MIT group had not planned to risk politicizing its seminar presentation by analyzing any of the existing financial arrangements proposals. Minister Evensen, however, was not at all averse to having his proposal examined — critically — as an example to "demonstrate the model's capability." The team easily showed several economic and technical scenarios under which Evensen's ad hoc compromise would severely reduce a project's profitability. At the conclusion of the presentations Evensen acknowledged the critique, thanked the group, and indicated that he might consider modifying his proposal.

Certain delegates expressed curiosity about the economic feasibility of other proposals. In particular, the eminent Indian representative, Dr. Jagota, praised the team at the end of the seminar and inquired as to the effect of the Indian proposal. The MIT group had already performed the analysis, and not surprisingly, the financial impact of a $60 million payment some five or more years before commercial production was to begin, along with a 20 percent royalty, was devastating. Jagota, too, indicated that a reconsideration might be in order. In neither case did Evensen or Jagota have to admit the correctness of the arguments of "opponents" in order to justify a possible move. Indeed, each could point to a seemingly objective, outside analysis as a reason for considering a new position. Offers by the MIT members to modify the model to handle future financial proposals as well as their offer to maintain constant contact with conference members were generally well received.

Evensen and members of the Norwegian delegation soon after made a trip to MIT, where they had a chance to discuss seabed economics more fully. While in Cambridge, Evensen asked team members to analyze several possible proposals. On his return to New York, Evensen made a new proposal that conspicuously leaned on the MIT analysis. Once again, he used a technique of movement toward consensus by offering a proposal that all sides found objectionable but that delegates could consider as a more central basis for negotiation.

Much of the subsequent discussion centered on Evensen's new proposal. By the end of the session, Koh felt for the first time that he could include specific figures within his financial structure and that they would offer a substantially improved prospect of consensus. Koh's system leaned heavily on Evensen's second proposal, but it tilted slightly more toward developing country positions. Koh did not include new proposals for finance of the Enterprise.

Koh had relied very heavily on the baseline case of the MIT study to fashion his scheme. As he stated in his report:

> There are two fundamental ways in which my compromise proposal can be evaluated. First, we can compare it with financial

provisions in national laws for mining contracts. The second way is to monetize my proposal. For the purpose of monetizing my proposal, I have looked at both the MIT cost model and the European Base Case. I have used the MIT model because it is a much more detailed and comprehensive study than the European Base Case. I think the majority in the Negotiating Group, both from developed and developing countries, will agree that the MIT model is the most reliable estimate we have of the costs, expenditures, and revenues of seabed mining.[7]

Paul Engo of the Cameroon, the politically adept chairman of the negotiations on the overall seabed regime, provided indirect but quite persuasive evidence on the extent to which the model had permeated the consciousness of the conference, and how the locus of political power was shifting to the technocrats. He lamented that "[we] have ourselves been dragged into adopting models and systems of calculations based on fictitious data that no one, expert or magician, can make the basis of any rational determination. We get more and more engrossed with each session and have been reduced to mere spectators in the inconclusive tournament among experts."[8]

Even though Koh asserted that his proposal would allow the contractor a 15 percent internal rate of return, the financial delegates grew increasingly conscious of the inherent limitations of the model's baseline analysis with respect to economic and technical uncertainty. In partial recognition of this changed perception, Koh included a so-called safeguard clause in his proposal. If the miner did not recover his investment within a certain time, the sharing rates would not increase, and if twice the investment costs were unrecovered by a specified later date, the lower rates would remain in effect. The currency gained by the notion of a safeguard clause reflected emerging understanding on the part of some delegates that uncertainty was a fundamental condition of seabed mining. As useful as the model was for increasing general understanding or allowing people to move from entrenched positions, it was not likely to capture the future of mining in a tidy set of scenarios, however artfully concocted on the banks of the Charles River in Cambridge. The introduction of the model may have early been a psychological prop to delegates who were uneasy about even discussing such an uncertain activity. Over time, however, the model highlighted rather than erased the unknowns.

The New York session ended, then, with great differences in profit probabilities and in versions of the correct ANP figure. A model was in place on which delegates relied heavily in the development, presentation, and evaluation of new proposals. Important mediation efforts by

Koh and Evensen had moved NG2 closer to a zone of possible agreement.

2.4 The 1979 Geneva Session

Springtime in Geneva saw very little in the way of new proposals. This session can best be viewed as a time for deepened understanding of the issues themselves and their relationships in any possible compromise. Negotiating Group 2 met a total of twenty-two times, and innumerable smaller groups held related sessions.

Koh focused major efforts on building a productive relationship between the formal NG2 process and the parallel, informal ones. A number of interested individuals and delegations generated ideas. Smaller groups explored underlying technical and economic factors related to particular proposals. Frequently, these small group meetings took the form of staff seminars, where promising ideas were explained and debated.

To the extent that an idea or proposal had the potential to shape NG2 consensus, technical members of Koh's staff would present it to a number of different interest or regional groups. As such ideas were introduced, tested, accepted, modified, or rejected in the smaller groups, the more promising possibilities among them could be introduced into NG2 proper. Koh tried to establish agreement among key people on a particular suggestion and then to have someone bring it up in the larger session. He attributed "ownership" of the ideas widely and sought to build momentum toward agreement. In the larger group Koh frequently used a technique that might be called creative summarizing, by which he would succinctly interpret often rambling and confused statements on unfamiliar technical matters. Through these clear summaries Koh could effectively draw out useful elements of the discussion, give credit to delegates for constructive comments, and direct the negotiation toward potential compromise and away from impasse. It was often difficult, however, to identify in such a large group the negotiators whose acquiescence was critical to general acceptance of a point. Moreover, as the promise of a settlement seemed greater, new (typically higher-level) delegates began to participate in NG2, necessitating frequent review and debate of relatively well established points.

Variations on this pattern, loosely orchestrated by Koh, characterized the eventual adoption by NG2 of many provisions in the text. Their evolution could be traced, despite frequent reversals and dead ends, along a path from generation and modification of ideas and potential solutions to small-scale education and dealing with the suspicious critiques of delegates. Large-scale introduction of surviving ideas followed where earlier skepticism, discussion, and education had a chance to engender familiarity with the new notions. Some fraction of these proposals passed into NG2's conventional wisdom and gained legitimacy. With luck, Koh felt able to incorporate them into the draft text, which itself would present new problems.

Delegates generally began to regard the uncertainty surrounding seabed economics as inherent. The MIT model offered less assurance about seabed economic outcomes than had seemed the case in NG2 shortly after the model's introduction. This perception of uncertainty was in part implicit in the general reaction to an extensive and direct attack on the MIT baseline case that was made by the Battelle-Institut in Frankfurt.[9] This new study suggested that the base figures MIT had used were quite optimistic. The new report did not discredit the earlier study; instead, many delegates regarded the Battelle projection as something that *could* happen, as indeed might a variety of other possibilities. Aside from causing its German government sponsors some awkward moments as they tried to explain in NG2 why their companies were so eager to pursue such "clearly uneconomic" ventures, the study generally came to represent a pessimistic scenario.

Several important concepts began to diffuse widely. An increasing number of negotiators came to see the problem of making a seabed investment as equivalent to purchasing a "profit (loss) lottery." Imposing fixed fees, royalties, or shares of profit would change the shape of this lottery. Appreciation grew of the importance of the time value of money in the context of thirty-year projects. The difference between *overall, project-long* profitability (net present value or internal rate of return) and *within-year* profitability (annual net income) became a frequent feature of the formal and informal NG2 discussions.

The specific debate centered around the concept of flexibility, or how responsive the financial terms of contracts were to the actual economic condition of projects. "Flexibility" came to mean the extent to which contractors would be protected in case of adverse outcomes and how the Authority would share more than proportionately in bonanza projects. Three mechanisms were proposed and widely discussed as being more flexible than Koh's proposal, whose rates climbed sharply and virtually automatically with the passage of time. The first, proposed by a French delegate, tied the rates to the return on miners' sales or the "gross margin." A second, put forth by a representative of the U.N. Conference on Trade and Development, used the ratio of annual cash flow to investment; a third system, offered by an MIT team member, suggested that change in the net present value of the project (calculated using a negotiated discount rate) should be the basis for changes in tax rates.[10]

Debates about the extent of the Authority's jurisdiction over seabed operations for revenue-sharing purposes (the so-called ANP) grew both in prominence and intractability. A variety of methods are used on land to make such a determination: cost ratios, "netting back" revenues to the primary sector after deducting costs and an agreed profit for the other segments, arbitrarily "presuming" revenues, and so forth. While the mechanics of these different alternatives became more evident, so did disagreement among the delegates. The model's analysis, moreover, was of an entire, vertically integrated operation, and therefore the effect of ANP changes on the financial complexion of the overall operation could be measured but could not reflect the intensely debated legal and political ramifications of the ANP choice. As conference participants in NG2 began to realize that nonintegrated but *independent* mining, processing, and transportation operations might characterize part of the seabed industry, the model's output declined in direct relevance.

Participants in NG2 strenuously debated the likely economic fitness of the Enterprise's first operation in terms of the cash/guaranteed debt mixture proposed for its financing. Acutely aware of debt service problems in many developing countries and worried that a new organization without a proven track record might have trouble raising money, delegates emphasized the financial terms of contracts as the real means for starting the Enterprise.

Although the contractual terms and Enterprise finance were discussed in the same group, most NG2 members treated them as independent *negotiation* issues. Many among the G-77 had assumed a *substantive* link between the issues, however, which was reflected in an early desire to fund the Enterprise by means of revenues raised from the "private" side of the system. Otherwise, there was no real negotiating linkage between the issues. With the negotiators treating the financial terms and Enterprise finance questions as separate, moreover, there did not seem to be a possible zone of agreement. As Koh noted, "The scheme of taxation preferred most by the developing countries is preferred least by the developed countries."[11] Some delegates from developed countries expressed reluctance to give higher cash contributions that would aid the Enterprise, which they saw as a potential competitor to their national companies. They held the provisions of the current text to be overgenerous.

Considering the issues one by one, then, the possibilities for solution looked dim. The developed countries could not accept a "rigid" financial arrangements system; the developing states would block a "flexible" system. The North felt that enough had been done to ensure the functioning of the Enterprise; the South saw much more as necessary. Discouraged predictions of an impasse filled the corridors. As a result, Koh made very few changes in his proposals: he lowered the royalty rates somewhat, reduced the ANP figure from 40 to 35 percent, and changed the nature of the "safeguard clause." In earlier versions the safeguard clause prevented higher taxation rates from coming into effect if the investment had not been recovered by a specific time; now the recovery of twice the investment triggered a set of higher rates. Koh's rationale for the change was based on the general realization that a quickly successful project might be able to afford higher payments earlier than a preset number of years, while a troubled project might be harmed by an automatic rate increase.

In a highly controversial move, Koh raised the cash contributions for funding the Enterprise from $33\frac{1}{3}$ to 50 percent of the requirements for its first operation. Instead of the cash grants ("interest-free loans") being required only to the extent necessary to secure Enterprise debt, the cash was now to be due regardless and was seen as equity in the Enterprise's debt-equity mix.

The 1979 Geneva session, then, involved formal and informal processes in an attempt to clarify the issues and build momentum toward a settlement. Koh used a process of small group consultations, trying to identify and win over key people to possible compromise ideas and then floating these suggestions in the larger NG2 deliberations. Delegates understood more fully that the Authority could expect a greater amount of revenue but with less certainty under a flexible system than under a rigid one and that contractors preferred the more flexible schemes. Extended discussion brought the issues underlying the ANP and Enterprise finance questions more into the open, but Koh lamented what he saw as a "hardening of positions" on all sides.[12]

2.5 The 1979 New York Session and Beyond

Near the start of the 1979 New York session, Koh had arranged for more informative seminars to be held under Methodist/Quaker auspices. A number of experts from diverse disciplinary backgrounds, organizations, and nations made presentations on the ANP question, the flexible/rigid character of the required payments, and the likely ability of the Enterprise to obtain needed funds from international capital markets. Once again a large number of delegates attended, asked questions, and detailed their criticisms. The seminars consolidated much of the understanding that had been achieved in Geneva.

In the belief that all outstanding seabed issues needed to be considered together, a so-called Working Group of 21 (WG21), consisting of ten developed nations, ten developing nations, and the People's Republic of China, had been formed near the end of the previous Geneva session. The WG21 members discussed financial questions in New York. This nominally new group was really a reconstructed NG2; the working relationships of the NG2 participants were too strong to be broken down by being combined into a new group. After a week Koh began presiding over a de facto NG2.

In an attempt to soften positions, Koh had his staff prepare a veritable flood of option papers on the various issues. Despite arduous debate on these analyses, delegates found it extremely difficult in the medium-to-large groups for any real movement to be made from established positions. If a negotiator indicated willingness to accept a compromise, he could feel no certainty about reciprocal gestures or about the relation of the proposed move to a final compromise.

Evensen tried again to bridge the gap with a compromise proposal on financial terms. The most distinctive aspect of his suggestion was that the ANP be set at 20 percent for ten years and 40 percent thereafter. Debate flourished on the merits of his idea, but its rationale was too clearly arbitrary. What was more important, it satisfied no one ideologically and seemed too favorable to the industrialized nations for the land-based producers or G-77 members to consider. The EEC, Japan, and the United States, meanwhile, proposed a set of figures that seemed a retreat from their earlier positions. They clung tenaciously to a capital-cost ratio (mining sector capital divided by total project capital, variable with each operation) rather than a set ANP figure as well as a profit-sharing system and low royalty. They did, however, suggest that one-third of the first Enterprise operation be financed by non-interest-bearing loans.

The negotiations showed little explicit movement for a period of weeks. Koh felt that the time was ripe for dramatic compromise. He quietly chose four individuals (from the United States, Mauritius, Pakistan, and Argentina) as being among the most articulate and knowledgeable about the financial issues. Over the two-year course of the negotiations, patterns of deference had emerged among the delegates that allowed these four informally to represent the developed countries as well as the Asian, African, and Latin American regional groups. They negotiated intensively for three days over a final compromise, amidst avid speculation about their whereabouts and activities.

COURSE OF THE FINANCIAL NEGOTIATIONS

Koh put forward the result of their deliberations as his own compromise, and each of the four negotiators undertook to sell it to his respective group.

The results of two years of NG2 education made the technical elements of Koh's compromise seem quite clear to a large number of key delegates in the regional groups. Although there were angry rumblings from India and the EEC (for opposite reasons), the main elements of the new Koh proposals survived widespread debate in the 1979 and the subsequent 1980 New York sessions. The sales efforts of the four delegates proved successful within the conference: a virtually unchanged version of the proposal survives in the final treaty which was opened for signature in December 1982. The proposal contains provisions both on the financial terms of contracts and on the means of financing the Enterprise.

The text specifies two alternative payment systems for contracts. Both systems require a $500,000 application fee and a payment of $1 million per year until commercial production begins. The first alternative contains a 5 percent royalty levied on the market value of the processed metals for the first ten years of production, with a 12 percent royalty assessed during the remaining years of the contract. This system was negotiated primarily for miners who are unwilling or unable to furnish detailed accounting data or who do not recognize the concept of profit; it is largely in response to Eastern bloc requirements.

Designing the structure of the second system and specifying its rates, of course, had occupied most of the attention of the negotiators. This alternative contains both royalty and profit-sharing provisions to be applied to the seabed portion of an operation (defined by the ANP). The ANP is defined as the fraction of the integrated operation that is equal to the proportion that the mining capital investment represents of the integrated operation's total capital. This fraction is not, in any case, allowed to go below 25 percent. Operations that are not vertically integrated have ANP figures calculated on an analogous basis.

Two basic payment schedules apply. In the first of these, a 2 percent royalty on the value of processed metals is to be assessed from the start of production. An incremental scale of profit sharing is also initially in effect. The Authority's share is 35 percent of those profits representing up to a 10 percent return on investment for the year; plus 42.5 percent of the profit increment representing from a 10 percent to a 20 percent return; plus 50 percent of remaining profits. A ten-year depreciation period is set for the purpose of calculating net income. The second profit-sharing and royalty schedule is triggered when the overall cash flow of the operation, cumulated forward with a 10 percent real rate, is sufficient to recover the preproduction investment (also cumulated with interest). The operation then shares its profits at rates of 40 percent for profits up to a 10 percent return for the year; 50 percent of the next profit increment, representing between a 10 percent and a 20 percent return; and 70 percent of the remainder. Royalties rise to 4 percent in years when there is at least a 15 percent accounting return on investment.

Other provisions deal with adjustments to the calculation of fees, costs, and revenues to remove the effects of inflation; accounting definitions; strict data requirements; and auditing procedures. Depending on the economic success of the operations, total undiscounted payments to the Authority per contract can range from a low of over $200 million (1976 dollars) for marginal projects to well over $2 billion for fairly profitable mines.[13]

Two sources will provide the funding for the first mining operation of the Enterprise. Half the total amount required to launch a single project will come in the form of non-interest-bearing loans from member countries, with shares to be assessed on the basis of the U.N. scale of contributions. Interest-bearing loans for the balance of required funds will be guaranteed by nations who are parties to the treaty.

The high hurdle posed by the financial questions had thus been surmounted, and the delegates' attention turned to the few remaining issues. When the original president of the overall conference died in 1981, Tommy Koh was elected to the top post, partly in recognition of the work he had overseen in the financial arrangements. Although the United States eventually presented a long bill of particular objections to the text in its rationale for not signing the convention, these financial terms largely escaped U.S. criticism and survived into the final treaty.

Appendix 1: The Detailed Financial Arrangements Proposals

Table 2.1 contains the details of the various financial arrangements proposals offered at LOS conference sessions from 1977 to 1979. The entries in the columns are as follows.

Proposal and session (col. 1): Country or individual making the proposal and the LOS session during which it was made. If more than one proposal was offered by the same sponsor, the number following the proposal indicates its order in the sequence. An "A" following the number indicates a profit-sharing-based proposal; "B" indicates a royalty-only alternative.

Application fee (col. 2): Fee due with application (in millions of dollars).

Table 2.1 Summary of proposals

Proposal/ session	Application fee	Fixed charge	Royalty	ANP	Profit share	Depreciation	Enterprise funds
US-1A NY, 1977	$0.5 mm	—	—	20%	15% of low increment (0–25% return), 25% of medium increment (15–25% return), 50% of high increment (>25% return)	6 yr	10%
US-1B NY, 1977	$0.5 mm	—	2% years 1–10, 10% years 11–25	—	—	—	—
INDIA-1 NY, 1977	—	$60 mm	20% plus $5/ton of mined nodules	100%	60%, once 200% of investment is recovered	10 yr	—
EEC GEN, 1978	$0.1 mm	—	0.75%	20%	10% if return <10%, 18% if return 10–14%, 26% if return 14–18%, 34% if return 18–22%, 42% if return 22–26%, 50% if return 26–30%, 58% if return >30%	6 yr	—
JAPAN GEN, 1978	—	—	0.75%	20%	25% years 1–10, 50% years 11–25	10 yr	—

(continued)

Table 2.1, *continued*

Proposal/session	Application fee	Fixed charge	Royalty	ANP	Profit share	Depreciation	Enterprise funds
US-2 GEN, 1978	$0.5 mm	—	2%	20%	30% of low increment (0–7% return), 60% of medium increment (7–20% return), 70% of high increment (>20% return)	10 yr	—
INDIA-2 GEN, 1978	—	$60 mm	10%	100%	50% until 200% is recovered, 60% thereafter	10 yr	—
USSR GEN, 1978	—	—	7.5%	—	—	—	—
NORWAY-1A GEN, 1978	—	—	3% years 1–10, 5% years 11–25	50%	50% years 1–10, 80% years 11–25	10 yr	—
NORWAY-1B GEN, 1978	—	—	8% years 1–5, 10% years 6–25	50%	—	—	—
KOH-O GEN, 1978	—	—	—	—	—	—	33⅓%
NORWAY-2A NY, 1978	$0.5 mm	$1 mm/yr creditable against royalty	2% years 1–10, 4% years 11–25	40%	40% years 1–10, 75% years 11–25	10 yr	—
NORWAY-2B NY, 1978	$0.5 mm	$1 mm/yr creditable against royalty	7.5% years 1–10, 13% years 11–25	40%	—	—	—
KOH-1A NY, 1978	$0.5 mm	$1 mm/yr creditable against royalty	2% years 1–6, 4% years 7–12, 6% years 13–25	40%	40% years 1–6, 70% years 7–12, 80% years 13–25	10 yr	—
KOH-1B NY, 1978	$0.5 mm	$1 mm/yr creditable against royalty	7.5% years 1–6, 10% years 7–12, 14% years 13–25	—	—	—	—

KOH-2A GEN, 1979	$0.5 mm	$1 mm/yr creditable against royalty	2% in "1st period," 5% in "2nd period"	35%	45% in "1st period" (until 200% is recovered), 65% in "2nd period" (after 200% of investment is recovered)	10 yr	50%
KOH-2B GEN, 1979	$0.5 mm	$1 mm/yr creditable against royalty	8% years 1–10, 13.5% years 11–25	—	—	—	50%
NORWAY-3 NY, 1979	$0.5 mm	$1 mm/yr creditable against royalty	2% in "1st period," 4% in "2nd period"	20% in "1st period," 40% in "2nd period"	40% in "1st period" until 200% is recovered, 75% in "2nd period" (after 200% of investment is recovered), 25% in "1st period" until NPV of investment is 0 at 15% discount rate	10 yr	—
US/EEC/ JAPAN, NY, 1979	$0.5 mm	—	1% in "1st period," 2% in "2nd period"	20%	50% in "2nd period" (when NPV of investment is positive at a 15% discount rate)	10 yr	33⅓%
KOH-3A NY, 1979	$0.5 mm	$1 mm/yr creditable against royalty	2% in "1st period," 4% in "2nd period" if return is 15%	capital-cost ratio, 25% floor	35% of low increment (<10% return), 42.5% of medium increment (10–20% return); 50% of high increment (>20%) in "1st period" (until NPV of investment is 0 at	10 yr	50%

(continued)

Table 2.1, *continued*

Proposal/ session	Application fee	Fixed charge	Royalty	ANP	Profit share	Depreciation	Enterprise funds
KOH-3B NY, 1979	$0.5 mm	$1 mm/yr creditable against royalty	5% years 1–10, 12% years 11–25	—	10% real discount rate); 40% of low increment (<10% return), 50% of medium increment (10–20% return), 70% of high increment (>20% return) in "2nd period" (when NPV of investment is positive at 10% discount rate)	—	50%

Sources: US-1A and US-1B are from "Statement by Ambassador Elliot L. Richardson to the Committee I Chairman's Working Group of the Whole," June 3, 1977 (mimeo); INDIA-1 was presented by Minister Shanti Bhushan on June 6, 1977 (mimeo); Descriptions of EEC, JAPAN, US-2, USSR, NORWAY-1A, and NORWAY-1B can be found in Third United Nations Conference on the Law of the Sea, "Reports of the Committees and Negotiating Groups on Negotiations at the Seventh Session Combined in a Single Document both for the Purposes of Record and for the Convenience of Delegations," Geneva, May 19, 1978, pp. 49–52; NORWAY 2-A, NORWAY 2-B, KOH-1A, and KOH-1B can be found in Third United Nations Conference on the Law of the Sea, "Report by the Chairman of Negotiating Group 2 to the First Committee," NG2/10, New York, September 13, 1978, pp. 1–5; KOH-2A and KOH-2B can be found in Third United Nations Conference on the Law of the Sea, "Second Report to the First Committee by the Chairman of Negotiating Group 2 Ambassador T. T. B. Koh (Singapore)," A/CONF. 62/C.1/L.22 25 April 1979, pp. 1–5; NORWAY-3, US/EEC/JAPAN, KOH-3A, and KOH-3B are contained in "Report to the Working Group of 21 by Ambassador T. T. B. Koh of Singapore, Chairman of Negotiating Group 2," New York, August 1979, pp. 1–6.

Fixed charges (col. 3): Additional specified payments (in millions of dollars).
Royalty (col. 4): Percentage of the gross proceeds of the integrated mining-transportation-processing operation.
ANP (col. 5): "Attributable Net Proceeds" or the percentage of the profits of the integrated operation upon which profit-sharing payments are levied.
Profit share (col. 6): Percentage of the attributable net proceeds. Effective rate on integrated operations is the product of ANP and this figure.
Depreciation (col. 7): Time period for (straight line) recovery of investment costs (in years) for purposes of calculating net proceeds.
Enterprise funds (col. 8): Percentage of requirements of first operation of the Enterprise that will be furnished by cash grants or interest-free loans by member states. Balance of Enterprise requirements will be from loans guaranteed by member states.

Appendix 2: Description of the MIT Model

A team at MIT under the direction of Professor J. D. Nyhart prepared the report entitled "A Cost Model of Deep Ocean Mining and Associated Regulatory Issues" in March 1978.[14] The Marine Minerals Division of the Department of Commerce's National Oceanic and Atmospheric Administration (NOAA) initially supported the project through the Sea Grant Program. Later sponsors included the U.S. Treasury and State Departments. The LOS Secretariat gave some financial support in return for particular work. The EEC Secretariat also licensed the model for its own analyses. Nyhart and the team members originally intended to develop means for comparing the economic performance of a hypothetical deep ocean mining system under different conditions. The resulting model permitted quantitative comparison of varying assumptions on physical, engineering, financial, and regulatory conditions.

The model is patterned on a hypothetical consortium operating in the near-equatorial Pacific Ocean which mines 3 million tons of manganese nodules annually over a twenty-five-year commercial recovery period. The engineering for the systems and methods used by this consortium were chosen to be representative of what would be used by a consortium interested in the recovery of three metals—copper, nickel, and cobalt. The design, however, was not identical to the plans of any of the existing deep ocean mining consortia.

The aggregated cost estimates serve as input for the financial analysis section of the model, which generates cash flow projections for the life of the projects. The cash flow data form the basis for estimates of the investment returns on the operation and for projections of annual federal, state, and local tax revenues over the life of the project.

More than 75 percent of the cost estimates of equipment components were developed independently of the major industry consortia. However, an industry-government-university workshop was convened in March 1977 to review the model and the first draft of the study. The team evaluated many of the resulting suggestions, found them to be useful, and incorporated them into the subsequent version of the model, which in turn had the benefit of detailed review by workshop participants. The remainder of this appendix describes the version of the model that was used in the financial arrangements negotiating sessions.

In the baseline model, costs were grouped into four types: research and development, prospecting and exploration, capital, and operating expenses. Much investigation and analysis went into the values assigned to the input variables. The following table summarizes the four types of costs estimated for the baseline model.

Summary of Cost Estimates
(in millions of 1976 dollars)

Research and development	50.00
Prospecting and exploration	16.40
Capital investment	493.05
Total capital and operating expenses prior to commencing commercial recovery	559.45
Annual operating expenses	100.50

The prospecting and exploration costs of $16.4 million are composed of four expenses: prospecting cost, exploration labor costs for the research team, the cost of conducting the mapping survey, and the cost of conducting the survey for discrete samples of nodules and soil. These prospecting and exploration costs are allocated over time and used as an input for computation of annual cash flows, as are the (highly speculative) research and development funds.

The $493 million total capital investment in the ocean mining project divides into costs from the three major sectors of the cost model: mining, transportation, and processing. The following table shows the division of capital investment among the sectors and subsectors of the ocean mining project.

COURSE OF THE FINANCIAL NEGOTIATIONS

Allocation of Capital Costs: $493 million
(in millions of 1976 dollars)

Mining sector		Transport sector		Processing sector	
Platform	54	Sector costs	55	Equipment	199
Pipe handling	21			Utilities	84
Lift	9			Site	20
Power plant	7			Buildings	20
Navigation	5			Waste disposal	19
Subtotals	96		55		342
Total capital costs					493

The estimated annual operating costs for the ocean mining project of $100.5 million are also allocated among the mining, transportation, and processing sectors. The costs of each sector are further divided into the annual expenses for energy, labor, materials, fixed charges, and miscellaneous items. These costs are shown below.

Estimated Annual Operating Costs of the Baseline Model
(in millions of 1976 dollars)

Mining sector		Transport sector		Processing sector	
Energy	3.7	Energy	3.1	Energy	19.3
Labor	4.0	Labor	7.5	Labor	23.8
Materials	9.4	Materials	2.2	Materials	12.8
Fixed	3.0	Fixed	1.4	Fixed	6.8
Miscellaneous	1.1	Miscellaneous	0.7	Miscellaneous	1.9
Total annual operating cost					100.5

The project goes into commercial production in its sixth year. Its annual production and revenues from that point through the thirtieth year are as follows.

Annual Production and Revenue

Product	Annual production (lbs. $\times 10^6$)	Revenue ($\$ \times 10^6$)
Nickel	85.5	171.0
Copper	74.1	52.61
Cobalt	8.64	34.56
Manganese	0.0	0.0
Total annual revenue		258.17

Three measures of economic return were routinely provided: net present value (NPV), internal rate of return (IROR), and payback period. The NPV for different discount rates applied to the baseline case is shown below.

Net Present Values for
Baseline Case at Different Discount Rates
(NPV in millions of 1976 dollars)

Discount rate	8%	10%	12%	14%	16%	18%	20%	22%	24%
NPV	349.1	230	144.6	82.4	36.4	2.1	−23.9	−43.6	−58.77

The IROR for the baseline project is 18.14%. The payback period is 5.4 years.

The team expended a great deal of effort in providing estimates of the more than 150 main parameter values (or vectors of values) for the model's base case. Of course, a great deal of uncertainty surrounded many of these values. The report dealt with these uncertainties primarily by sensitivity analyses for individual variables or groups of variables. Project costs turned out to be particularly sensitive to metal price assumptions, ore grade, rate of ore recovery (and its component elements), indirect construction costs, water depth at the mine site, pump submergence depth, efficiency of separation of nodules from lift discharge, distance from port facility to processing plant and waste disposal site, use of U.S. ship construction facilities and crews, design assumptions on reliability (one mine ship or two; number of ore carriers), scheduling and delays, capital structure, level of depletion and depreciation allowances, and whether foreign or domestic tax treatment is allowed. Users of the model, of course, could provide their own input value assumptions. Although uncertainty pervaded discussions of the results, the model was explicitly deterministic; no formal means (such as Monte Carlo methods) were employed to analyze stochastic elements directly.

In its initial form, the model did not include provisions for payments to an eventual International Seabed Authority (nor was there a discussion of whether such payments would be creditable or deductible against domestic taxes). Subsequent analyses included such revenue-sharing effects, as well as differences in operation under the tax codes of various nations; likely differences between Enterprise and private operations with respect to tax status, banked site requirements, training obligations, and so forth; numerous refinements of parts of the basic model, particularly in the areas of transportation, processing, and waste disposal; and differences in legal organizational forms and in "venture types," such as pioneering, new entrant, or later joint venture. (Nyhart's group finished another revision of their model in 1981 after the financial discussions had effectively concluded. Some of these results are presented in Chapter 4.)

3 Elements of Agreement

3.0 Diverse Factors in Agreement

That such a negotiated compromise resulted from the politicized atmosphere of the Law of the Sea conference is remarkable; its relatively sophisticated provisions make the result even more so.[1] A number of factors contributed to the outcome. The informal mediation techniques used by Koh and Evensen in this fluid, multilateral context deserve a large share of credit. The use of a "single negotiating text" procedure was relevant. The financial arrangements were among a small number of issues on which the Group of 77 did not develop a common position; this may have added flexibility to the talks.

The cast of negotiators who handled the financial questions — Koh, Richardson, Evensen, and many others — was an extraordinary one in terms of intellectual capacity, experience, skill, and temperament. The personal relationships that developed as the conference continued ultimately proved quite important. In an atmosphere where the audiences for statements and positions were often outside political groups or home foreign ministries, the growth of personal familiarity and trust among numerous delegates as a result of many in-conference and out-of-conference contacts provided a basis for loosely binding commitments. In the earlier days of the conference it was not uncommon for a delegate to make one statement privately or in a small group, only to contradict it shortly thereafter in a formal statement. The later stages of the Negotiating Group 2 deliberations, however, saw greater mutual accountability of the delegates.

The sophisticated arrangements for the financial terms of contracts were heavily inspired by trends toward greater risk sharing in land contracts, some negative consequences of renegotiation of those contracts, and the virtual impossibility of renegotiation of the financial terms in an eventual LOS treaty. In the face of this difficult situation, the invention and acceptance of a new technical solution to these problems owed much to the time available and the educational aspects of the negotiations that Koh orchestrated.

The length of the financial negotiations (over two years) permitted the genuine diffusion of knowledge on the subject. The delegates who were most involved in the final deliberations were fully conversant with topics such as the time value of money, the risk analysis of investments, and the capital market access of international entities. Unlike the situation in many bilateral mineral negotiations, where provisions such as those in the LOS financial arrangements have proved difficult even to discuss, the multilateral quality of NG2 permitted provisions rejected by one party to reappear at the prompting of another. Although this quality of "reincarnation" of ideas made it difficult to dispose of some unhelpful notions, it also allowed some good ideas, even once denounced, to continue to play a part in the deliberations. The two-year life of these negotiations also permitted patterns of deference among the delegates to emerge. Based on perceived expertise and loyalty to group goals, these patterns enabled Koh to construct small negotiating groups whose agreements stood a good chance of larger group acceptance.

Three aspects of the financial arrangements negotiations merit special discussion as they relate to the process of reaching agreement in a large group. First, the use of the MIT model stands out and holds the promise of illuminating the role of outside information in multilateral negotiations. Second, a case can be made that agreement on the financial arrangements was facilitated by *differences* among the participants — in preferences, in forecasts and beliefs, in attitudes toward risk and toward time (discount rates) — rather than by similarities among them. Finally, the way in which different issues were combined — financial terms of contracts and Enterprise finance — created a potential for agreement where continued separate treatment might have precluded it, even among the identical groups of negotiators with their same sets of interests.

3.1 Use of an Outside Model

3.1.1 *Acceptance and Role of the Model*

The MIT cost model played an extensive role in the work of NG2. At a minimum, the model's widespread acceptance depended on perceptions of its independence, credibility, and accessibility.

Many NG2 negotiators accepted the study in part because they judged it to be independent. Several factors enhanced this perception: the model's extended and special construction procedure, the fact that it obviously was not designed for direct use by the conference (recall the model's assumption of a U.S. tax system and scant mention of the conference), as well as its reliance on outside sources for the bulk of its figures. The fact that its implications about seabed profitability fully pleased no delegation, though a fortuitous event, made broad acceptance easier.

The negotiators had a chance to assess for themselves the independence and competence of the model's builders on the neutral turf of the New York Quaker/Methodist seminar. The claims of the team appeared modest but firm. Criticism from all sides during the seminar and the nature of the team's responses simultaneously helped to build confidence in the technical credibility of the effort and to dispel the impression that the model was merely a partisan tool.

Conference members had full access to the documented version of the study, and a member of the MIT team was frequently present at the negotiating sessions in Geneva and New York to answer questions and run analyses. Although the model was primarily used by Koh, Evensen, and some members of the U.S. and EEC delegations, continued access to it in conjunction with its perceived technical competence and independence contributed greatly toward its broader acceptance.

The model was a vehicle for educating the negotiators. It provided a coherent framework in which to consider the myriad interacting factors affecting the economic and technical success of ocean mining. Sensitivity to general or sectorial inflation, to the range of equipment alternatives, to different quality and abundance of nodules, and to dozens of other variables could be and was readily queried.

The model also offered measures to evaluate the negotiations themselves, measures that supplied a precise language for the debate and that came to frame the issues in a clear, nonideological form. Of the economic indicators built into the model—the net present value at several discount rates, the internal rate of return, and the simple payback period—conference delegates began frequently to refer to the internal rate of return, or at least to its tortuous acronym, IROR. At the same time, the magnitude of payments to the Seabed Authority became a central measure of the international attractiveness of the proposals.

There were important limitations to the use of these two indicators, however. Since the model was deterministic, its point estimates of IROR and Authority payments did not reflect their inherent variability. As the sessions progressed, delegates became less and less satisfied with the baseline assumptions that early on had seemed to offer some certainty about the economic profile of this as yet unborn industry. Increasing challenges to the baseline results invoked several factors: the uncertain capital costs of a new high-technology venture proposed to operate for twenty or more years in a hostile physical environment; uncertain operating costs that depended on energy, chemical, and labor prices; and uncertain revenues that were at the mercy of notoriously volatile metal markets. Gradually, the apparent certainty that had attracted delegates to the study in the first place gave way to appreciation of the fact that uncertainty was inescapable. As a result, the negotiators began to turn their attention from payment schemes that were based on relatively fixed charges to more contingent methods that could be adapted to a variety of economic circumstances. While the specific numerical results of the model became less important, its structure and method for project evaluation (using discounted cash flow analysis) were increasingly important and ultimately influenced the shape of the final compromise.

When the model was perceived as independent of adversarial negotiation elements, it could more readily foster the communication and learning that pointed to mutually beneficial agreement. But whether real learning occurred or genuine joint gains in fact were found, negotiators could also use the model to escape frozen positions. A closer look at the way commitments to positions are made often reveals them to be conditional implicitly on the party's current information about issues and interests. Appeal to powerful norms of rationality by offering "new independent analysis" or "superior information" may unstick commitments and reduce the costs of movement. The treatment of Evensen's initial proposal at the MIT seminar, his subsequent trip to Cambridge, and his return with a new compromise proposal exemplified this facilitating role. Beyond a greater understanding of mining economics, Evensen could use the model as a reason for moving from his prior position without appearing to have been influenced by one or another partisan argument. Other delegates used this tactic with varying success.

Many future international conferences and negotiations will confront largely nontechnical participants with technical questions to be resolved in charged political contexts. The LOS experience suggests that outside analysis can be remarkably useful if certain conditions are met.[2] The reason that many academic and government seabed mining studies appeared to have little impact on the conference proceedings is perhaps that they were not perceived as relevant, competent, independent, or accessible for interpretation and modification. Avoiding these pitfalls, needless to say, is neither a necessary condition nor a guarantee of a study's use in a political setting.

It may be that the LOS need and the MIT study merely enjoyed a lucky confluence as long as the "parallel system" formula appeared to compromise the conflict between international and private exploitation of the seabed's "common heritage" resources. As long as this formula was maintained as a basis for agreement, negotiations could proceed over crucial subsidiary issues like the financial arrangements; the MIT model could offer an artificial common ground for proposals to be developed and tested, differences to be dovetailed by ingenious analysis, and disputants "convinced" to move to new-found accommodation. Yet the model could only function as a pragmatic tool within a larger, agreed-upon framework. The existence of the MIT model may even have deflected the minds of some delegates away from more fundamental differences that were latent in this framework and toward the less ideological questions that the model could handle. The resurgence of American misgivings about the entire parallel system/common heritage formula, however, not only signaled a reevaluation of policy but also pointedly reminded modelers of their derivative role.

3.1.2 Quantitative Dynamics of the Negotiations

Something of the dynamics of this emergent compromise can be seen in Figure 3.1. For a middle-range economic scenario of the MIT model, this chart displays the effects of different financial arrangements proposals on the internal rate of return (IROR) of a mining-transportation-processing venture.[3] These effects come from the reduction in the IROR that would be caused by imposing international revenue sharing. Only profit-plus-royalty schemes are shown, since most negotiating attention focused upon them.

Before NG2 was formed, two delegations offered highly divergent proposals. The pure profit-sharing U.S. proposal (point A) caused a small IROR drop, while the Indian suggestion (point B) would have reduced the return of the integrated project by almost two-thirds. Negotiating Group 2 was set up at the 1978 Geneva session, and Koh substantially restructured the text. His subsequent call for positions is reflected in the three somewhat more forthcoming proposals of the EEC (point C), Japan (point D), and the United States (point E). India (point F) also moved marginally from its position toward a more central range. Evensen's entry into the NG2 debate shows up as the last proposal (point G) of the 1978 Geneva session. With attention focused on this middle range, the negotiation could proceed apace.

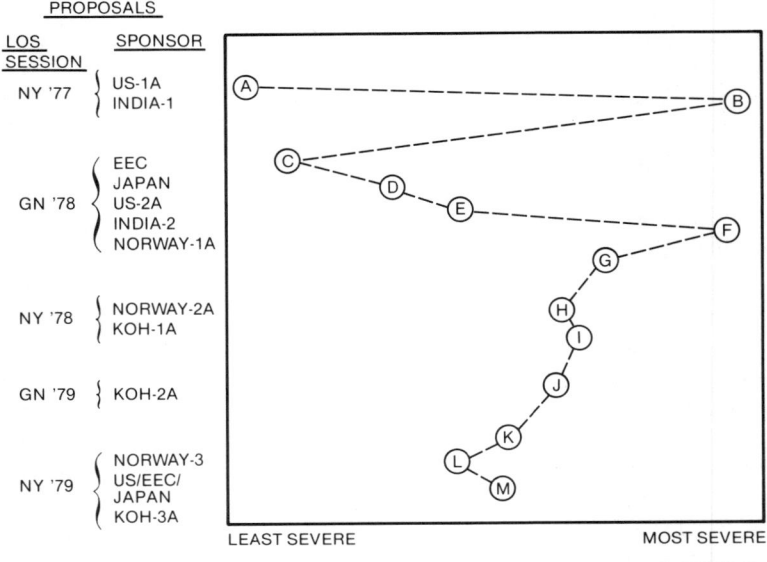

Figure 3.1 Bargaining dynamics: Financial terms of contracts

The MIT/Quaker/Methodist seminar took place during the 1978 New York session. Shortly thereafter, Minister Evensen made a trip to MIT. Upon his return, he offered his new proposal (point *H*), with a much milder negative effect on the project's economic return. Here Evensen was true to his usual style of moving step by step toward his perception of a compromise. The support he seemed to garner by this proposal enabled Koh, for the first time, to offer his own specific numbers. Koh's proposal (point *I*) verged somewhat more toward the Indian position than did Evensen's.

The 1979 Geneva session saw little overt movement but a greatly deepened appreciation of the issues of the time value of money, uncertainty and risk aversion in project evaluation, the ANP determination, and Enterprise finance. Koh modified his proposal somewhat (point *J*), but a serious impasse persisted on the financial terms. Despite the session's discouraging rhetoric, Figure 3.1 seems to show clear possibilities of reconciliation within an emerging zone of agreement.

In the 1979 New York negotiations, Evensen offered a third compromise (point *K*). The EEC, Japan, and the United States pulled back from earlier positions, with a qualitatively different sharing structure and lower percentages (point L). In conjunction with the Enterprise finance issue (on which Section 3.3 focuses), Koh put forth an intensively negotiated "final compromise" (point M). This compromise survives in the treaty text.

The chart appears to show the evolution of a genuine negotiation conducted by a single text procedure, once the bargaining range was suitably narrowed, in this case, by Evensen's first proposal (point G). From that point on, the pattern appears as incremental bargaining toward a central solution. This one-dimensional measure of the proposals' economic effects does not show the considerable risk differences among them, however, nor does it reflect the intense legal and political character of the ANP debate. Different economic cases would yield different graphic values of offers and counteroffers, but only relatively extreme cases show qualitatively different patterns. It is perhaps worth noting that the negotiators themselves did not appear to use such a schema directly in evaluating their proposals. It is also interesting that the chart seems to reveal a *bilateral* structure of offers and counteroffers in a negotiation that was quite multilateral in character. Identifying the predominant players as "North" and "South" (including two mediators) seems warranted on the basis of this graphic representation.

3.2 Agreement as the Result of Differences

Suppose that a vegetarian and a carnivore each know the other's habits and are trying to divide a quantity of meat and vegetables. Differences in their relative preferences for the same items should render agreement easy. It would hardly be useful for the vegetarian to attempt to convince the carnivore of the desirability of vegetables, or vice versa. Seeking a common ground of preference or interest in this manner could be self-defeating. Agreement can be fashioned as a result of the difference.

Negotiations by countries over disputed lands are often thought of as archetypical zero-sum confrontations. Such bargaining is typically seen as an adversarial exercise in boundary drawing, with the presumption that one side's gain is the other's loss. Roger Fisher and William Ury, however, offer a twist to such an interpretation when they cite the Egyptian-Israeli negotiations over the disputed Sinai. Over and over again, their negotiators drew maps with different boundary lines to apportion the Sinai between the two countries. If Egypt really wanted sovereignty and Israel were primarily interested in security, however, a clever agreement might "unbundle" these differentially valued attributes and give each side its most valued attribute (sovereignty or security). In fact, a method for achieving this result involved the creation of a demilitarized zone under the Egyptian flag, thereby giving Egypt sovereignty and Israel security.[4] Of course, searching for creative ways to unbundle differentially valued attributes is only a variant on the use of preference differences. When such differences are discovered, however, they can serve as the raw material for agreements.

Section 3.3 illustrates the role of such preference differences in reaching the accords on financial arrangements. It examines how the North and South each valued the terms of contracts relative to the Enterprise finance issue in a manner that led to resolution of both questions.

Other differences facilitated the subsidiary agreement on the financial terms of contracts. The next subsection develops the proposition that creative dovetailing of differences in beliefs, risk attitudes, and time preference offered the NG2 negotiators possibilities for impasse-breaking joint gains. Furthermore, the MIT model proved useful in bringing out such differences and pointed to ways for their use.

3.2.1 Differences in Probabilities

If the owner of an investment property believes that its price will go down and a potential buyer thinks it will rise, the resulting sale is facilitated by the difference in probability assessments, or beliefs about the uncertain event. In the LOS negotiations there was a sharp divergence of opinion about the likely profitability of seabed mining. Despite the widely discussed results of the MIT model, many G-77 delegates seemed to believe that mining would prove enormously profitable (if its accounts could be accurately monitored). Representatives from developed countries saw less chance of such an outcome, consistently projecting relatively more modest returns. Delegates frequently articulated these views in the NG2 discussions.

The negotiated outcome in effect used this difference creatively, with relatively low rates (a 2 percent royalty and 35 percent tax rate) applying for low-success projects, and high rates (a 4 percent royalty and 70 percent marginal profit share) applying to very successful operations. This contingent arrangement is analogous to a bet on seabed profitability that could be set up as a result of forecast differences.

When the delegates restricted their deliberations to finding a single schedule, either the industrialized countries found its rates too high or the developing countries criticized them as too low. Without a contingent approach, the rates for a noncontingent or single schedule proved difficult or impossible to negotiate. Rather than denying the uncertainty of seabed mining by trying to pick a single set of rates, however, the compromise scheme adapted to it in a way that all sides saw as advantageous given their different expectations about the future. The developed countries seemed to expect a modest level of profits; accordingly, the high rates that apply for bonanza projects were not much of a concession. Many developing countries professed to expect high profits; agreeing to low rates of sharing for normal profit levels was no great concession. Giving each side an advantage for the outcome it thinks most likely is the principle behind the use of probability differences.

One might reasonably inquire whether using differences in probabilities to fashion agreements will favor the side with apparently "better" forecasts or more information. In the LOS case, the views of each side were formed after hearing the other's views and discussing the MIT analysis. Despite the commonality introduced by the model, wide room remained for divergent opinions. (Of course, deliberate misrepresentation is always a possibility for one side or the other. Had the announced probability beliefs been reversed, however, agreement on a single system of higher rates should have proved fairly easy.) If, however, the divergence of opinion persisted after full discussion and access to similar information, why not use it to help fashion a settlement?

The participants knew that as the profit uncertainties were resolved, the nodule regime would have to withstand pressures generated by any seeming unfairness in the workings of the financial arrangements scheme. Thus, delegates had to consider likely perceptions of ex post fairness. Rate schedules involving, say, no royalty and a 5 percent profit share for low- or medium-profit operations and a 20 percent royalty and a 95 percent profit share for successful projects would contain the seeds of their own destruction, even if they accorded strictly with the parties' ex ante probability beliefs. Use of different probability distributions to fashion agreement should be intelligent, and appropriate consideration should be given to the relationship of the parties after the uncertainty is resolved.

3.2.2 Differences in Risk Aversion

A second difference among the participants may have involved differences in attitude toward risk. Seabed divisions of mining firms would be investing large sums relative to their corporate assets. In particular, the managers of these divisions would likely have a stronger concern with "low-end" protection from the effects of high, relatively fixed taxes than with the tax effects if the mining projects proved very successful. This group could be said to be risk-averse. On the other side, the international coalition of more than 150 countries would likely receive modest shares of seabed revenue relative to their national incomes. Arguably, this group should be concerned with maximizing the *expected* amount of seabed revenue they could receive, rather than ensuring for themselves a smaller amount. They could be said to be more neutral toward the variability in income streams from operations. A system that offers low-end protection to the miners in return for much higher rates on successful projects would use this difference in risk preferences among the parties.

A straightforward chain of reasoning suggests a rationale for a coalition to act relatively more neutral toward risk than would its individual members. Consider one person's decision to accept or turn down a lottery with a one-half chance at winning a certain amount of money and a one-half chance at losing a possibly different amount. The decision obviously would depend on the magnitudes of the gain and loss, the state of the person's finances, and his or her attitude toward risk. Figure 3.2 displays such lotteries for a range of gains and losses.[5] The horizontal axis measures the magnitude of the gain; the vertical axis shows the size of the loss. A point on the graph, say *AB*, represents a lottery with a one-half chance at winning an amount *A* and a one-half

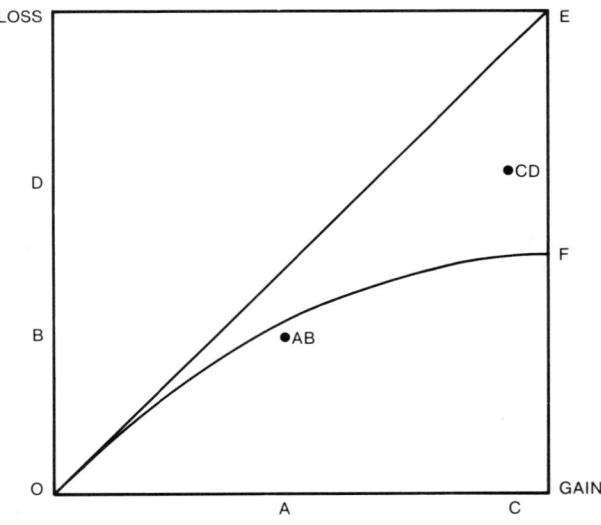

Figure 3.2 Risk sharing

chance at losing an amount of magnitude B. Each point in the rectangle represents such a lottery, with the horizontal component indicating the gain and the vertical component showing the possible loss.

The diagonal running from the southwest corner to the northeast corner of the graph represents the set of lotteries with equal gains and losses (since the horizontal and vertical components of points on the diagonal are equal). The "expected" or actuarial value of these lotteries is zero, given the same chance at equal losses or gains. Someone who acts according to expected value would be indifferent about accepting any lottery on the diagonal, would accept lotteries below the diagonal (which have greater gains than losses), and would reject those lotteries represented by points above the diagonal (which have greater losses than gains). Many people would be risk-averse; that is, to accept a lottery with the risk of a large loss, they would require an even larger possible gain. A risk-averse individual might divide the set of such lotteries into acceptable and unacceptable ones, as indicated by the curve below the diagonal in Figure 3.2: acceptable lotteries would be below the curve, unacceptable ones would be above it. For low gains or losses, such a person might be relatively neutral toward risk (that is, would act in accord with expected value or be willing to "play the odds"). To accept lotteries with the chance of higher losses, however, would require the lure of more than proportionately higher gains (implying greater risk aversion).

The same risk-averse individual would not accept the lottery indicated by point CD, since it is above the curve (the possible losses are too large for the gains). If, however, there were two individuals whose attitudes toward such lotteries were captured by this same curve, it is intriguing to ask whether the pair would ever accept the lottery that each of them would reject individually. The answer is yes, since they could divide the CD lottery into two component lotteries, each with half the gains and half the losses. Each of the two individuals would be willing to accept an AB lottery, which has exactly half the gains and losses of CD. With respect to lottery CD, the pair could happily act more risk-neutral, less risk-averse, or more as if the diagonal described their attitudes toward risk than could either of the single individuals. The more the lottery can be divided, the closer the resulting sublotteries fall in a region where the individuals are closer to risk neutrality. Arrow and Lind have shown that this result generalizes quite nicely to a large group of individuals, even if they have different attitudes toward risk.[6]

In the case of seabed mining under the LOS treaty, the miners would share revenues with a large group of countries. In return for bearing more of the risk of fluctuating revenue shares, the international community—which should be relatively risk-neutral—could expect a higher return. In exchange for protection from high taxes at the "low end"—when there is substantial risk associated with the operation (that the investment itself plus its opportunity cost will go unrecovered) —the more risk-averse miners should be willing to offer a greater sharing rate when higher profits are assured. When the second schedule of the payment system is triggered, the investment (cumulated forward with 10 percent real interest) will have been recovered, signaling a substantial reduction in the original perceived risk of the project. The higher sharing rates that would thereby be triggered in effect serve as a contingent "premium" against the risk of high rates on unsuccessful projects. Thus, this scheme profitably dovetails the parties' different risk attitudes.

3.2.3 Differences in Time Preference

The financial compromise also reflected different attitudes toward the passage of time. The companies would evaluate their investment decisions using private, after-tax discount rates. Sovereign nations that would receive their income shares before taxes, that were expressly trying to create an enduring system, and that in the negotiations frequently voiced concern about the welfare of future generations might evaluate the revenue streams using relatively lower discount rates. A sharing system whose rates rise over time, giving a higher proportion of the early money to companies who then value it the most and much higher amounts later to the international community, offers a creative use of such differences. Although this is hardly an argument for social optimality, it does offer a way to reach agreement that builds on what was an often-articulated variation in time preference. Public/private negotiations often exhibit this characteristic.

By requesting and examining simulations of the MIT model, some delegates became rather good at analyzing which factors decisively influenced the companies' rates of return and which ones affected the timing and amounts of the payments to the Authority. In the words of a former U.S. negotiator, "It should be noted, however, that the idea of raising the figures over time was in part based on the MIT analysis, which gives far greater weight to dollars paid earlier than to those paid later in the contract. By raising the royalty rate over time, the Chairman—in a constructive attempt to combine Western economics and Group of 77 politics—has created a system which requires the lowest payments at the greatest time of risk and the highest payments in the cheapest dollars."[7]

ELEMENTS OF AGREEMENT

3.2.4 Agreement from Dovetailed Differences

At least three possible differences thus potentially divided the international community and the would-be miners of the deep seabed. Remarkably, however, these differences complemented each other in pointing to a similar resolution of the contractual terms. As described in Section 2.5, the chosen system employs tax rates that increase with the economic success of the project over time (its accumulated present value) and annually (its yearly return on investment).

First, the scheme with a high and a low payment schedule offered joint gains once the different profit expectations of the parties were taken into account. The terms of the contingent agreement, however, show a pragmatic concern for the future relationship between the parties: whether high, low, or medium profits come about, the sharing scheme should appear to be fair.

Second, the projects would pay taxes on a relatively low schedule as long as the invested funds were still at risk; a significantly higher schedule would come into effect after investment and interest charges were recovered. This arrangement takes advantage of the apparently higher risk aversion of companies (whose mining investments would be significant in relation to corporate assets) than that of the international "syndicate" of recipient countries (whose revenue shares would be modest relative to their national incomes). In return for "insurance" against the risk of high tax rates on marginal projects, companies in effect would pay an attractive (contingent) "premium" in the form of stiffer charges on very successful operations.

Finally, since the profitability of normal projects is expected to increase with the passage of time, the higher schedules would come into effect later. Thus, an expressed difference in time preferences (or discount rates) is recognized by allowing the companies to get more earlier, and the International Authority to get much more later on.

Thus these three factors — belief, risk attitude, and time preference — which often could imply divisive conflict in negotiations were implicitly dovetailed by means of an agreement that is more sophisticated than traditional approaches. (Chapter 5 elaborates these ideas in considerably more detail.)

3.3 Combining Issues

Until the 1979 Geneva session, delegates effectively separated the question of Enterprise finance as a negotiating issue from the bargaining over the financial terms of contracts. Many G-77 members conceptually linked the two issues, however, as a result of their desire to finance the Enterprise from private contractors' financial payments. The only prior national proposal whose provisions dealt simultaneously with the two issues was the 1977 U.S. proposal. It suggested that up to 10 percent of the cost of the Enterprise's first project be contributed in cash by states ratifying the treaty. With this sum in hand, the U.S. sponsors argued, the Enterprise could secure the balance of its monetary requirements through loans. Six delegations made proposals (two Indian proposals, another U.S. proposal, and one each from the EEC, Japan, and Norway) concerning the financial terms of contracts before anyone again approached the question of Enterprise finance. At the first 1978 session, held in Geneva, Koh suggested a one-third cash contribution (without simultaneously making a recommendation on the financial terms of contracts). Indeed, the subsequent New York session passed without new Enterprise finance proposals; it was not until the 1979 Geneva session that the two issues were generally seen as linked in a bargaining sense. It is quite probable that no settlement could have been reached on either issue had delegates continued to consider them separately. Virtual impasse threatened each issue.

Ultimately, Koh suggested a level of 50 percent cash contributions for the Enterprise's initial requirements, a proposal that many industrialized countries declared unacceptable. By the 1979 New York negotiations, the United States, the EEC, and Japan appeared to pull back from their earlier financial proposals while tacitly agreeing to Koh's earlier one-third cash contribution proposal. The compromise outcome ultimately involved relatively flexible financial terms, with the first Enterprise operation to be half financed with cash contributions. Figure 3.3 displays the sequence of Enterprise finance proposals.

If the schematic of Enterprise finance proposals is overlaid on the pattern of financial terms proposals, the lack of connection of the two issues until the 1979 Geneva session becomes immediately evident (Figure 3.4). From that session on, delegates considered the two issues together. The proposals on financial terms pull toward the Northern countries' preferred side (left side of the chart); the Enterprise finance proposals move in line with Southern preferences (on the right side). This reduction of the negotiation to two simple dimensions, of course, suppresses many important economic considerations (for example, risk) and political considerations (for example, ANP).

This joint pattern illustrates the principle that combination of issues may create a joint zone of possible agreement even where separate resolutions of the issues might be impossible. For this result to occur, it is usually necessary that the parties differ in their relative preferences

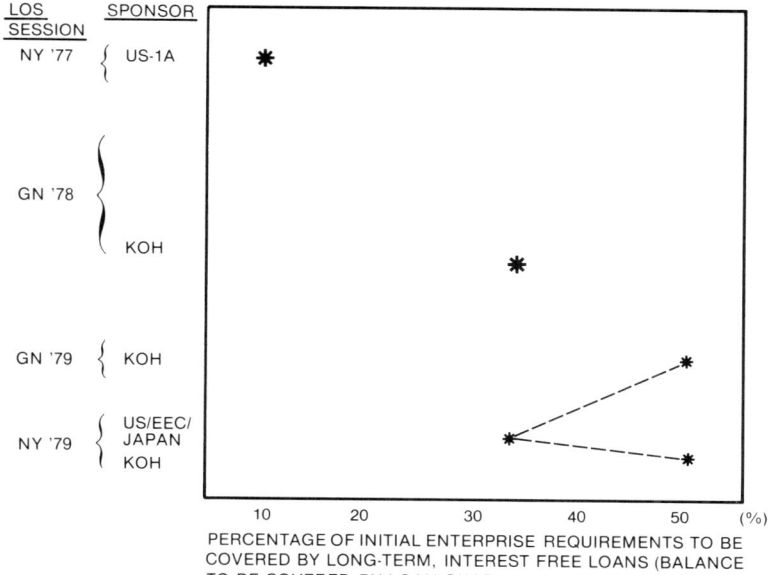

Figure 3.3 Bargaining dynamics: Financing of the Enterprise

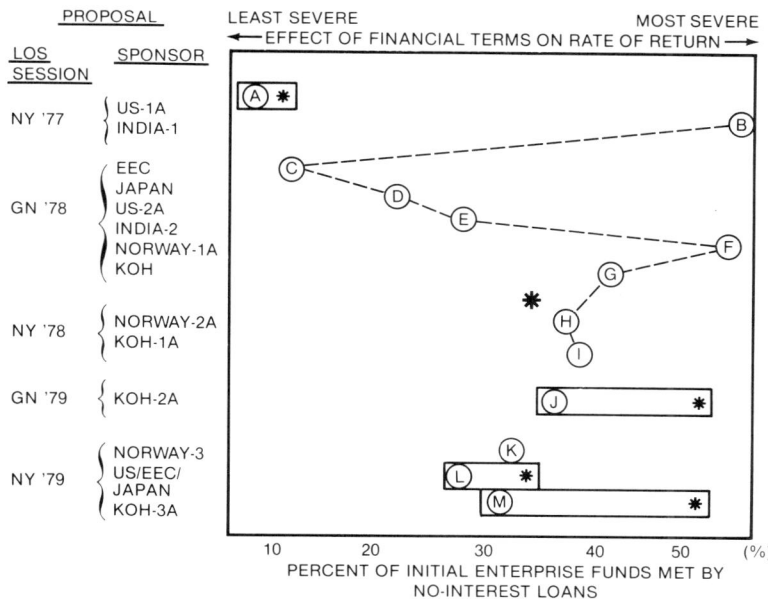

Figure 3.4 Bargaining dynamics: Financial terms and Enterprise finance

NEGOTIATING THE LAW OF THE SEA

for the items under discussion (as was the case in the earlier vegetarian/carnivore and Egypt/Israel examples). Figure 3.5 offers a highly simplified abstraction as analogous to what occurred with these issues in NG2. Here, a stylized less developed country (LDC) and developed country (DC) bargain over two issues, the financial terms of contracts (issue 1) and Enterprise finance (issue 2).

Issue 1 poses a simple choice between a flexible or a rigid system. Illustrative subjective payoffs to each side as a result of agreement on either alternative are indicated. The payoffs are set with reference to a "no-agreement" alternative in which each party's payoff is zero. Clearly, relative to the no-agreement status quo, the LDC would always block a flexible system and the DC would never agree to a rigid system. By itself, no agreement on financial terms could be forged.

Issue 2 requires the parties to agree on a value of, say, X, which can range from zero to three. The DC "pays" X and the LDC "receives" X in the form of Enterprise finance. The DC's payoff is minus X and the LDC's is X. Again, if this is considered as a single issue, the DC would always block a settlement at any positive value of X, considering its alternative of zero at the status quo.

A combination of issues 1 and 2, say a flexible system with X equal to two, obviously generates a zone of possible agreement. In this particular settlement the DC gets a total of one (plus three for flexibility, minus two for X) as does the South (minus one for flexibility, plus two for X). Each party is better off with such a settlement than with a failure to agree. In fact, any settlement on flexibility with X ranging from one to three is better than the status quo. The issues, insoluble separately, can be combined to realize joint benefits.

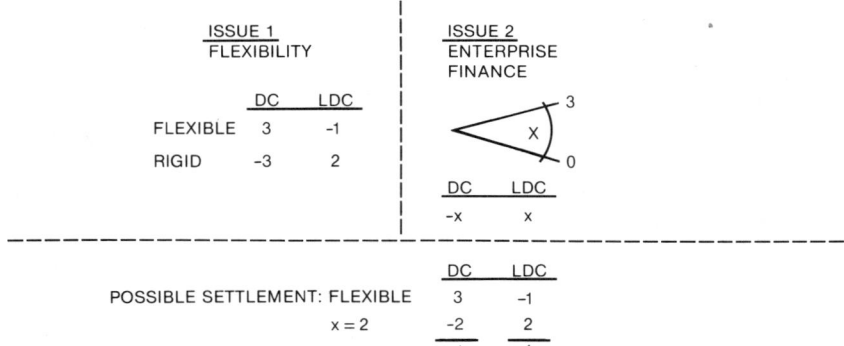

Figure 3.5 Combining issues: Stylized example

ELEMENTS OF AGREEMENT

Figure 3.6 shows the value of possible settlements to each player on a pair of axes. The origin—point O, coordinates (0,0)—represents the value to each player of the status quo without agreement. Points in this plane correspond to subjective values of particular settlements of the issues. No interpersonal comparisons of value are required, only each side's valuation of a proposed settlement relative to that side's valuation of no agreement. Both players are better off with a proposed settlement only if it falls in the northeast quadrant; all other points would be opposed by at least one of the parties, which could do better without agreement.

By itself, the "rigid" alternative gives the DC minus three and the LDC plus two. It is located at (−3,2) in the northwest quadrant. Similarly, the "flexible" choice is at (3,−1) in the southeast quadrant. Possible settlements of issue 2 are represented by points along the solid line segment OA in the northwest quadrant, from the origin (where X equals zero, the amount each side gets without agreement) to the point where X equals three, where the DC gives three ("gets" minus three) and the LDC gets three.

Only points in the northeast quadrant offer both the DC and the LDC gains over the status quo. Singly, no settlement of either issue offers such a northeast point. But if the two issues are joined together (done graphically by attaching the lower end of the solid line to either the "rigid" or "flexible" points, as in Figure 3.7), a possible solution is evident on the hatched segment in the northeast quadrant, corresponding to the "flexible system with X negotiated anywhere from one

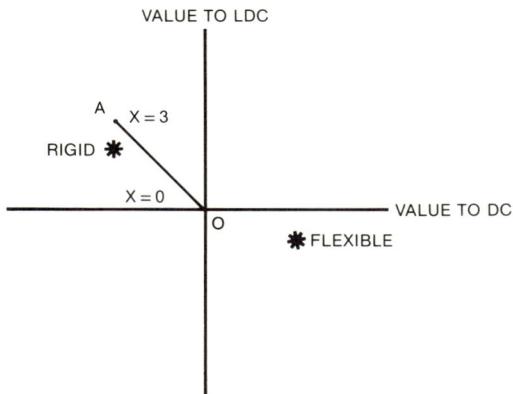

Figure 3.6 Combining issues: Graphic representation

NEGOTIATING THE LAW OF THE SEA

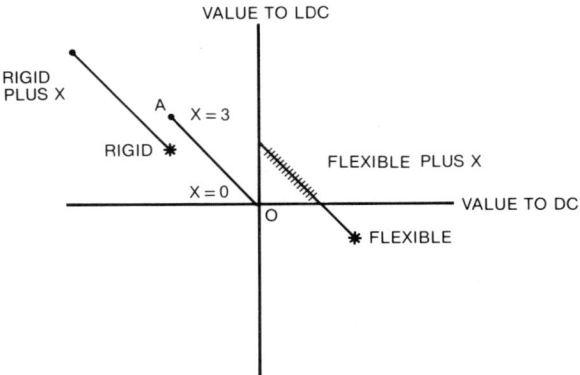

Figure 3.7   Graphic combination of issues

to three" choices. Points on this segment (representing jointly beneficial solutions) are thus created from individually unacceptable points.[8]

This stylized argument illustrates the point that the structure of the negotiations and the separation or combination of issues can critically affect the results. It is sometimes implied that the outcome of a negotiation is due to the underlying "interests" or relative "power" of the participants. Although these factors are certainly relevant, the organization of the negotiations can also be critical. Regardless of interests or power, separate negotiation in this simple example would preclude beneficial agreement. (In fact, this analysis suggests that effective separation of LOS issues first into different committees and then into essentially autonomous negotiating groups, while possibly critical for managing the complexity involved, could have reduced the opportunity for beneficial compromise.)

When policy is formulated across several issues, or when "bottom lines" are drawn for negotiating purposes, the decisions are often made on an issue-by-issue basis. What appears incontestably to be an "unacceptable" settlement on this or that issue may be quite acceptable when combined with favorable settlements on other questions. Of course, only a more senior official concerned with the overall negotiations would be most likely to concur with this conclusion. A policy formulation system in which different entities, say the Commerce, State, and Defense Departments, are primarily concerned with different sets of issues may result in the drawing of bottom lines that prevent a settlement with acceptable overall utility. If integration of the issues is supposed to occur at a higher governmental level, but only contested

ELEMENTS OF AGREEMENT

issues are the subject of higher-level decision, the process may unduly restrict the range of possible settlements that would be found acceptable to higher officials.

This simple example also suggests that if a negotiation proceeds *sequentially* to resolve issues, this may lead to an impasse. For example, an early agreement on a rigid system would not be compatible with any bargained value of X (northwest quadrant of Figure 3.7). This may be one of the reasons why a "single negotiating text" procedure (used at Camp David as well as in the LOS conference) often proves useful. The conventional alternative of making incremental concessions from far-apart positions in the hope of stimulating reciprocal concessions, but without knowing where the final settlement will lie, risks impasse by settling the "wrong" issues first.

Of course, this argument does not suggest that one should always combine issues in a negotiation. Figure 3.8 displays the utility values of two dichotomous issues, A and B, which may be settled between two parties, say, DC and LDC (again). Issue A may be settled as A' or A''; issue B may be similarly resolved into B' or B''. Both sides would prefer A' or A'' to the no-agreement alternative represented by the origin. LDC would prefer B' and DC would prefer B''. But if the two issues are combined (coordinate values added for DC and LDC), and if resolution

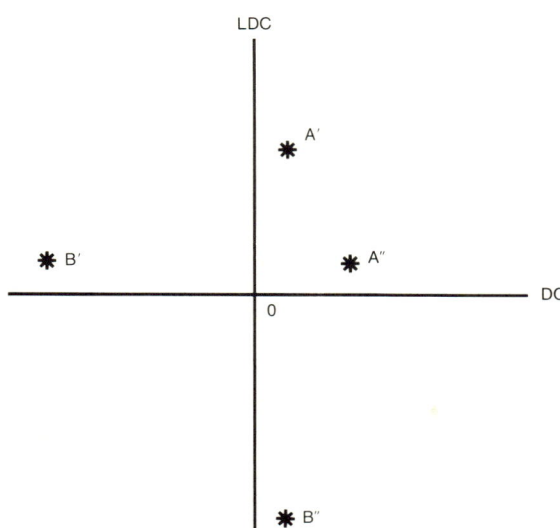

Figure 3.8 Separate discontinuous issues

NEGOTIATING THE LAW OF THE SEA

of each issue is required, none among the four outcomes, $A'B'$, $A'B''$, $A''B'$, or $A''B''$ (Figure 3.9), lies in the northeast quadrant. (This conclusion need not be altered by including the possibility of randomizations between the joint outcomes. These are shown by dashed lines in Figure 3.9.) Agreement here would be precluded by combining the two issues, since each outcome of issue B, while mildly preferred by one of the parties, is sufficiently disliked by the other to preclude any joint settlement. The parties are better off limiting their negotiations to issue A, or separating the two without a requirement of joint settlement.

The combination of the financial terms of contracts issue (of relatively greater concern to the North) and the Enterprise finance question (relatively more important to the South) may well have been decisive in creating the possibility of a settlement. When the two were effectively joined, a zone of agreement opened that did not seem possible when the issues were negotiated separately. The previous stylized example suggests a mechanism by which this could have occurred. Independently of the LOS case, it suggests reasons that the structure of negotiations, the creative association or dissociation of issues, and the order of settlement may be critical. This may explain some of the advantages of a single negotiating text as well as suggesting that the process of defining bottom lines (negotiating instructions)

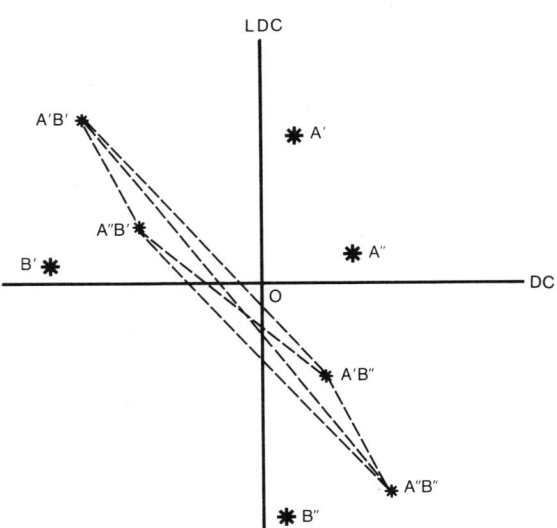

Figure 3.9 Adding issues to destroy possible zones of agreement

should focus on whole packages, not just single issues that are contested by different bureaucratic entities. (Chapter 6 elaborates these ideas and extends them to the "addition" and "subtraction" of negotiating parties as well.)

3.4 Summary

Within the Law of the Sea negotiations, the task of constructing a regime for mining manganese nodules involved a large group with divergent interests and ideologies dealing with contentious and uncertain issues. That a settlement was reached at all is remarkable; that its terms are fairly sophisticated is intriguing. Regardless of the overall treaty's fate, the financial arrangements may influence future bilateral mineral contracts on land as well, perhaps as deliberations on regimes to govern other, arguably "common" resources.

Intense use of the oceans, conflicting claims, and inadequate law were among the factors that led to a new LOS conference and the inclusion of nodules on its agenda. Compromise between preferences for international and private exploitation of the seabed's "common heritage" resources produced the parallel system within which the financial arrangements were negotiated. Numerous divergencies in political philosophy and substantive interest, along with the fundamental uncertainties of mining and the difficulty of renegotiation, complicated the negotiators' task. Trends in Third World mineral contracts — greater risk sharing, costly renegotiation, and the desire for effective "control" of natural resources — offered at least some guidance in how the mega-mineral contract at hand was to be negotiated.

Tracing the negotiations themselves brought out a number of points. From initially disparate positions, a set of negotiating dimensions gradually emerged. More or less incremental bargaining could then take place. Graphic analysis revealed the extent to which this multilateral negotiation could usefully be regarded as bilateral.

Koh had difficulty identifying the key people in a large group, convincing them that certain ideas might engender consensus, and then seeking to build an atmosphere in which commitments could be made. His mediation techniques ranged from requesting "positions" (a questionable tactic), to operating an intensive informal process in tandem with the larger group, to building momentum in a variety of ways. The evolution of key textual provisions followed a common path: small group invention, modification, testing, large group familiarization, passage into conventional wisdom, legitimation, and inclusion in the draft. Evensen's dramatic entry into the NG2 deliberations and his subsequent proposals toward compromise complemented Koh's efforts.

The financial negotiations suggested the proposition that differences among participants — in values, in attitudes toward time and risk, and in forecasts of the future — may be the ingredients for agreement rather than a source of bargaining friction. The MIT model helped to highlight such factors and held out the possibility of joint gain from their sophisticated use.

Finally, the artful combination or dissociation of separate issues, along with the order of settlement of issues, proved critical to the negotiated outcome. These observations suggest lessons for the manner of preparing for negotiations and forming bottom lines, and they offer clues as to why the use of a single text may be a fruitful procedure.

Here, then, was a complex negotiation that did not proceed in ignorance. Rather, the deliberations of dozens of delegates from various foreign, mining, and finance ministries constituted a lengthy mutual education process. A great deal of information was exchanged, and a powerful computer tool was generally available to analyze proposals, to help invent new ones, and to lay out implications for the parties' economic interests. While pure bargaining necessarily took place in tandem with analytic investigation, it is hard to imagine more elements of rationality injecting themselves into such a negotiating process among so many nations. Yet this rationality could only produce lasting results within a larger, agreed structure. As it began to fracture, even the most carefully contrived subsidiary agreement, replete with modeling-inspired joint gains, could not sustain consensus.

The financial deliberations illustrate a series of propositions about negotiations. These propositions, once suggested, may be developed independently and applied far beyond their original context. Part II of this book undertakes this general task. Before embarking on that elaboration, however, it is instructive to step back and examine the course of the overall LOS conference.

4 Disagreement in the Large: Explanation and Evaluation

4.0 A Framework for Negotiation Analysis

Detailed examination of the financial deliberations yielded a number of observations about the elements of negotiated agreement. In order to concentrate on this part of the LOS conference, however, the preceding chapters merely sketched the major forces leading to the overall negotiations, the place of the financial issues in the parallel system, and the relationship between the seabed and nonseabed regimes. In effect, an analytic circle was tightly drawn around the NG2 deliberations, maintaining the larger factors in the background along with the complex bureaucratic politics among the many interests that make up each national "side."[1]

Agreement in the small, however, gave way to disagreement in the large. Elliot Richardson's assessment that it was "all but certain" that the text would be ready for signing in 1981 hardly foreshadowed Ronald Reagan's resounding rejection of virtually the same treaty two years later. This chapter provides an account of the radical switch in the expressed U.S. stance toward the LOS negotiations.

An explanation of this nature can be greatly aided by an analytic framework. Although the financial arrangements discussion suggested elements of such an approach, a fuller set of considerations offers more power to the analysis. This chapter proceeds, therefore, by sketching a simple framework for explaining the results of negotiations.[2] It then traces the broad evolution of U.S. negotiating strategy toward the LOS conference up to the point where agreement appeared likely. Examining the shape of the proposed treaty brings its central elements—a trade-off between navigational freedoms and the regime for seabed resources — into sharper focus. The elements of the Reagan policy may then be conceptually disentangled and evaluated both in substance and for their implications about negotiation analysis.

To make sense of a negotiation, one must obviously understand the structure of the parties' *interests*. If a side is monolithic — that is, if it has no internal divisions — this task is equivalent to specifying its utility function, or the ways in which trade-offs among the various interests will be made. In negotiations over erecting a building, the relevant attributes may be cost, time, and quality; in a more complex setting, the interests may include less tangible aspects such as precedent, reputation, and the relationship among the parties. When individuals or groups with different concerns nonetheless constitute a negotiating "side," it is no longer possible in general to specify an overall utility function; however, carefully tracking which set of interests is ascendant in the internal bargaining continues to provide insight. In short, a sophisticated conception of the interests in a negotiation constitutes basic data for analysis. It is often important to distinguish parties' underlying interests from the *issues* under negotiation, on which positions or stands are often taken.

Parties generally engage in negotiation with the expectation that their interests will be better served by a joint agreement than by the unilateral alternatives each side would pursue in the case of no-agreement.[3] This observation focuses central attention on the parties' perceived *alternatives to a negotiated agreement*. The extent to which no-agreement serves a party's interests provides the benchmark against which any proposed agreement must be compared. The more favorably that negotiators perceive and portray their best alternative course of action — whether this means a course that is less costly, more efficient, less risky, with earlier benefits, with more desirable linked attributes (such as reputation) or fewer undesirable ones (such as bad precedents) — the smaller is their ostensible need for the negotiations and the higher the standard of value that any proposed accord must reach to be acceptable.

Alternatives to agreement may take many forms: they may have one attribute or many; they may be certain or uncertain; they may be static or changing; they may be unilateral or coalitional; they may involve simply walking away from the negotiation to an independent status quo ante; or they may critically depend on moves and countermoves among the original negotiators as it becomes clear that no-agreement will result. A tactical and strategic commonality cuts across these possible characteristics of alternatives; that is, at any point comparison of the expected utility of agreement with that of no-agreement can heavily influence the way a party will act in the negotiations. Careful monitoring of bargainers' perceived unilateral alternatives — which, of course, may be hazy and in conflict — suggests the limits of any joint action and thus implies the zone of possible agreement.

The lure of negotiations, of course, lies in the prospect of doing better than the alternatives. It is therefore crucial to understand the basis for joint gains from cooperation and to envision possible agreements. In some cases negotiators want the same result, and their mere agreement has the power to produce it. Acting in accord with a shared vision, ideology, or norm of equity may sometimes provide the basis for agreement. Where economies of scale, collective goods, alliances, or requirements for a minimum number of parties exist, this condition may lead to agreements among similar bargainers. Less well understood is the fact that differences among the participants — in relative valuation, forecasts, risk aversion, time preference, and so forth — often constitute the raw material for joint gains. As the financial negotiations suggested, when such differences can be discovered and creatively dovetailed, mutual benefits can result.

Some negotiations are primarily "distributive" or constant-sum; that is, what one party gains the other gives up. Others possess an "integrative" or variable-sum character, wherein shared information or creativity points the way toward joint gains. Of course, once the pie is cleverly and cooperatively expanded, there remains the more adversarial question of dividing it. In other words, integrative bargains engender distributive ones. If interests make up a negotiation's basic data and alternatives place limits on it, then joint gains from agreement, regardless of how they are shared, constitute its potential.

Thus far the parties, the issues, and the evaluations of the issues have been treated as constant for analysis. Yet in setting an agenda, including or excluding groups from the bargaining, or seeking to link or separate different attributes or issues, these "givens" may become variable. The parties' attempts to *reconfigure the negotiations* by varying one or more of these aspects become central to understanding the process.

With these elements in mind — interests, alternatives, agreements, and reconfiguration of the bargaining — this chapter proceeds by considering the evolution of U.S. negotiating strategy in the LOS conference. From a description of the shape of the proposed treaty, the central trade-off — between navigational freedoms and the seabed regime — can be identified. It is then possible to account for the changes in the American position, to evaluate them substantively, and to draw out implications of this episode for negotiation analysis.

4.1 Evolution of the U.S. Negotiating Strategy

When the United Nations convened the 1958 Geneva Conference on the Law of the Sea, a majority of states claimed territorial waters of 3 nautical miles. A decade later, the percentage of states claiming this limited jurisdiction had dropped to just over one-third, while the percentage of states asserting broader jurisdiction seaward from 12 to 200 miles more than doubled (from 18 to 43 percent). Beyond outright territorial claims, such as Brazil's 200-mile zone, a number of countries asserted claims for special purposes such as fishing (Iceland), pollution control (Canada), or security (North Korea). Further, archipelagic states such as the Philippines, Indonesia, and Fiji claimed the equivalent of sovereignty over the vast waters "within" their widely dispersed islands. If this trend of creeping jurisdiction ran its full course, close to 40 percent of the world's oceans — an area larger than that of the combined continents — would be subject to sovereign regulation of navigation, overflight, fishing, scientific research, and other activities. Even if territorial seas only extended to 12 nautical miles, traditional activities in 116 international straits less than 24 miles in width could be restricted. These areas include the straits of Gibraltar (between the Atlantic and Mediterranean), Bab el Mandeb (linking the Indian Ocean with the Red Sea and Suez), Hormuz (at the entrance to the Persian Gulf), as well as Malacca and Singapore (between the Pacific and Indian Oceans).[4]

The coastal, straits, and archipelagic states that led this territorialist trend did so for a variety of reasons: to extend control over living and nonliving resources (for example, fish and oil); to stop any foreign research leading to commercial "exploitation"; to prevent pollution and accidents; to protect their security from real or imagined threats; and to respond to nationalist sentiments and internal political promptings. Although the more extensive claims could not be fully maintained in the face of opposition by major maritime countries, several coastal states developed substantial military capabilities to support their jurisdictional assertions (patrol boats, sophisticated missiles, small destroyers, maritime patrol aircraft, and so forth).

A somewhat belated recognition of the potential importance of this dynamic of expanding claims came in the late 1960s.[5] According to international law, ships sailing through territorial waters do not enjoy full "high seas" freedoms. Submarines must navigate on the surface. Moreover, as is the case over land, aircraft must obtain permission to fly over territorial seas. Of course, the U.S. Navy had powerful interests in unimpeded and submerged passage for its nuclear submarines; in conventional force projection, overflight, "showing the flag," rapid and routine deployment, and resupply missions; and in exerting influence in a variety of situations for which seapower is particularly suited. Unfettered commercial transport of commodities such as oil also had a security component.

To Defense Department planners, a widely accepted international agreement offered the potential for halting this troublesome jurisdictional creep. A Law of the Sea treaty that promoted consensus on these traditional rights could avert the need for choosing between their apparently inevitable erosion in customary law and an uncertain series of politically and diplomatically costly assertions of force. A universal agreement that shaped norms and expectations also seemed preferable to negotiating a network of bilateral navigational treaties that always depended on the current state of relations between the United States and the particular coastal or straits state.

Chapter 1 sketched several broader factors that combined to generate worldwide agreement on the need for new Law of the Sea negotiations. These included technological change; increasing conflicts among ocean users as the scope and intensity of maritime activity burgeoned; an inadequate (and, for some new states, illegitimate) structure of international ocean law; and fears of overfishing, pollution, and accidents (on the average, somewhere in the world, a 60,000-ton merchant ship sinks every day).[6] There was also the new prospect of great benefit from manganese nodules. The United States shared concerns with other nations in many of these areas, but it was the intense interest of the Defense Department in unrestricted naval mobility and continued freedoms of the high seas that centrally and powerfully influenced U.S. policy toward the LOS negotiations.[7]

By the late 1960s the Soviet Union came to share U.S. concerns over this tightening net of maritime restrictions. After two and a half years of discussions between the two countries and with their respective allies, both governments began actively promoting a single international negotiation to deal with territorial sea questions.[8] In return for an early agreement to guarantee passage through straits, the United States was willing to "concede" recognition of 12-mile territorial seas along with carefully specified preferential fishing rights for coastal states in order to induce them into the bargain.[9]

Meanwhile, negotiations concerning the regime for mining the deep seabed had been inconclusively mired in the U.N. Seabed Committee, formed after the Maltese initiative in 1967. The United States and the Soviet Union nominally preferred to *separate* the seabed negotiations and the territorial seas/fisheries negotiations (into "manageable packages").[10] Three major factors prevented this outcome. First, the obvious physical linkage between the seabeds and other parts of the ocean lent intellectual and political plausibility to a bargaining linkage. Second, many developing countries (especially Latin American countries) powerfully pressed for negotiations over the full range of ocean issues; they expected concessions on seabed questions in return for any accommodation of the navigational demands of developed countries. Among these developing states were several with the most troublesome 200-mile claims. This ensured that the maritime countries would strongly consider a comprehensive conference. Other developing countries supported the coastal states in part because the prospective seabed concessions seemed to offer great benefits to the Third World in general. Lured by the promise of vast undersea treasure (nodules) and mindful of their technological disadvantage, developing countries "doggedly introduced consideration of other maritime legal regimes related to the breadth of the territorial sea, rights of passage through straits and fishing practices 'in order to strengthen their bargaining position.'"[11]

The third factor — and perhaps the decisive reason for the addition of seabed issues to the other questions — can be found in the bargaining within the U.S. government. The nascent seabed mining industry and its bureaucratic ally, the Interior Department, were the main forces that pressed hard for the separation. As Defense Department interests in preventing "territorial" claims in the ocean strengthened, a strong international seabed authority seemed the best means of assuring that the equivalent of coastal jurisdictional "creep" would not spread to the open ocean. Without a treaty, it appeared likely that national mining sites would be staked out, and, inevitably, assertions of rights in the superjacent waters would proliferate. Beyond this substantive preference for an international authority — and what was perhaps most important — national security officials hoped that generous seabed provisions in a comprehensive negotiation would favorably affect the resolution of navigational questions.[12] Thus physical linkage, LDC coastal state pressures, and the results of internal bargaining led to U.S. acquiescence in the crucial General Assembly decision to commence negotiations on a full range of ocean issues.[13]

On a separate but related issue, defense interests ran strongly counter to the preferences of the Interior Department and the oil industry. Consistent with its attempts to halt creeping jurisdiction and impediments to navigation, the Department of Defense preferred that coastal states have jurisdiction only over narrow slices of their continental shelves. However, wide continental margins, like those of the

United States, promised to contain rich oil and gas resources. An early U.S. proposal reflected this Defense preference in calling for renunciation of national claims beyond a depth of 200 meters. From this 200-meter isobath seaward to the edge of the continental margin, the coastal state would act as a "trustee" for the international community, and, in return, would receive a share of revenues from hydrocarbon development in the zone.[14] The oil industry, however, wanted U.S. jurisdiction to encompass the entire continental margin and argued that internationalizing this area would be a "giveaway of rights already confirmed to this nation."[15] Though the industry and the Interior Department opposed the trusteeship idea, they lost the early bureaucratic battles.[16]

The petroleum industry continued to attack this U.S. policy. As fears of an energy crisis were followed by the 1973 embargo, the importance of offshore oil resources climbed. Petroleum interests began to carry more weight in the internal bargaining. Domestically, the Interior Department began leasing areas beyond the 200-meter isobath and indicated that the provisions of such leases would not be subject to future international agreements. Internationally, the cool reception accorded the previous "trusteeship" zone proposal led the United States to drop the idea and veer more toward "economic or resource zone" proposals that heavily favored coastal states.[17] By proceeding with its resource claims on continental shelves, however, the United States effectively sanctioned similar claims by other countries without respect to how the LOS deliberations came out.

Early U.S. negotiating strategy also counted on the lure of preferential fishing rights to help secure desired provisions on navigation. A number of developing countries had asserted fisheries jurisdiction out to 200 miles, but the major maritime powers, especially those with large distant-water fishing fleets (the United States, the Soviet Union, Japan), opposed these claims. Their opposition derived both from interest in continued access to worldwide coastal fisheries and from a fear that claims of fishing jurisdiction would expand to limits on navigation. By contrast, coastal states energetically sought in the negotiations to obtain universal recognition of their rights to "manage" these fisheries and catch what they could.

Although the differences in relative valuation of navigation and fishing interests seemed to contain the elements of jointly beneficial agreements, U.S. domestic politics undercut this promising possibility. Constant complaints by coastal fishermen that foreign fleets (Soviet and Japanese) were fishing important species to the point of extinction prompted the U.S. Congress to enact legislation in 1976 that created a

200-mile fishery conservation and management zone. This legislation closely resembled LOS conference proposals. Tight primary politics led Gerald Ford to sign the legislation over the vigorous opposition of the State and Defense Departments. Once a great power had unilaterally enclosed some 2.2 million miles of hitherto open ocean, coastal nations worldwide judged that a Law of the Sea treaty was no longer needed to assert similar claims. "Resource" zones quickly proliferated. The developing countries' interest in the LOS fisheries provisions virtually evaporated, and with this interest went any utility that the fisheries articles had as a possible "trade" for navigational concerns.[18]

With hydrocarbons and fisheries thus reduced in negotiating importance, the regime for mining manganese nodules remained the principal item of generalized interest to developing countries that could be linked to navigational rights. By 1976 the outlines of an eventual treaty were clear, with seabeds as the only significant unresolved issue. Conditional on its satisfactory resolution, the LOS convention would call for a 12-mile territorial sea, a 200-mile exclusive *economic* zone for coastal states (but with virtual freedom of international navigation in the zone), coastal state jurisdiction over the continental margin beyond 200 miles, and provision for unimpeded transit through straits and archipelagic waters.

From the beginning of the seabed negotiations, developing countries pressed hard for a single international entity to mine the "common heritage of mankind." In contrast, countries who expected to develop mining technology generally preferred an international authority that would act mainly as a claims registry, preventing overlapping claims, providing for orderly development of mining, and perhaps sharing some revenue with the international community. These polar positions largely persisted until 1976, when Henry Kissinger agreed to a "split-the-difference" compromise which became known as the parallel system. As discussed in Chapter 1, private miners and state companies would be able to conduct operations on one side of this system, while an international Enterprise would itself (or in joint ventures) mine on the other side.

4.2 The Shape of the Final LOS Treaty

Negotiations through the end of the conference centered on two key issues: defining the rights and obligations of those who would mine on the private side of the system, and ensuring that the Enterprise actually could undertake mining-transportation-processing operations. To do so, the Enterprise needed assurance of mine sites, funds, and technology. The final treaty signed in December 1982 dealt with these items, along with a host of other seabed and nonseabed issues.[19]

Under the treaty, those who made application to the International Seabed Authority to mine on the private side of the system would be required to present the Authority with two prospected sites. The Authority would choose one site and "bank" it for later Enterprise operations; the private party would be able to mine the other site. LOS treaty signatories would provide funds sufficient for the Enterprise's first venture (estimated to be upwards of one billion dollars). Half the funds would be in the form of long-term, interest-free loans; loan guarantees by participating states would cover the balance. If the Enterprise were unable to obtain mining technology, private miners would be subject to a temporary obligation to transfer it on "fair and reasonable commercial terms and conditions." All these provisions favorable to the Enterprise were in line with Kissinger's early offer to get this international entity under way "either concurrently with the mining of state or private enterprises or within an agreed timespan that was practically concurrent."[20]

Other provisions of the seabed texts included a limit on the production of seabed minerals, intended to protect land-based producers. This limit was tied to the rate of growth of the nickel market. As described in Chapter 3, private miners would pay fees, royalties, and shares of profit to the International Authority in respect of the "common heritage" principle. The Authority would either distribute this money to treaty members or reinvest it in further Enterprise operations. The International Seabed Authority would govern this system by means of a one-nation, one-vote assembly and a smaller executive council whose membership would be determined by a complex formula based on economic, geographic, and political factors. In order to protect the interests of the minority of industrial countries, the most important actions of the council would require consensus. Large majorities (three-quarters, two-thirds) would be required for other central decisions. Twenty years after the first mining, a review conference could make changes in the treaty by a three-quarters vote. (These provisions are further described and evaluated in Section 4.5.2.)

Apart from the seabed provisions, the treaty would replace the jumble of conflicting ocean claims by coastal states by a universal 12-mile territorial limit, within which foreign ships would have the right of "innocent passage," that is, passage that does not threaten the coastal state's security. Straits less than 24 miles wide would not become territorial waters but would be subject to a new regime of "transit passage" that would allow overflight as well as submerged and surface travel. The adjacent states would be given some protection from pollution, accidents, and security-threatening activities. A similar regime would be in effect for archipelagic sea-lanes. Beyond 12 miles, coastal states would gain a monopoly (1) on fish and other living resources to a distance of 200 miles and (2) over oil, gas, and other minerals on their continental shelves out to a distance of 350 nautical miles. Some international revenue sharing from hydrocarbon operations beyond 200 miles would take place. Other provisions would give landlocked states limited access to the economic zones of neighboring states.

Beyond navigational, resource, and jurisdictional issues, the treaty contained rules on the conduct of marine scientific research. These provisions were designed to promote research expeditions while reassuring coastal states about possible commercial or military espionage. The new treaty also addressed the need to preserve and protect the marine environment from pollution. Further, the text set extensive mandatory and binding dispute resolution mechanisms for parties to the convention.

Apart from the various substantive features of the new treaty, however, lie a variety of other motives and interests. Some people see the treaty's prime virtue in its express attempt to narrow the gap between wealthy and poor nations, at least for one class of unclaimed resources. Many participants and observers regard the LOS conference as a powerful example of how diverse states can peacefully accommodate their competing interests and extend the rule of international law. As Henry Kissinger said in 1975, "We are at one of those rare moments when mankind has come together to devise means of preventing future conflict and shaping its destiny rather than to solve a crisis that has occurred or to deal with the aftermath of war."[21]

4.3 The Central Trade: Navigation and Nodules

In addition to the welter of provisions just described and manifold appeals to different parties, the treaty's more than 400 articles deal, for example, with the prohibition of slave transport by sea, the treatment of underwater objects, the laying of submarine cables, and the particular status of ships flying the flag of the International Atomic Energy Agency. In order to explain and evaluate these complex negotiations, however, analytic attention must focus on the dominant issues: navigation and ocean resources. As Ambassador Elliot Richardson explained, "Although the Conference has . . . dealt with issues ranging all the way from piracy to vessel-source pollution, its participants understood from the outset that the accommodation of navigational and resource issues must be at the core of any eventual 'package deal.'"[22]

As discussed earlier, de facto resolutions *outside* the LOS framework were effected by U.S. actions on certain key resource questions (living resources in the 200-mile zone and mineral resources on the continental shelf). These questions, though the subject of energetic discussion, were classic "easy issues": a substantial number of the LOS participants preferred that they be resolved identically. With their effective removal from the comprehensive LOS package and the consequent reduction in joint gains available uniquely from the treaty, however, a great deal more pressure built up around the nodule regime, the major remaining element of the "trade" for mobility rights.

Coastal, straits, and archipelagic states of the Third World generally do not possess the means for harvesting the deep seabed. Developed maritime nations perceived that these states had been restricting and could continue to limit valuable navigational freedoms. Given these twin conditions, navigation and seabed questions became inseparably linked in what would rise or fall as a package.[23] It is significant that one of the earliest threats of retaliation for the Reagan policy decisions came as an attack on the treaty's provisions guaranteeing navigational mobility.[24]

That the early stance by the United States for a seabed claims registry system gave way to near-acceptance of a parallel system is readily understandable by the linkage to navigation rights and the relatively higher priority that the latter issue consistently enjoyed. In his 1970 "State of the World" message, President Nixon said, "The *most pressing* issue regarding the Law of the Sea is the need to achieve agreement on the breadth of the territorial sea to head off the threat of escalating national claims over the ocean" (emphasis added).[25] Throughout the rest of the decade, stopping jurisdictional creep and achieving legal guarantees of transit freedoms were predominant in U.S. policymaking and became virtually nonnegotiable positions in the LOS conference.[26] When an announced absolute requirement on one issue is linked with an apparently flexible position on another, it should not be surprising that concessions on the latter issue are the currency with which the former demand is bought, probably at a high price. The negotiating progression through the Nixon, Ford, and Carter years leading toward acceptance of the parallel system exemplifies this proposition.

4.4 What Happened? Explaining the Reagan Decision

How, then, can one account for the Reagan administration's choice against the treaty? Two elements of the framework discussed earlier (interests and alternatives) provide a means for understanding this apparent anomaly when they are applied to the "core trade" offered by the LOS treaty. First, administration *preferences* (or perceived *interests*) shifted, giving relatively greater (negative) weight to the seabed side of the balance. Second, the new administration judged its *alternatives* to a treaty, both with respect to navigational freedoms and to the seabed, as being much more favorable than had many previous American policymakers like Elliot Richardson. If the price of an agreement appears to rise and the benefits seem largely available without joint action, the bargain looks poor. To be sure, important members of previous administrations had pressed this view of the LOS treaty; it is uncertain whether President Carter would have chosen to sign. Nonetheless, this negative evaluation of the overall treaty officially ascended after the 1980 U.S. elections.

In establishing these assertions, it is useful to distinguish between two important attributes of the parallel system for seabed mining under the treaty, namely, (1) the purely commercial implications and (2) those deriving from principle, precedent, or ideology. Richard Darman, once the vice chairman of the U.S. LOS delegation and subsequently a senior policy adviser in the Reagan White House, explained in an influential *Foreign Affairs* article, "The most important issues at stake in the deep seabed negotiations, however, are not merely questions of manganese nodule mining. What is fundamentally at stake is a set of precedents with respect to systems of governance."[27] In drawing a distinction between the adverse "precedential elements of the seabed *regime* (as distinguished from seabed *mining*),"[28] Darman singled out production controls, technology transfer, special rights of the Enterprise, and the workings of the Seabed Authority.

It is useful to compare the shift over time in the importance accorded (1) the commercial and precedential implications of the seabed provisions and (2) the navigational articles. The perceived U.S. alternatives to the LOS treaty with respect to each of these areas can then be examined.

In contrast to the earlier predominance of naval mobility interests in the treaty, the seabed provisions assumed much more weight in the new administration's calculations. In fact, after noting that "those extensive parts dealing with navigation and overflight and most other parts of the convention are consistent with United States interests," President Reagan said that he rejected the treaty because of his "deep conviction that the United States cannot support a deep seabed mining regime with such major problems."[29] This reduced emphasis on the importance of the texts' navigational gains derived in part from political and military analyses that challenged traditional thinking.[30] For example, submerged transit through straits was arguably more pressing for strategic submarines in the late 1960s and early 1970s before the longer-range Trident class vessels were deployed. Moreover, the new administration's heightened concern about assured access to "strategic minerals" (including manganese nodules and other potential ocean resources) translated into a greater emphasis on the workability of the seabed provisions.[31] The President emphasized that the treaty would "deter future development of deep seabed mineral resources."[32]

Moreover, the Reagan administration attached heightened importance to the adverse precedential implications of the seabed regime. Richard Darman's earlier prescriptions for a greatly altered U.S. negotiating strategy were offered from "the perspective of one who would weigh these precedential elements heavily."[33] In the same vein, the deputy chairman of the U.S. delegation to the final LOS negotiating session contended that "the primary U.S. objective, in fact, was the eradication of ideological impurity. As a result, when the time came for compromise, the United States did not make ideological concessions to the Third World in exchange for pragmatic improvements."[34] Other observers share the view that the "dangerous precedents" in the treaty were the "major forces shaping U.S. policy."[35]

Along with a shift in relative preferences or *interests* came a change in attractiveness of the perceived *alternatives* to a negotiated agreement. In the earlier days of the LOS negotiations the official view generally held that, in the absence of a treaty, navigational rights would erode and conflict would generally increase. Further, without universal legal recognition of their claims, seabed miners would find capital unavailable and proceeding too risky. A typical, if overblown, assessment of the no-treaty alternatives came from the U.S. Secretary of State in 1975: "The current negotiation may thus be the world's last chance. Unilateral national claims to fishing zones and territorial seas extending from fifty to two hundred miles have already resulted in seizures of fishing vessels and constant disputes over rights to ocean space. The breakdown of the current negotiation, a failure to reach legal consensus, will lead to unrestrained military and commercial rivalry and mounting political turmoil."[36]

By the early 1980s, however, the alternative to an LOS seabed mining regime appeared more promising. The United States had passed interim legislation in 1980 allowing its citizens to go forward with ocean mining.[37] Similar legislation was passed in West Germany and a few other countries.[38] Although this legislation only grants exclusive mine site rights vis-à-vis other U.S. citizens, its supporters hope that this unilateral regime can expand to include other key mining nations, and a number of states have taken steps in this direction. Such a "mini-treaty" outside the framework of the convention presumably would have few of the drawbacks of the LOS regime.[39]

The nontreaty alternatives for navigational issues also seemed brighter. Far from heralding the onset of chaos and continued erosion of maritime freedom, the new treaty's navigational provisions — which were negotiated on the basis of consensus and which commanded nearly universal support — arguably establish favorable customary international law.[40] A policy had been undertaken in the Carter administration to send ships through and planes over waters that the United States maintained were open to such transit. After the dramatic Gulf of Sidra incident, in which two Libyan planes challenging the U.S. presence in the gulf were shot down,[41] the perceived need for and value of treaty provisions guaranteeing transit freedoms seemingly declined. Moreover, Navy Secretary John Lehman asserted that "customary international law is well established on rights of passage through straits and we have very amicable relations with those littoral states with whom there may be differing interpretations of existing law." Although he denied having stated that the United States could always shoot its way through straits if transit permission were refused, his perceptions of the attractiveness of the nontreaty alternatives were clearly more positive than many earlier views.[42]

In brief, the original "navigation for nodules" proposition no longer offered the lure of joint gain. The interests of the United States had shifted to place a relatively heavier emphasis on seabed access and, in particular, a much greater weight on precedential aspects of the seabed regime. In addition, the alternatives to a negotiated agreement — assertion of customary law with the threat of force in the background, along with the mini-treaty option — looked far more tolerable than earlier assessments had held. "Paying dear" (with seabeds) for "something cheap" (navigation) looked like a bad bargain.

4.5 Evaluating the Decision to Reject the Treaty

The explanation in the preceding section of the U.S. rejection of the LOS treaty was couched in the terms of negotiation analysis — changes over time in the effective terms offered by the LOS treaty, shifts in the relative weights accorded different interests, and changed perceptions of the desirability of nontreaty alternatives. The following sections seek to complement this approach by sketching a substantive evaluation of the treaty's "core" elements, navigation rights and the seabed regime.

In exploring these issues substantively, moreover, a number of broader *negotiation* questions emerge as central to understanding the implications of the LOS process and result.

4.5.1 Navigational Freedoms with and without the Treaty

As discussed earlier, the marked trend toward increased territorial claims by coastal, straits, and archipelagic states accelerated from the adoption of the 1958 Geneva conventions through the early 1970s. If previously open ocean came to be regarded as sovereign territory, a number of commercial and military interests might be imperiled. The right of strategic submarines to pass submerged through international straits need not exist under a territorial regime. Spain, Morocco, Indonesia, and Malaysia are among the key straits states that had expressed unhappiness with traditional rules of submarine passage. Many analysts hold such unimpeded submarine transit to be strategically vital,[43] though its importance may be declining.

Passage in archipelagic sea lanes has related military value. Of increasing significance are restrictions on surface commercial and military navigation. The restrictions may be direct, such as Egypt's denial of commercial passage to a vessel in the Gulf of Aqaba on grounds of its Israel-bound cargo,[44] or indirect, such as conflicting or onerous regulations, requirements for prior notification and permission, navigational tolls and taxes, or prohibition of particular cargoes or of cargoes headed for certain destinations. There is high military value to unquestioned and unchallenged rights to deploy ships and forces rapidly or routinely, to steam through, to take up station, and to undertake supply missions.[45] Beyond submarine transit through straits and navigational mobility, however, is the legal right of overflight, which does not exist in the airspace above territorial seas and which could be subject to restriction or revocation if national jurisdictions extended seaward.

The exercise of these and related rights seemed increasingly jeopardized by many incidents and the creep of territorial claims. Indeed, despite its navigational interest, the United States itself led this trend with the 1945 Truman Proclamation of control over the continental shelf and the 1976 assertion of fishing jurisdiction out to 200 miles. Although such U.S. actions were formally drawn so as to leave high-seas freedoms unaffected, other nation-claimants had no compelling reasons to respect the old rules. Maritime nations, of course, have often argued for a global commonality of interest in maximum ocean freedoms. At least in the short term, however, developing coastal states do not profess strong concern with unfettered rights of submarines, merchant vessels, warships, and planes. Given fairly straightforward environmental and accident protections, ship and aircraft movements are generally not inconsistent with coastal states' sovereignty and basic interests. This apparent asymmetry of interest in preserving ocean freedoms together with the obvious political advantages of expanded claims, however, suggest that, absent consideration of something else of value, the sequence of restrictions and claims observed over many years will continue.

The new LOS treaty, of course, offers the conditions under which this expansionist dynamic could be restrained and, in fact, under which many claims would be rolled back. President Reagan acknowledged as much even while rejecting the treaty on the basis of its seabed provisions. This is not to imply that the LOS treaty would have much bearing on actions taken in crisis situations or in cases where vital interests were directly challenged. At the point of armed conflict, divergent interpretations of international ocean law are likely to be irrelevant. The major advantages of widespread agreement on maritime rights, however, seem to come in the vast range of important intermediate situations — commercial transport and routine operational deployment of ships and planes, often acting in preventive, supporting, or deterrent capacities. Without such consensus and the legitimacy it confers, exercise of these key functions cannot be as certain, predictable, or costless. By institutionalizing this consensus and rendering its characteristics more precise, a widely accepted LOS treaty would tend to strengthen it and increase its applicability.

The high value attached to this complex of ocean activities is practically uncontested; the policy question turns in part on the degree to which the nontreaty alternatives realize this value in comparison with the LOS convention. The following three subsections, therefore, consider the leading alternative — but not mutually exclusive — policies to the treaty, namely, (1) counting on good relations with coastal states, (2) forcibly contesting coastal state restrictions on navigational or overflight prerogatives, and (3) relying on customary law as fostered by the LOS process itself to secure the desired rights. To presage the implications of this examination, the treaty appears to offer considerably more certainty about the exercise of these rights than do these prominent alternatives.

4.5.1.1 MAINTAINING GOOD BILATERAL RELATIONS WITH COASTAL STATES TO PRESERVE FREEDOMS

To repeat the statement by Navy Secretary John Lehman quoted earlier, "We have very amicable relations with those littoral states with whom there may be differing interpretations of international law." There are a number of instances in which the state of bilateral relations or a special accommodation of American interests could have rendered a universal sea treaty inessential. For example, pursuant to its interpretation of waters "enclosed" by archipelagoes as having internal rather than international status, the chief of staff of the Indonesian Navy reportedly threatened that "our armed forces will attack any foreign submarines entering territorial waters without permit, because it means a violation of Indonesian's sovereignty."[46] Although Indonesia (along with Malaysia) reaffirmed this stance when the convoy including the U.S. carrier *Enterprise* passed through the Malacca Strait on the way to the Bay of Bengal during the 1972 Bangladesh crisis, some accommodation was apparently reached with the United States that avoided a dispute.[47] Similarly, the president of Brazil reportedly took the position in 1971 that the U.S. Navy was welcome in Brazilian territorial waters (claimed to 200 miles) but that no such accommodations would be made for Soviet ships.[48]

Of course, making the exercise of desired rights in the first instance squarely conditional on bilateral relations with particular states risks a change in the relationship. For example, an influential 1974 analysis of U.S. security interests in ocean law (which generally discounted the need for an LOS treaty) noted that "considering the more than $2 billion in arms the United States has provided Iran to bolster its claim to paramountcy in the [Persian] Gulf, Iran's forward policy [to seek control of shipping in the Gulf and Straits of Hormuz) should not be inconsistent with America's broad security interests in the Gulf."[49] The subsequent reversals in U.S.–Iranian relations underscore the vulnerability of the arrangement and help to explain Vice Admiral James Doyle's admonition: "As to bilateral agreements with coastal states on navigation and overflight, anyone familiar with the political, military and economic implications of base rights negotiations would avoid this alternative like the plague. The bargain is often fragile and temporary: witness the history of bases around the world. Moreover, the concessions and costs are generally high."[50] Furthermore, if transit rights are accepted as discretionary, it is possible that competing maritime powers may find themselves in expensive and risky "bidding wars" over quite insecure arrangements (as, for example, in 1971 when Malta played Britain and the NATO countries off against Libya and the Soviet Union to increase dramatically the rentals paid for naval base rights).[51]

Even where bilateral relations are otherwise good, third-party pressure or particular policy disagreements may lead to the denial of rights enjoyed by virtue of treaty. United States support for Israel in the 1973

Middle East war provides a case in point. That the NATO allies did *not* grant overflight and refueling rights to the United States deeply impressed Defense Department analysts.[52] Since only Portugal allowed U.S. overflight, the need to fly over Gibraltar was accentuated. This experience further underscored the value of overflight above international waters as a nonsuspendable right and suggested the adverse consequences had Gibraltar been considered, say, Spanish territory (in which case overflight would have been a discretionary privilege). Echoes of this situation came in January 1979 when the United States decided to send F-15 fighters to Saudi Arabia, presumably to reiterate support for that regime and send messages to "audiences" in Iran and the Soviet Union. Spain refused permission for the jets to refuel at U.S. bases located in Spanish territory.[53]

The distinctive function of a widely accepted LOS treaty, in contrast with country-by-country understandings, is its tendency to lift transit rights out of the domain of the discretionary, tradable, and disputable. Instead of an ongoing bilateral bargain, which may be affected by substantively unrelated items in the joint relationship or by third parties, the LOS rules help to diffuse and remove the issues of passage to questions of worldwide, multilateral understanding.

4.5.1.2 FORCIBLE CHALLENGE OF RESTRICTIONS
Rather than facing the gradual loss of valuable ocean rights, the United States could follow a policy of routine challenge to claims and restrictions. Certainly, direct military confrontation—as in the Libyan case described earlier—in crisis situations is likely to be answered in kind. Difficulty arises with less obviously provocative cases, in which the claim of jurisdiction takes the form of a demand for notification, permission, or delay; a regulation based on environmental, safety, or resource grounds; or any of a large number of restrictions that could lead to the erosion of rights as a result of state practice.

Although the United States has sometimes adopted such a stance (most recently begun during the Carter years), this approach has often been unsuccessful and will likely continue to be ineffective over the long term in preserving the desired freedoms. Take the hypothetical example of a South American country that for one reason or another objects to a small U.S. naval training exercise scheduled to take place in waters that it claims as territorial but that the United States holds to be high seas. To the country, "imperialistic" insistence on the maneuvers close to its shores can loom large and be publicized as a visible, powerful affront to its sovereignty and pride. Beyond economic and political retaliation, there is the possibility of a military response. To patrol "their" waters and protect themselves against hostile neighbors, a number of Third World countries have added planes, sophisticated missiles, small and medium-sized fighting ships, and mine-laying capabilities to their arsenals.[54] Moreover, especially if the country's territorial claims are widely regarded as legitimate, a vocal and sympathetic regional and general Third World response may be expected.

To decision makers in Washington, this issue is often likely to be viewed as a proposal by the Navy of a militarily inessential action in order to assert a somewhat abstract principle in a far-away location. Opposing it will be the spokesmen for any number of tangible, immediate issues involving the coastal country.[55] That country may be contemplating the purchase of a major telephone system from a U.S. or a German firm, as well as a dozen American-made or French Mirage jets. Tax policy involving the operations of hundreds of U.S. firms may be in flux and subject to adverse change. Unrelated diplomatic initiatives may be under way involving human rights, O.A.S. policy toward Cuba, or grain sales to the Soviet Union. The U.S. decision will often go against asserting a desirable principle (high-seas freedom) and in favor of not prejudicing a complex of linked issues. As Richard Darman observed, "In the overwhelming majority of cases, the United States has treated the state of 'relations' with the country involved as more important than the high seas freedom that may have been lost."[56]

This should not be surprising. Many postwar analyses have concluded that the use or threatened use of force by large states has become increasingly costly over time.[57] The norms and linkages that would have inhibited the United States from challenging the 1973 European denials of overflight rights are obvious. In the 1950s, when Ecuador and Peru regularly seized and fined U.S. fishing vessels in their claimed territorial waters, the United States did not respond with gunboat protection for its injured citizens; it seemed much more important to ensure the sympathy of Ecuador and Peru toward the anti-Communist alliance. Accordingly, the United States made legislative provision to reimburse the fishermen's fines. In an analogous situation, the forceful British response in the "Cod Wars" with Iceland was considerably tempered by the threatened expulsion from Iceland of a critical NATO base.[58] A number of other cases in which the United States did not use force for one reason or another can be found; examples include the North Korean seizure of the *Pueblo* and the continuing series of denials by coastal states of permission for U.S. marine scientific expeditions.

In short, a policy of routine challenges of any coastal state restrictions will often pose choices that appear to involve either insistence on an abstract principle or not jeopardizing a complex of substantively unrelated but politically linked, concrete issues. To the state, the challenge can stand as immediate and significant. The entirety of its political and economic ties to the United States can be called into question. To the United States, however, restriction can appear marginal in the context of its overall relationship with the state. In some cases, of course, the United States will decide to challenge the restriction—when, for example, "vital" interests are immediately at stake, when there is direct military action accompanying the restriction, or when the set of linkages that might otherwise inhibit reaction is small. (When Libyan planes tried to keep U.S. craft out of Libya's claimed waters, the United States responded forcibly, but against a direct attack and from a "terrorist" country with whom the United States had practically no diplomatic relations.) In many less dramatic cases, as has been the case in the past, the challenge was not mounted, and an apparently inexorable erosion of traditional rights has continued. This possibility appears to be inherent in a policy that mainly relies on the threat of military challenges.

In the late 1970s and early 1980s, however, the trend toward increasing jurisdictional assertions slowed considerably. During this time the Carter administration reactivated a policy (continued by the Reagan navy) of periodically sending ships and aircraft through and over waters that were nominally restricted by coastal states. The relative paucity of incidents associated with this practice was encouraging for the traditional interpretations of high-seas freedoms. Nevertheless, such restraint by coastal countries occurred while the LOS conference had provisionally settled the navigation articles pending resolution of the vigorous seabed debate. It is impossible to disentangle the extent to which the observed claims slowdown was a function of forceful U.S. policies as opposed to countries acting in accord with their tentative LOS agreements. (The durability of the treaty's navigational articles given the U.S. stance is discussed in Section 4.5.1.3.) Uncertainties about the long-term future of such a policy are notable given the history of similar approaches and the inherent unattractiveness of overt reliance on force. How long such a U.S. policy might be sustained is unknown, as are the post-LOS reactions of the other coastal countries.

Somewhat ironically, a policy of forcible challenges can be counted as successful only if actual force is rarely employed. To be fully valuable, transit rights need to be sufficiently clear and widely accepted that their routine operational exercise may be counted on. As John Norton Moore observed, "If the exercise of a right is to be accompanied by a severe political dispute about the existence of that right, then the value of the right itself is impaired."⁵⁹ With territorial seas and resource rights conditionally established through an extensive multilateral process, the LOS treaty largely undercuts the basis for conflicting claims and restrictions. If virtual consensus is attained and maintained on rights, obligations, and dispute resolution mechanisms, the occasional confrontation that arises under the treaty should look more like the taming of an international outlaw than a great power provocation.

4.5.1.3 LETTING MOBILITY "RIGHTS" BECOME CUSTOMARY LAW; IGNORING SEABED "OBLIGATIONS"

Beyond counting on bilateral relations or forcible challenge, a third navigational alternative to U.S. participation in the new LOS treaty would take the nonseabed provisions as "establishing" customary international law or providing the best evidence of its status.⁶⁰ Since the convention was negotiated over several years on the basis of consensus and was signed by a preponderance of states, why not simply accept the benefits contained in the navigational provisions and ignore the undesirable features of the seabed regime? Moreover, it seems impracticable for coastal or straits states to discriminate between signatories and nonsignatories. Given these realities, should not the United States be a "free rider" on the political consensus and the legal pronouncements of treaty signatories?

Protracted litigation involving the United States before the International Court of Justice is entirely possible over whether the desired mobility rights are "contractual" in nature (that is, only those who assume the treaty's obligations can enjoy its rights) or whether the treaty provisions are the best evidence of customary international law. In his synthesis of the statements of 120 delegations after the LOS convention was signed, conference president Tommy Koh remarked on the widespread position to the contrary: "This convention is not a codification convention. The argument that, except for Part XI [the parallel seabed system], the Convention codifies customary law or reflects existing international practice is factually incorrect and legally insupportable. The regime of transit passage through straits used for international navigation and the regime of archipelagic sea lanes are two examples of the many new concepts in the Convention."⁶¹ Good legal arguments can apparently be made on both sides of this question, however, implying considerable uncertainty about whether the desired navigation rights might be jeopardized by the Court's decision.⁶² If these rights were lost in this manner and the United States still opted to remain outside the convention, its alternatives would come back to those considered earlier, namely good bilateral relations with coastal states backed up by force. Of course, the then-weakened international legal basis for such actions could affect both coastal states' decisions to restrict navigation and U.S. willingness to contest them.

Beyond legal ramifications, it is useful to consider the nature of the emergent political consensus on mobility rights (to which legal pronouncement contributes). Before the LOS process began, of course, a powerful and worrisome trend toward increased coastal state assertion had accelerated considerably, with no apparent end in sight. This trend originally led the maritime powers to negotiate. Apart from the final agreement's seabed provisions, the LOS convention essentially validates many of these enlarged jurisdictional claims while subjecting them to strict limits and qualifications. Territorial seas are held to 12 miles, and their extension to straits is qualified by the new right of "transit passage" allowing submerged passage and overflight; the new "sea lanes" provisions qualify the concept of archipelagic waters; and the exclusive economic zone provisions set a 200-mile limit for the resource jurisdiction of coastal states while generally leaving international high-seas freedoms intact in the zone. Legal declaration and political consensus on these new limits and qualifications represent a major part of the treaty's lure for developed maritime states.

The viability of the free-rider option turns on the extent to which this postnegotiation consensus on these limits and qualifications is *independent* of or *conditional* on the full realization of international seabed expectations. In the short run, of course, any consensus emerging from the exhaustive LOS process will have an inertial quality. A brief assessment of whether this widespread agreement will remain intact, however, suggests several grounds for doubt.

As discussed earlier, Soviet and American preferences originally kept navigational and seabed issues apart. They were combined in the new LOS conference after no progress was made on them separately during the late 1960s and early 1970s. Throughout the conference, however, strenuous efforts were made and abandoned to segregate the two areas of negotiations. The "package" nature of the text involving a generalized navigation-resources trade seemed too firmly embedded in delegates' understandings and expectations to permit "delinkage."[63] It was, of course, precisely the apparent differences of maritime and coastal state interests in the navigational and seabed issues that seemed to provide the elements of a mutually advantageous bargain when the two subjects were combined. At the signing of the new convention, Ambassador Satya Nandan of the archipelagic state of Fiji stated: "To attempt to rationalize parts of the Convention as being simply customary international law is to ignore the fact that what was customary international law has been clarified or modified and if [parts] have been preserved it was done as a *quid pro quo* for other provisions. This selective use of the Convention, therefore, will be unacceptable."[64] President Koh's summary of delegations' statements similarly noted that "the provisions of the Convention are closely interrelated and form an integral package. Thus it is not possible for a State to pick what it likes and to disregard what it does not like. It was also said that rights and obligations go hand in hand and it is not permissible to claim rights under the Convention without being willing to shoulder the corresponding obligations."[65]

A policy to ignore the seafloor resource provisions of the treaty and count on the benefits of the navigational portions is analytically equivalent to an ex post attempt at separation or unlinkage of the seabed from the nonseabed issues. The original strong trend toward coastal state assertion contained no tendency toward limits or qualifications; early negotiations seeking such limits made scant progress when separated from the seabed talks; once the link was forged in the overall conference, it proved unbreakable; finally, the convention's signers vigorously declared that rights depended on obligations. Little, therefore, seems to suggest the longevity of the navigational provisions if seabed aspirations go unrealized.

Nonparticipation by the United States would seem inevitably to weaken the LOS treaty apparatus in general and, in particular, to attenuate the seabed-related parts of the organization. To the extent that the political consensus on navigation is conditional, various U.S. actions further threaten its prospects. A generalized unraveling of the consensus, of course, is possible even with a convention in force. But if the United States moves from merely rejecting the treaty to withholding financial support (as President Reagan announced in 1982),[66] to active challenge (setting up a rival seabed regime and mining under it), this "barefaced attempt to have it both ways" would almost certainly strain the consensus on navigational freedom and might well provoke retaliation in this domain.[67]

Participation in the convention by the United States offers the strongest legal and political support to the navigational consensus. Staying outside the treaty risks legal rebuff. It is also conceivable that certain states would seize on U.S. repudiation of the convention as an excuse to impose selectively special costs, taxes, requirements, or regulations on vessels flying the U.S. flag. This might occur as an adjunct to another Middle East crisis or during an unrelated confrontation between other nations. Beyond outright discrimination, however, lies the prospect that without its support for the whole treaty, the very consensus the United States is relying on will erode. In the face of resurgent navigational restrictions, vulnerable bilateral relations and force would be the fallbacks.

The final version of the LOS treaty presented the United States with a central trade-off between navigational rights and the regime for seabed mining. Breaking with the views of many in the Nixon, Ford, and Carter administrations, President Reagan rejected the treaty. The explanation for this action includes a shift over time in perceived national interest from legal mobility rights to nodule resources, along with more favorable estimates of the nontreaty alternatives in both domains. The last three sections have evaluated the LOS navigational regime with respect to three leading alternatives for the United States: relying on good bilateral relations, forcibly challenging any restrictions, and taking advantage of the navigational consensus without actually joining the convention. Of course, these alternative policies could be employed singly or in combination. In fact, they would also have a role should the United States join the treaty. In that case, however, the treaty should diminish the need for the alternatives while increasing the legitimacy of their exercise, when required. None among these choices guarantees the continued enjoyment of mobility freedoms. Yet compared with exclusive dependence on the alternative policies, the LOS treaty improves the odds that the desired rights will be more extensive and secure.

4.5.2 *Evaluating the Reversal: The Seabed Regime*

Relative to the alternatives, the treaty promises a higher probability that the United States would enjoy valued ocean freedoms. The coin with which this advantage would be bought lies in the deep seabed. As discussed earlier, this seabed price has at least two dimensions: the strictly commercial ramifications of the regime and its precedential features. In continuing to evaluate the Reagan reversal, one needs to compare each seabed dimension to the relevant nontreaty alternatives.

Frustrated by the slow pace and inhospitable direction of the LOS talks, the United States in 1980 enacted legislation allowing its companies to proceed unilaterally. Other potential mining nations could join with the United States to set up a "reciprocating states" or "minitreaty" regime that would act both as a spur to the LOS deliberations and as a more palatable alternative in the event of an unsatisfactory negotiated outcome. Unhappy with practical and precedential aspects of the draft LOS convention (for example, the governance system, seabed production limits, mandatory provisions of sites and technology to the Enterprise, and so forth), the United States attempted through April 1982 to negotiate substantial changes. Although the parallel-system provisions of the convention remained largely immune to these efforts, conference delegates did pass a resolution guaranteeing special rights to "pioneers" in the ocean mining industry.

At least three possible regimes — the full-blown LOS treaty, unilateral U.S. legislation, and its possible expansion to a mini-treaty — thus confront would-be nodule miners. Each system carries a distinct set of precedential and commercial implications. The next section briefly surveys the economic outlook for an unfettered mining operation and compares the treaty's commercial aspects with those of the leading alternatives. The following section then discusses the precedents set by the seabed regime.

4.5.2.1 COMMERCIAL IMPLICATIONS OF THE SEABED REGIME

To evaluate the fundamental economic attractiveness of seabed mining, a look at subsequent results of the MIT model is in order. The original model was developed between 1976 and early 1978. The systems design, cost, and revenue estimates dated from the first quarter of 1976. The baseline case of the model showed positive (after-tax) net present values at real discount rates of up to 18.1 percent. Such rates of return could sustain interest in ocean mining but certainly did not promise a bonanza in view of the risks involved.

The MIT group revised the model in 1981. Design changes along with new cost and revenue estimates, updated to the second half of 1980, were made with the assistance of industry experts. The estimates showed a substantial increase in real costs over those in the original model.[68] As a result of prototype tests conducted in 1979 and 1980, the new model used more complicated and expensive designs than were believed necessary in 1978. Moreover, the average metal content of nodules in the mine site was lower in the revised model, reflecting the results of later exploration. As illustrated by changes in the model over the five years from 1976 to 1981, the economic outlook for ocean mining is not particularly good at present and does not promise significant improvement in the near future. Other researchers generally share these conclusions.[69] The high costs of ocean mining are due largely to the bulk and complexity of the equipment involved. There do not seem to be major improvements on the horizon. Although it is likely that real metal prices will increase, resulting in an increase in revenues, it is also likely that capital and operating costs will increase. Increases in metal prices would also raise the attractiveness of competing land-based mineral deposits.

These results, of course, do not predict the doom of the ocean mining industry. There is enormous uncertainty in such estimates. If a miner can obtain equipment at a lower cost, for example, if metal prices increase at a relatively higher rate, or if higher-grade deposits are found, ocean mining could represent the new lower-cost source for these minerals. If an investor or a government places a premium on obtaining direct assured access to a supply of manganese, say, then a lower financial return may be acceptable. Moreover, there may be early entrants that wish to position themselves strategically in the new industry or to develop an advantage in deep ocean technology. Thus, while ocean mining in general does not now seem to be a financially attractive investment, it is plausible that in the future investors may wish to proceed with the enormous commercial-scale investments required for seabed production.

The primary advantage of the LOS regime for deep seabed resources lies in its potential to grant widely recognized exploitation rights and its procedures to resolve claims and other conflicts in an orderly manner. When ocean mining beckons as an economically attractive proposition, the legal certainties of an international treaty would facilitate planning, capital raising, and operating activities. Nevertheless, miners will encounter a number of costs and regulatory uncertainties associated with operating under the LOS convention. Several of the treaty's provisions stirred intense controversy both within the Reagan administration, as noted previously, and beyond. In a fairly typical example, a *Wall Street Journal* editorial entitled "Cartel of the Sea" indicated that

> UN bureaucrats, meanwhile, see the Law of the Sea as a gold mine. They hope to establish a perpetual mining empire which will set production limits and thereby provide a price floor to keep on-land producers happy. It would also exact a hefty tax on Western mining ventures. The draft Treaty calls for application fees of $500,000, annual operating fees of $1 million and a scaled-up tax on mining operations as high as 70% of net proceeds. If production limits don't stop development of the seabed, it can always be taxed into oblivion.
>
> If the mining does produce any funds, they would be used for any number of UN boondoggles. One plan, for instance, is to set up a U.N. mining "enterprise" using technology that Western companies might be forced to hand over without adequate compensation.[70]

Such statements of the treaty's onerous commercial implications do not bear up well when analyzed. The most significant of the treaty's burdens are evaluated in the following paragraphs. Mining under the LOS regime is then compared with mining under the alternatives of U.S. law or a mini-treaty.

Uncertainty over contract approval and other actions of the Seabed Authority. According to the treaty, all qualified applicants must be issued a contract for exploration. A determination of qualification is made by a Legal and Technical Commission according to the rules, regulations, and procedures of the International Authority. This causes two uncertainties for a potential investor. First, the rules, regulations, and procedures have not yet been written but will be drafted by a Preparatory Commission before the convention comes into force. The second uncertainty involves the Legal and Technical Commission, which is to consist of experts in the fields related to ocean mining. Commission members are supposed to base their decisions on objective criteria established by the treaty and by the rules of the Authority. The commission does, however, possess considerable discretion, and there can be no ironclad assurance except through the treaty's dispute resolution procedures that abuse of this discretion will not occur.

Reservation of a mine site for the Authority. A basic element of the convention is that an applicant for a mine site must propose two areas for exploration and exploitation, one of which will be selected by the Authority and reserved for the Enterprise. This requirement increases the effort that must go into prospecting the seabed for exploitable deposits, but the costs involved (almost certainly less than $10 million) are small with respect to the capital costs of more than $1 billion required for an operation.

Financial payments to the Authority. The greatest burdens for a miner operating under the convention regime are the financial payments that must be made to the Authority. As discussed extensively in preceding chapters, the convention provides alternative systems of determining the payments required. One system, a simple royalty payment based on gross revenue from the sale of metals from nodules, is included for use primarily by the centrally planned economies such as the Soviet Union that do not calculate profits. A second system, which combines a reduced royalty with a profit-sharing system, is generally favored by market economy countries.

The financial provisions of contracts are designed to function well in the risky environment of ocean mining. Operators pay a base royalty equal to 2 percent of gross revenues and a base tax equal to 35 percent of any mining profits. For projects that are extremely successful, payments include a 4 percent royalty and a 70 percent share of the marginal profit dollar from mining operations during later years of the operation. (There is also a series of intermediate rates.) Two things should be kept in mind about these figures. First, all financial calculations are done in constant (deflated) terms, implying that only real profits are taxed — not paper profits, as is common in inflationary times under domestic law. Second, although rates such as 70 percent may appear high, they apply *only* to the mining portion — about 25 percent — of an integrated project, and then only to the highest profit increment after a significant discounted cash flow return has been reached by the entire project. Thus the maximum effective marginal tax is 17.5 percent — equal to a 70 percent rate applied to 25 percent of the net profit of an integrated operation. The highest rate takes effect only late in the life of a very successful project. By similar reasoning, the base tax rate is 8.75 percent of the net profits of an integrated operation.

The magnitude and nature of payments made under the convention compare favorably with those made in many developing countries by land-based mining operations, but unlike many such terms, the LOS rates are unlikely to be renegotiated upwards. Although the seabed payments may be substantial, their effects are somewhat mitigated by the progressivity of the tax system.[71] In addition, the financial burden on investors can be greatly reduced if the investor's parent government allows all or part of the payments to be credited against its taxes.

Production limits. The convention will establish a fifteen-year limit on the annual production of seabed nickel. Although the principle of a production limit has drawn much criticism, in practice the limit is unlikely to have much effect. The limit is calculated as the sum of the growth of nickel consumption over the five years prior to the first commercial mining operation plus 60 percent of the growth of nickel consumption thereafter. To protect against exaggerated restrictions during periods of low market growth, the treaty imposes a growth rate floor for the calculation. Analysis of allowable production under the limit, based on plausible starting dates for the first mining operation and a wide range of future growth rates of world nickel consumption, suggests that between ten and seventeen sites should be available in the first decade of the industry.[72]

Based on these projections, on the uninspiring economic forecasts for early ocean mining, and on the small number of prospective entrants (three to eight), it is quite likely that the production limit would have little practical effect, with the possible exception of the first five years. Then, however, all pioneer investors would be allowed to apply for production authorizations under the special conference resolution discussed later in this section. Ironically, the low-growth scenarios in which the production limit could "bite" are those that imply the worst underlying economic climate for the industry, and hence should cause the least worry about the production restrictions.

Technology transfer. Provisions mandating the sale of technology by the private miner to the Enterprise and to developing states have aroused the greatest opposition of all of the convention's provisions. In large part these objections draw force from the principle that technology should be sold only by the decision of the owner, and then on freely negotiated terms. As with the production limit, however, the technology transfer provisions are unlikely to have a significant effect in practice.

The treaty forbids the Enterprise to invoke the mandatory transfer obligation unless and until it has failed to obtain the technology by other means, including tenders for bids. Beyond tenders, the Enterprise has other highly potent but noncoercive means at its disposal. Its problem likely will be less that of prying technology loose from reluctant owners than of choosing from among the many eagerly proffered systems. Under the financial provisions of the treaty, member governments promise to supply the Enterprise with funds sufficient for an entire integrated project. This amount of money will be at least two or three times the total spent to date by all existing consortia in developing their mining systems. It should more than suffice for the Enterprise to contract for and build its own system, if desired. Some consortia, however, may wish to spread their development costs by licensing their techniques. Moreover, a contract study by the Interior Department indicates that there is a relatively large number of suppliers for each component of an ocean mining system as well as for the design and construction of the system itself.[73] Beyond outright purchase, the Enterprise may also acquire needed technology under a joint venture arrangement, for which it can offer strong inducements. As a result of these several factors, forced technology transfer probably will not occur. In the unlikely event that purchase and joint arrangements do fail, however, any mandated sale must take place on "fair and reasonable commercial terms and conditions." If the terms offered by the miner are challenged by the Enterprise or by developing countries, the dispute can then be referred to commercial arbitration for resolution.

There are, however, inhibiting aspects of the transfer provisions. Firms that supply technology not available on the open market must provide written assurance of their willingness to negotiate the sale of the technology to the Enterprise. Failure to live up to this assurance would probably bar the supplier from future ocean mining operations but would not affect contracts that were already approved.

It is also worth noting that these potential technology transfer obligations do not apply to transportation or processing technology; they apply only to mining technology, the proprietary parts of which make up significantly less than a third of an operation's capital cost. Moreover, the entire transfer requirement expires ten years after the Enterprise has begun commercial production. Hence the overall practical effect of this obligation, as compared with its possible philosophical and precedential implications, is likely to be modest.

Joint ventures with the Enterprise. In addition to the private side of the parallel system, the convention provides the opportunity for the Enterprise to enter into joint venture agreements with private firms. Joint venture operations may be particularly attractive during the early years of the industry. At that time, before ocean mining technology has been proved in full-scale operation, private firms might find investment capital hard to acquire. The Enterprise, on the other hand, will have no experience in ocean mining, and its investment capital will be sufficient to finance only one mine site. A joint venture would offer advantages to both parties: the private investor would acquire a partner with capital with whom to negotiate for financial incentives and reduction of requirements for banking of sites; the Enterprise would gain access to the technical and managerial skills of firms already involved in ocean mining, thereby reducing the risk of failure due to inexperience and speeding the entry of the Enterprise into commercial exploitation. In addition, partial equity participation would enable the Enterprise to spread its investment capital over several projects and thus to reduce the risk of loss.

Resolution on pioneer investment. In addition to the convention, which establishes the future mining regime, the conference adopted a resolution to deal with ocean miners that have already made substantial investments toward nodule recovery. The purpose of the resolution is to provide the stability and certainty necessary to encourage continuation of development activities already under way.

The resolution requires the Preparatory Commission to recognize the exclusive right of a pioneer investor to conduct exploration activities on its mine site. Further, the commission must accept the application of every pioneer investor. Before submitting an application for a site, the pioneer investors must resolve overlapping claims. If conflicting claims cannot be resolved through negotiation, they will be brought to arbitration.

Investor fears about possible actions by the Legal and Technical Commission should largely be mitigated by the requirement that the Authority approve applications for mining contracts submitted by pioneer investors. The commission can only ensure that the applications are filed in accordance with the convention and the rules of the Authority. In this way, the discretion of the commission will be curtailed.

As noted earlier, the constraining effects of the production limit could only plausibly occur during the first five years of commercial production. Although such a case is unlikely, the resolution establishes procedures for the allocation of production authorizations if requests exceed the allowable allocation. In this case the authorizations are issued in order of the date of application, except for the Enterprise's first application, which will be given priority. If two or more applications are received at the same time, the applicants must attempt to negotiate a settlement. If negotiations fail, then a decision will be made, probably by the executive body of the Seabed Authority, in accordance with criteria specified in the convention and the resolution.

Review conference. Fifteen years after the first operation has successfully tested its systems and has started commercial nodule production, the convention requires that a conference be convened to evaluate the workings of the parallel system. This review conference has five years to decide what changes, if any, should be adopted. If consensus is not achieved by the end of this period, alterations to the system may be made by a three-fourths vote. If, as seems likely, ocean miners begin commercial production in the mid-1990s, the review conference would be convened sometime between 2010 and 2020. This review would present the United States government with the potentially unpleasant prospect of either (1) being bound by the uncertain results of this procedure without formal Senate reconsideration or (2) withdrawing from a treaty which, by then, could be accepted as governing a wide range of ocean uses other than nodule mining.

As long as a contract is signed, however, between the entry into force of the LOS treaty and the end of the review conference, the convention provides that the rights under the contract over the life of the mining operation will remain unaffected by actions of the review. Thus, investment decisions that result in contracts issued before the end of the review conference are immune from the effects of future changes.

This period of stability (for the contract, the mining provisions of the treaty, and, effectively, the accompanying rules and regulations) compares favorably with that in mining agreements in many developing countries, which are constantly subject to the possibility of renegotiation or expropriation. Even in developed countries where investment conditions are usually regarded as stable, taxes along with environmental and safety regulations are subject to unpredictable changes — witness the dramatic increase in North Sea oil tax rates as well as the imposition of a windfall oil profits tax and the reduction in the depletion allowance in the United States. The LOS treaty provisions, however, are effectively frozen in such respects. Thus, relative to mining regimes on land, the LOS regime offers a stable investment climate for operations commencing before the end of the review conference and continuing through the mid-twenty-first century. After that, the terms facing prospective miners will be determined by the results of the review and the countries' reactions to them.

United States law. Under the provisions of the Deep Seabed Hard Mineral Resources Act of 1980, an American citizen, corporation, partnership, or other business entity controlled by an American citizen must obtain a license for exploration or a permit for exploitation before conducting ocean mining activities on the seabed beyond the limits of national jurisdiction. Issuance of a license or permit would exclude all other Americans from conducting exploration or exploitation activities within the specified mine site. The conduct of such activities would be subject to domestic environmental and other regulations, and, in addition to normal corporate taxes, miners would be required to pay a tax equivalent to 0.75 percent of the gross revenues from the sales of metals produced from nodules.

While the advantage of operating a seabed mine site under domestic law is the certainty about how it will be enforced, the disadvantage is the uncertainty over the value of the rights recognized by the law. The right to mine is exclusive only with respect to other U.S. miners or miners of reciprocating states; claims could be challenged by any miner that operates under the convention (including, for example, Canada, Australia, France, Japan, the Soviet Union, and India). In addition, the right to conduct any exploration or exploitation activities outside the treaty regime may be challenged by nonseabed mining countries either individually or collectively. In fact, Ambassador Koh of Singapore, president of the LOS conference, announced that if a mini-treaty were established among seabed mining countries, he would ask the U.N. General Assembly to refer the question of legality of mining the seabed to the International Court of Justice.[74]

There is also uncertainty as to which other countries may be able to participate with U.S. citizens. When a country signs the convention, it is required to recognize the convention regime as the only legitimate system for seabed exploitation. The provisions of the Resolution on Pioneer Investment will temporarily allow signatories to work with nonsignatories until the convention comes into force. At that time, ratifying countries must forbid their citizens to operate under laws of nations that do not sign the convention. This could cause severe, possibly fatal, strains on the multinational mining consortia by forcing companies to change nationality, withdraw from the consortia, or buy out the U.S. participants and apply for contracts under the convention.

The disincentive to investment might be significantly decreased if mining consortia could obtain political risk insurance from the U.S. government, loan guarantees, or other financial protection from the losses that could result from the United States being outside the convention. If such protection were made available, it is likely that it would be available only to the U.S. participants in the consortia. Therefore, political risk protection would probably be attractive only to the consortia with majority participation by U.S. companies.

The possibility of disputes over exclusive rights to a mine site, the lack of agreed provisions for the resolution of such conflicts, and the threat of international legal action combined with the extremely large capital investment and long payback periods make ocean mining solely under domestic law relatively unattractive. The situation improves to the extent that other mining nations can be persuaded to establish a mini-treaty for seabed exploitation. However, given that France, Japan, the Netherlands, Australia, Canada, and the Soviet Union, among others, have signed the LOS treaty, a mini-treaty regime could not offer complete legal certainty to its members. Of course, U.S. legislation and any legislation by reciprocating states would inject similar uncertainties into the LOS mining framework. Particularly under a mini-treaty, however, it is quite conceivable that banks and large corporations would find the risks of conflict, delay, and harassment too high to justify the investments required for commercial-scale operations.

For straightforward economic reasons, ocean mining is not likely to commence for seveal years. When the economic outlook improves, investment decisions will be greatly affected by questions over the legal right to exploit deep ocean resources. A domestic or mini-treaty regime can go part of the way toward granting that right, but substantial uncertainties will remain. A widely accepted LOS treaty would assure that right and eliminate most conflicts. The price of such international certainty would be banked sites, financial payments, limited production, technology transfer, and related convention requirements. On purely commercial grounds, then, the foregoing analysis suggests that the amount of U.S. mining under the probable nontreaty regimes would not likely be much different than if the United States joined the LOS treaty, at least through the first two decades of the next century.

4.5.2.2 PRECEDENTS SET BY THE SEABED REGIME
The issue of the seabed regime exhibits at least two primary attributes: its commercial workability and its precedential implications. As de-

scribed earlier, questions of adverse precedent and ideology weighed much more heavily in the Reagan administration's decision to reject the treaty than they had previously. Richard Darman sounded a note common to thoughtful treaty opponents when he drew a sharp distinction between the "precedential elements of the seabed *regime* (as distinguished from seabed *mining*)" and argued that "what is fundamentally at stake is a set of precedents with respect to a system of governance."[75] The most frequent objections on precedential grounds are aimed at the treaty's provisions on "mandatory" transfer of technology, production limitations, required financial payments, the Authority's discretion over access to the seabed, the review conference, the creation of the Enterprise, and the composition, structure, and voting rules for the International Authority.[76]

Precedent from earlier situations can certainly shape thought and expectations, especially in minds of a legal cast. It can offer an economical way of handling new but similar situations. Those concerned with the principles and institutional features of the Law of the Sea treaty contend that these precedents will affect arrangements for non-nodule ocean resources; international airspace; electromagnetic spectra; geosynchronous satellite orbit allocation; outer space; the moon; Antarctica; international commodity agreements; and the governing structures of the World Bank, the International Monetary Fund, and the Common Fund.[77] More generally, it is argued, U.S. acquiescence in the precepts of the New International Economic Order (NIEO) that are contained in the LOS treaty will generally advance the cause of undesirable principles of economics and world government.[78]

Concern with the precedent implied by the language of the LOS treaty has been a feature of ocean policy debate for some time. Yet the foregoing analysis of the commercial workability of the seabed regime suggests that the real precedent set by the treaty is one of NIEO rhetoric overlaying a system that is generally compatible with conventional economical operation. For example, "production controls" are temporary and calculated in such a way that they are unlikely to be a constraint. Although "mandatory transfer of technology" figures heavily in the calculations of many treaty opponents, this obligation is tightly circumscribed in extent and duration; the likelihood that the Enterprise will need or even be able to invoke it seems minimal. Similarly, the confiscatory-sounding rates ("70 percent of profits") that are contained in the financial provisions turn out, on analysis, to apply at much more tolerable levels, and then only late in the lives of extremely successful projects. (See the analysis in Section 4.5.2.1.)

The actual workings of these provisions *could* have been far more detrimental to future mining operations. In fact, American and other negotiators spent much energy improving the workability of these and other provisions from the standpoint of would-be commercial miners. It is probably fair to characterize the U.S. negotiating strategy during the Ford and Carter years as a sophisticated effort to dovetail differences of apparent preference between the developing and developed worlds. If the North wanted a commercially viable system and the South wanted affirmation of NIEO precepts (including a functioning Enterprise), then the resulting system—whose rhetoric was NIEO-inspired but whose workings generally accommodated private and state miners—seemed to meet both needs simultaneously.

At least two ironies attend this interpretation. The first is common to negotiations in which the principals have constituencies that are some distance from the proceedings. Although mandatory technology transfer, production limits, and 70 percent tax rates may have "sold" the treaty to Third World constituents, the same apparent properties sparked great criticism in the United States and may have inflamed many potential opponents. (Recall the quoted editorial from the *Wall Street Journal.*) This difficulty of keeping different "faces" of the issue separate can be found in the example of a conglomerate's president who, without prevarication, highlights the economic *potential* of a division to its would-be buyer while playing up its *flaws* in a closed-door session of the conglomerate's board of directors. A second irony in the interpretation of a commercial system couched in NIEO terms may be the actual precedent that it does set. Rather than the precedent of a model NIEO arrangement settling in over two-thirds of the earth's surface, as feared by many treaty opponents, the real precedent set may be for major rhetorical but modest substantive concessions to the Third World.

Although the set of precedents established by the LOS treaty may act as a lightning rod, another consideration should rank as more fundamental. The deeper concern should be with negotiating *linkages,* not precedent per se. If one asks why the United States should even consider a treaty with anything substantially less than its preferred commercial and institutional arrangements for seabed mining, the answer lies mainly in the supposed advantages of the nonseabed portions of the treaty. As discussed in Section 4.1, the American and Soviet position prior to the LOS negotiations was for separate consideration of these questions. Had this view prevailed, the likelihood is high that the seabed negotiations would have ended up much closer to a relatively minimal claims registry than to an involved parallel system. Similarly, it is probable that navigational questions would have been settled far less to the liking of maritime countries. As it happened, the negotiating link between these issues was fostered by (1) the combination of the physical and intellectual connection between the high seas and the sea floor; (2) dogged Third World insistence on combination; and (3) internal U.S. bargaining influenced by a Defense Department preference for an international seabed (likely to be immune from jurisdictional creep) and the hope that seabed concessions could lead to navigational gains.

Although these observations are unexceptionable in themselves, they do suggest that the existence of adverse precedents in future situations may be less important than the *structure* of the situations themselves. If a demand for the creation of an LOS-like mechanism for some other purpose is linked in a bargaining sense to issues in which the demanders have leverage, then the United States may agree to such a mechanism. Agreement would *not* primarily derive from the precedent, however, but from the possibility of joint gains or avoidance of losses. U.S. agreement in principle to LOS production controls was no more influenced by its domestic policies to restrict agricultural output than a future conference on world grain production would feel compelled to accept an International Grain Authority given the LOS precedent.

The critical element leading to extensive seabed concessions was the U.S. perception that developing nations held the key to stopping jurisdictional creep. Only in North-South dealings following the OPEC embargoes has the South been possessed of genuinely greater leverage. The implied lesson for those concerned with adverse economic and institutional precedents, however, should be one of caution when trying to influence the configuration of future negotiations. Avoiding precedent may be much less the issue than avoiding expensive links.

4.6 Summary and Conclusions

Financial agreement in the small hardly foreshadowed larger disagreement over the rest of the LOS treaty. This chapter has offered an explanation and evaluation of the U.S. decision, emphasizing a variety of negotiation-analytic precepts. A simple framework for analyzing negotiations can start by probing the *interests* both within and among the competing sides. Perceived *alternatives* to joint action serve as hurdles that proposed *agreements* must continually surmount. Common interests as well as differences among the negotiators provide the bases for mutually beneficial arrangements. The processes for reaching agreements include cooperative moves to create value in tandem with competitive ones to claim it. And, of course, the *configuration* of a negotiation—the attributes, issues, parties, and alternatives—is not immutable; negotiators seek advantage by *reconfiguring* these elements.

Arvid Pardo's stirring vision of the "common heritage of mankind" led to the creation of the U.N. Seabeds Committee, which debated the regime for nodule mining. At the same time, growing Soviet and American concern over vastly increased jurisdictional claims by coastal, straits, and archipelagic states prompted these maritime powers to propose separate negotiations to enhance navigational freedoms. Neither deliberation by itself apparently held out the prospect of joint gains to all the participants and, consequently, neither advanced. The physical link between nodule mining and the seas, along with Third World pressure and complex internal negotiations, led the United States to reconsider the separation of the issues. When the Nixon administration consented to a reconfigured negotiation involving the whole range of ocean questions—in retrospect, a critical choice—the U.S. defense establishment in particular envisioned an agreement for continued navigational freedoms mainly brought about by accommodating Third World interests in continental shelves, fishing rights, and the nodule regime.

As the negotiations progressed, the United States took unilateral actions with respect to oil on its outer continental shelves and fishing out to 200 miles. These claims conferred increased legitimacy on similar actions around the world and significantly reduced the importance of these subjects in the LOS forum. Pressure correspondingly increased on the trade between the nodule and navigational regimes. Although the final treaty deals with a vast range of ocean issues and broader interests, this chapter has argued that the core LOS bargain concerned these two questions. An explanation of the Reagan decision, therefore, could be constructed with primary reference to the seabed and the high seas. In contrast to perceptions of many officials during the Nixon, Ford, and Carter years, the succeeding administration gave seabed *interests* more weight. Moreover, between commercial and precedential ramifications of the nodule regime, the latter rose in importance. In further contrast to much previous American thinking, the Reagan negotiators judged their *alternatives* to an LOS treaty—in the realms of both mining and mobility—as being far more attractive than before. These shifts over time in the perception of interests and alternatives culminated in the 1982 decision against signing the treaty.

Evaluating the rejection required a comparison of policy attractiveness between the treaty and likely nontreaty alternatives. To counter the LOS trend toward loss of ocean mobility rights (submerged, surface, and overflight), the United States will have to rely primarily on good bilateral relations with littoral states, forcible challenge, and the treaty consensus of others. The analysis of each of these alternatives highlights important negotiation concepts.

Reliance on good bilateral relations, as with base rights, can represent a fragile and renegotiable arrangement. International consensus on the LOS treaty, by contrast, tends to take mobility rights out of the realm of the tradable, suspendable, and insecure.

Policies of forcible challenge to mobility restrictions have suffered a generally unsuccessful history, largely because of the kind of bargains they engender. In the case of many coastal state restrictions — often framed to protect the environment, resources, or security — an offshore challenge by a superpower can loom as a central political event. Attributes of pride, sovereignty, and the whole of a country's relationship with the United States may be called into question. Since the American view of the legal principle at stake will often be much more circumscribed, policies of relying on such encounters have failed and probably will continue to fail to halt the erosion of such freedoms. The attributes of the resulting bargains tend to escalate in a manner inherently unfavorable to the challenger.

A third alternative to U.S. participation in the LOS treaty involves being a "free rider" on the consensus of others. Analytically, this option turns out to be equivalent to determining whether the treaty's limits on jurisdictional extensions are independent of or conditional on the seabed provisions. A number of considerations lead to the conclusion that ex post reliance on effective delinkage of the navigational from the nodule issues will not likely be rewarded. These include pre-LOS trends, the lack of progress when the issues were treated separately, the numerous failed attempts at delinkage during the negotiations, and the statements of delegates at the end of the conference emphasizing the treaty's "package" nature. In fact, U.S. actions outside the treaty framework, especially toward the seabed, may hasten the breakup of the navigational consensus that emerged from the conference process. In sum, exclusive reliance on some mix of the three leading treaty alternatives — good bilateral relations, forcible challenge, and free riding — offers inferior prospects for retaining mobility benefits.

Alternatives to the treaty's seabed regime include U.S. law and its extension to a mini-treaty. Such an arrangement could avoid treaty obligations for banked sites, controlled production, technology transfer, financial payments, and the like. Yet, on analysis, these LOS provisions do not appear to be commercially onerous. Moreover, since a mini-treaty cannot offer legally secure rights or conflict resolution procedures, it is not clear that significantly greater mining would occur under its auspices than under those of the LOS convention.

A mini-treaty plainly avoids the costs of seabed precedents that are deemed adverse. Yet consideration of the necessary role of precedent in future negotiations points to other factors as being more fundamental. The existence of an adverse precedent need not be determinative except in future encounters configured to include issues that are both of concern to the United States and subject to the exercise of leverage by others. The lessons of sea law warn of such linkage.

Several benefits from the treaty add to the case in favor of signature by the United States. These benefits, though only discussed briefly in this chapter, include generally approved measures on the marine environment, dispute resolution, and the like. There is obvious appeal to U.S. affirmation of this ambitious effort to accommodate competing interests and to extend international law. Yet substantial negative weight given to the commercial and precedential disadvantages of the seabed — compared to a mini-treaty — is consistent with the Reagan team's choice against the treaty. For the decision to be good policy, that weight should exceed the enhanced prospects for mobility rights to be eroded, the commercial risks of a mini-treaty relative to a consensus regime, and, apart from navigation and nodules, the foregone advantage of more universal ocean law.

PART TWO

Agreement in Negotiation:
General Propositions

5 Differences and Joint Gains

5.0 Beyond Common Ground for Negotiation

The hope of doing better by joint action than would be possible unilaterally often lures people to the bargaining table. What is it, though, that enables individuals to gain mutually from negotiation? In some happy circumstances each party independently prefers the identical settlement on an issue, and their agreement has the power to produce this result. Suppose, for example, that a husband and wife discuss what color to paint their house and discover a shared preference for red. Or two nations bargain and derive value from an agreement to oppose their common enemy. Acting in accord with a shared vision, ideology, or norm may provide the basis for agreement. Where scale economies, collective goods, alliances, or requirements for a minimum number of parties exist, mutually beneficial accords may flow to identical parties. But beyond such coincidences of interest or advantages in number, why are there joint gains to devise and divide through negotiation?

This question, once asked, is easily answered: joint gains from negotiation often exist because negotiators differ from one another. Since they are not identical—in tastes, endowments, capacities, or in other ways—they each have something to offer that is relatively less valuable to them than to their bargaining partners. Though infrequently expressed directly, this "differences" idea is not new; it is implicit in the traditional description of the motivation for economic exchange as well as negotiation. What is the special advantage, then, of describing a fundamental force behind negotiated agreements in terms of differences between the parties?

There would be little advantage to such an approach if all negotiating possibilities were known fully and in advance; it would be enough to observe that joint gains exist. But in assuming that the full cooperative potential is known, an important part of the problem is defined away. Most negotiating partners do not automatically know what opportunities they have to exploit. They must explore — imperfectly — the arrangements they may jointly be able to create. From their perspective, the statement that through negotiation they can or will realize joint gains is unhelpful, because they face the prior problem of figuring out what possible joint gains there are to exploit. For example, a frequent diplomatic approach to negotiation — first to reach a common ground of facts, assumptions, and forecasts and then to bargain hard over this agreed terrain — may not lead the process in the most useful direction. Instead, the observation that the set of *differences* between the negotiators is often the engine that drives their ultimate exchange may fruitfully focus attention on how to identify the potential gains.

The observation that differences lie at the heart of many joint gains follows readily from the fact that in the usual economic world, identical individuals cannot jointly improve their positions by trading: their interests conflict diametrically and any bargaining will be purely distributive.[1] If differences are admitted along many dimensions, however, negotiation holds out the prospect of joint gain. For example, gains may arise from differences in *valuation* or preference, in *probability assessment* or forecast, in *risk aversion* or attitude toward uncertain consequences, and in *time preference* or attitude toward the passage of time, as well as in several other areas.

Since joint gains often derive from such differences, a primary orientation of negotiators and mediators should be toward discovering and dovetailing them. Of course, many good negotiators almost automatically seek to discern what is relatively important to each side — what the parties' "real" interests are. The best negotiators then find creative ways to weave these different strands into agreements of mutual benefit. To those who do not, who do so only vaguely, or who may not have considered some specific dimensions of difference, this chapter offers a possible reorientation of approach. Its premise is that to give form, precision, and prominence to difference methods is to give them more power in theory and application.

Robert Axelrod has proved that the "conflict of interest" in a game has an intuitive and unique measure that satisfies five strong axioms.[2] It is obtained by normalizing the game on the unit square and calculating the area above and to the right of the feasible negotiating set. For a game of maximal conflict, as in Figure 5.1(a) this measure is equal to one-half. Such a game can be called a zero-sum or purely "distributive"

DIFFERENCES AND JOINT GAINS

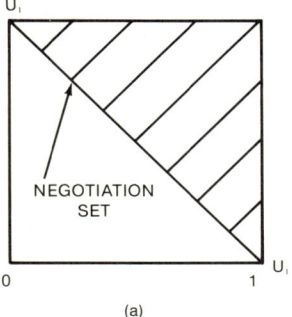 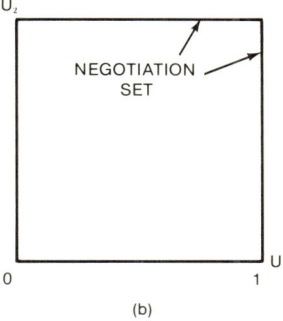

Figure 5.1 (a) Game of maximum conflict of interest; (b) game with no conflict of interest

bargain. A game with zero conflict in this sense is shown in Figure 5.1(b). This might be called a variable-sum or "integrative" bargain.[3] There is less conflict of interest in the game in Figure 5.2 than in that of Figure 5.1(a), and more than is in the game in Figure 5.1(b). Loosely, the more this set bulges up and to the right, the greater are the possible joint gains, the more integrative the bargaining, and the less the conflict of interest. The analysis of this chapter can be considered as a guide to reducing conflict of interest in negotiations by offering various methods to expand this set in a northeast direction. By precisely characterizing the optimal ways to use a number of differences, this chapter should help to bring about the realization of joint gains.

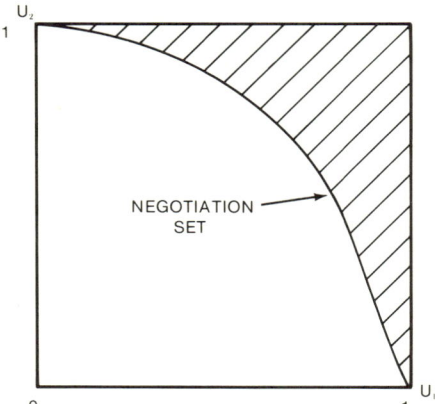

Figure 5.2 Conflict of interest (hatched area)

Intuition suggests, moreover, that negotiations are likely to be more successful when they are more integrative, offer greater joint gains, or, equivalently, have less conflict of interest. Indeed, in a series of carefully controlled experiments, Roth and Malouf found that agreements took longer to achieve as the conflict of interest rose.[4] Axelrod found a strong positive relationship between conflict of interest in prisoner's dilemma games and the probability of defection (rather than mutually beneficial cooperation).[5] Reviews of the social psychological literature lend support to the propositions that more integrative bargains (1) lead to speedier settlements, (2) have higher agreement probabilities, especially where aspiration levels and reservation prices are relatively high, (3) reduce the danger that one or more parties will repudiate the agreement, (4) tend to strengthen the relationship between the parties, thus facilitating later agreements, and (5) contribute to organizational effectiveness where subunits (individuals, work groups, departments) with distinct needs and values engage in intraorganizational bargaining.[6] Beyond offering an analytic account of the nature of joint gains, therefore, this chapter's discussion of how differences can usefully be dovetailed may also point the way toward easier, more advantageous agreements.

The analysis of this chapter is in two parts. The first part (Section 5.1) is a generally nontechnical introduction to the main ideas of a "differences" orientation. It commences with a brief look at preference and endowment differences and moves to a longer development of the implications of differences in probabilities. Major ideas behind using differences in attitude toward risk and time follow. The negotiation over financial terms for seabed mining serves as a unifying case in which these differences contributed to shaping an advantageous agreement.

Since the creative use of these particular differences may imply the need for contingent agreements, two qualifications deserve consideration. First, what if one party has "better" information; should such agreements still be undertaken? Second, what happens to an agreement that is advantageous to all parties on an ex ante basis, but whose ex post results strongly favor one side? How should such possibilities affect the original formulation? After this survey of the differences terrain, the nontechnical discussion concludes with ways to extend the orientation to dimensions that are possibly less quantifiable, but ones that may also be important in fashioning negotiated settlements.

The remainder of the chapter (Section 5.2) poses a number of underlying and related questions in a more formal manner. It offers a precise formulation of some of the ideas in the Introduction, lends them theoretical support, and suggests directions for their extension.

(The more and less technical sections are intended to complement each other but may read independently.)

5.1 Elements of a Differences Orientation

5.1.1 *Differences in Preference and Endowments*

If a vegetarian and a carnivore are bargaining over the division of meat and vegetables, it is the difference in their known preferences that facilitates reaching an agreement. No one would counsel the vegetarian to persuade the carnivore of the zucchini's succulent taste. Other negotiations may concern several items. Although the parties may have opposite preferences on the settlement of each issue, they may feel strongly about different issues. An overall agreement may reflect these different strengths of preference by resolving the issues of relatively greater importance to one side more in favor of that side. A "package" can be constructed in this manner so that, as a whole, it is better for all sides than the results of no agreement.

Individuals may have different *endowments* consisting of goods in different mixes, at different times, or in different states of the world. They may also differ in *interests, tastes,* or *preferences,* that is, in relative valuations of possible consumption bundles. Once tastes and endowments are given, the economic theory of pure exchange indicates that trading opportunities will exist. Even if individuals have the same endowments, they can trade if they have different tastes; similarly, with identical tastes, they can trade if they have different mixes of goods or goods at different times or in different states of the world. For mutually advantageous exchange, it is sufficient that their combinations of endowments and tastes—what might be referred to as "endowments relative to tastes"—differ, so that they have different relative valuations of goods.

Introductions to economic theory, and particularly introductions to general equilibrium theory, often begin with discussions of the two-person pure exchange problem illustrated by a device known as an Edgeworth box. Given presumed tastes (indicated by indifference curves for each individual) and an "endowment point" describing the initial allocations of commodities, it is noted that both individuals can be made better off by reallocating their joint endowment between them to a point where their indifference curves are tangent. It is frequently remarked that the relative valuations of the two commodities by the two individuals at the endowment point will typically not be the same. Since the valuation of one commodity relative to the other for one individual — the so-called marginal rate of substitution of the commodities — differs from that of the other, the two can trade with each other at rates of substitution of the commodities that improve the welfare of each individual. The reference in the theory to differing relative valuations or marginal rates of substitution of the commodities is a recognition of the fact that the traders must be "locally" different — that is, at the initial endowment point they must have tastes that differ relative to their endowments — in order to trade profitably. Rather than stating this presumption explicitly, however, the theory merely assumes implicitly (and by the way the Edgeworth diagram is normally drawn) that marginal rates of substitution will generally differ. Observing that it is precisely these presumed underlying differences that provide the opportunity for mutual gains leads to a search for how to exploit them.

Analogously conceived, negotiation is a special case of the economic theory of exchange, wherein parties "trade" differentially valued items for mutual gain. This is distinct from the view that negotiation is merely "war by other means."[7] This theory applies not only to trading discrete issues but also to constructing agreements that are responsive to different underlying interests. One party may primarily fear the precedential effects of a settlement; another may care about the particulars of the current question; and both may profit by contriving a unique-looking agreement on the immediate issue. One side may be keen on a political "victory" or international visibility of the result; the other side may want specific accommodation or "points" for a domestic constituency. Whether the differences are over form and substance, ideology and practice, or reputation and results, cleverly crafted agreements may often allow realization of both interests.

From an economic viewpoint, then, differences in relative valuation can lead to joint gains. It should not be surprising that such circumstances can facilitate joint gains. This contention is consistent with a proposition of the noted analyst of social behavior, George Homans: "The more the items at stake can be divided into goods valued more by one party than they cost to the other and goods valued by the other party than they cost to the first, the greater the chances of a successful outcome."[8]

Such valuation differences, which will underlie much of the discussion in the following chapter on adding and subtracting issues, are often key ingredients of agreements. Many other differences, however, also provide opportunities for joint gain. The next sections consider differences in probability assessments, risk aversion, and time preference as means to enable the advantageous resolution of certain negotiations.

5.1.2 *Probability Differences*

At the heart of the sale of an investment property may be the buyer's belief that its price will rise and the seller's conviction that its price will drop. The deal is facilitated by differences in belief about which state of the world is likely to occur. A performer may be negotiating with the owner of an auditorium over payment for a proposed concert. They may have reached an impasse over the size of the fee, with the performer's demands exceeding the owner's highest offer. In fact, no zone of agreement (in fixed payments) may exist at all. Suppose, however, that the basis for the performer's position is that the house will certainly be filled with fans, while the owner projects only a half-capacity crowd. This difference in their beliefs about attendance need not divide them; a contingent arrangement might be agreeable in which the performer would receive a small fixed fee plus a set percentage of the ticket receipts. The expected value of this percentage feature of their contract may be worth more to the performer than its expected cost to the owner, given their divergent projections of attendance. This arrangement may thus permit the concert to occur, leaving both parties feeling better off and fully willing to live with whatever outcome ensues.

Probability assessments of uncertain events derive from the combination of prior beliefs and observed evidence; discrepancies in either of these factors may form the basis for contingent agreements, even where endowments and tastes are similar. Much as the last section observed that value differences can lead to horse trades, Mark Twain noticed that "It is difference of opinion that makes horse races." When assessments differ, each individual will want to "move" his endowment (relatively) toward the states of the world he regards as more likely, and will be able to do so by offering his partner a portion of his endowment in states he regards as less likely (and which his partner feels are more probable). Thus probability disagreements may be the building blocks for more desirable agreements.

The first part of the discussion on probability differences (Section 5.1.2.1) offers a basic theoretical explanation of their attractiveness. Section 5.1.2.2 argues that contingent agreements with divergent assessments are quite common in practice. The implicit principle behind them is that of randomization, and having made the mechanism explicit, it is easy to see that probability disagreements can frequently be used to the advantage of all parties. After an example from the Law of the Sea negotiations is discussed, these ideas are qualitatively extended to more complicated cases (Section 5.1.2.3).

In practice, contingent agreements based on divergent beliefs seem quite common. In theory, however, Harsanyi argues that individuals share the same informational heritage, and thus that different assessments should be traceable exclusively to differences in observed information.[9] Aumann shows that posterior probabilities should be identical for events that are "common knowledge."[10] This tradition carries the implication that agreements based on different probabilities are "irrational." Sections 5.1.6 and 5.2.6 discuss the conditions under which this should and should not be the case.

5.1.2.1 RANDOMIZATION WHERE PROBABILITIES DIFFER

Imagine a mediator trying to assist two parties, 1 and 2, who are trying to decide between two possible outcomes, A and B. (These outcomes may themselves contain uncertain elements.) Party 1 greatly prefers A to B; party 2's preferences are opposite. Figure 5.3 displays this situation. Let the origin (O) represent the expected utility to each side should no agreement be reached. Neither settlement A nor B provides a simple resolution of the dispute.

If parties 1 and 2 act on the basis of an expected utility criterion, however, a zone of agreement could easily be created by the device of randomization. The mediator could flip a weighted coin with an r chance of coming up heads (H) and a $1 - r$ chance of coming up tails (T), where $0 \leq r \leq 1$. If the outcome were H, the parties would agree to

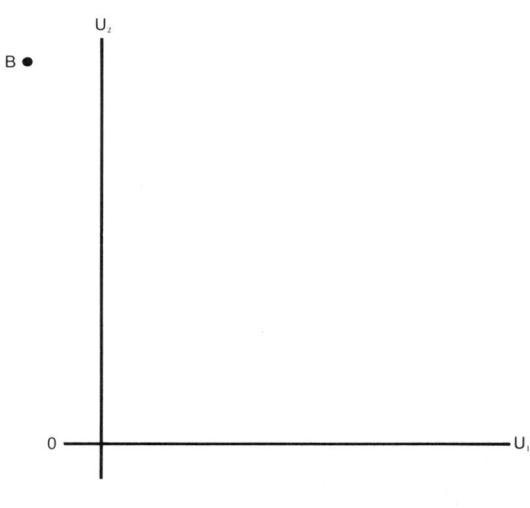

Figure 5.3 Basic negotiating situation

DIFFERENCES AND JOINT GAINS

A; if T, they would agree to B. On an ex ante or expected basis, this solution creates the zone of agreement that is represented by the segment connecting A and B in Figure 5.4. Points on the segment are obtained by varying the value of r. Notice that if $r = 1$, A is the (certain) solution, and if $r = 0$, B is chosen with certainty. The mediator's randomized solution procedure produces a *contingent* agreement, "A contingent upon H, and B contingent upon T," henceforth denoted $\langle A/H; B/T \rangle$.[11]

Suppose now that the event upon which the outcome is contingent is not a simple weighted coin flip but instead is another event that has two possible outcomes, E and E'. For a variety of reasons, parties 1 and 2 may disagree on the chances of these possible outcomes. If the mediator knows of this difference, he may use it to open the possibility of joint gains by means of what might be called "randomizing on the uncertain event."

Take an extreme case of divergent beliefs. Party 1 is certain that E will occur; party 2 is sure that E' will be the result. If the contingent agreement $\langle A/E; B/E' \rangle$ is chosen by the parties, their *expected* utilities are as high for party 1 as if A were definitely chosen and as high for party 2 as if B were the sure result. Figure 5.5 illustrates this situation. In this example, there is no ex ante conflict of interest between parties 1 and 2; each gets the desired result contingent on an ironclad belief

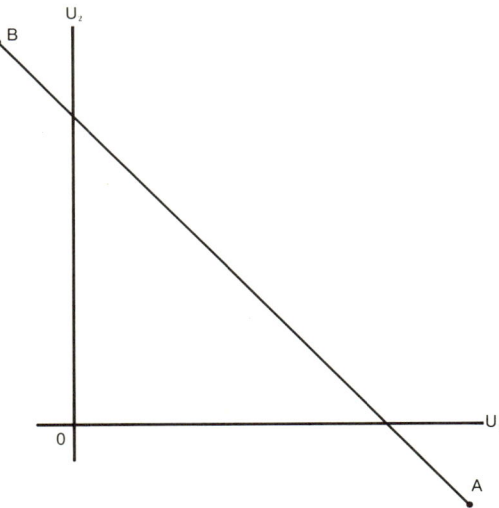

Figure 5.4 Basic negotiating situation with randomization

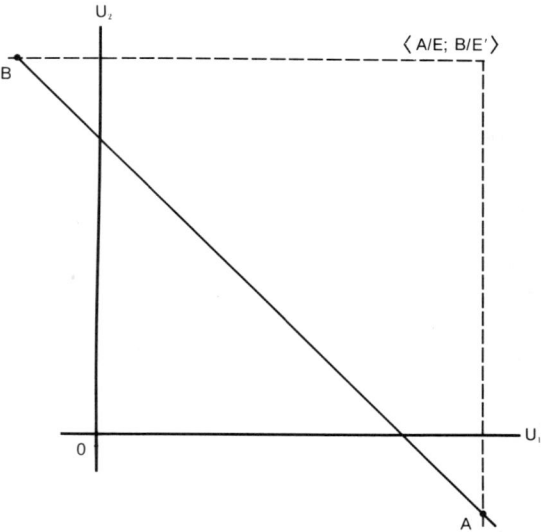

Figure 5.5 Contingent agreement with total disagreement on probabilities

about the outcome E or E'. (Notice that further randomizations could achieve any point in the triangle with vertices at points A, B, and $\langle A/E; B/E' \rangle$.) The possible zone of agreement is enlarged by use of divergent probability assessments.

If the divergence of belief is not total, as might normally be expected, the zone of agreement can still be enlarged over the possibilities offered by a simple randomization between A and B that uses agreed-upon probabilities. For example, if party 1 thinks the probability of E is $\frac{3}{4}$ and party 2 thinks it is $\frac{1}{4}$, an agreement $\langle A/E; B/E' \rangle$ will look something like the diagram in Figure 5.6. (If party 1's utility function is $U_1(\cdot)$ and party 2's is $U_2(\cdot)$, the coordinates of $\langle A/E; B/E' \rangle$ will be $(\frac{3}{4}U_1(A) + \frac{1}{4}U_1(B), \frac{1}{4}U_2(A) + \frac{3}{4}U_2(B))$. The greater the divergence in assessment, the greater is the possible joint gain from contingent agreements. Conversely, if the beliefs are very similar, there is less to be gained by a contingent agreement over a straight (objective) randomization.

5.1.2.2 RANDOMIZATION WHERE PROBABILITIES DIFFER: EXAMPLES
It is sometimes alleged that randomization is merely an academic trick, appropriate only for game theorists or other-worldly strategists. As a "real" option, goes this assertion, it is inconceivable that one would relegate an important decision to a mere chance mechanism (for exam-

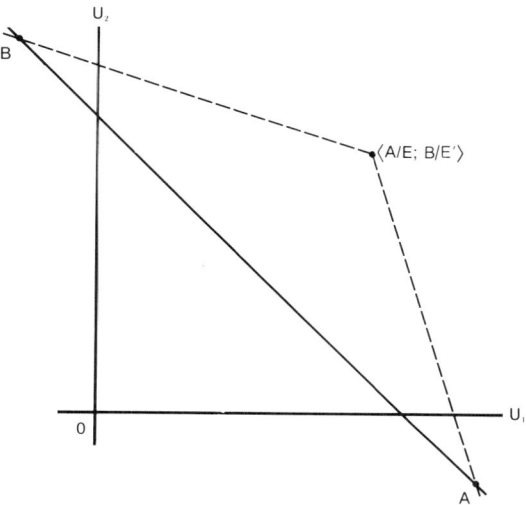

Figure 5.6 Contingent agreement with partial disagreement on probabilities

ple, an executive delivering a postmortem on a failed project to the irate board of directors: "We couldn't decide between projects X and Y and we weren't sure of our competitor's decision. So we flipped a (cleverly) weighted coin"). In fact, randomization to create or enlarge zones of agreement in negotiation may be fairly common. The case in which there is disagreement on probabilities may even be typical. Three classes of situations suggest themselves in which a de facto randomizing mechanism may produce joint gains: (1) the items under negotiation are uncertain and are themselves subject to different probability estimates; (2) each party feels that it will fare well under and perhaps can influence a proposed but uncertain resolution procedure; and (3) the parties believe that they can avoid negative aspects of the negotiation process itself by an effectively randomized outcome.

In the first case, the outcomes of the event under negotiation may be uncertain and subject to different probability estimates. Contingent agreements can effectively represent randomizations using different probabilities. Economic agreements frequently have this character. Suppose that the profit of a joint venture is uncertain. The partners can formulate sharing schedules that are contingent upon different levels of profitability, with each party given a schedule that will be advantageous if its most likely profit projections are realized. For example, assume that one partner is convinced of the venture's high profitability, while another partner sees more modestly profitable outcomes. To be enticed into investing, this second partner must receive the lion's share of the market profits that he expects will come about. But the first partner finds such a high overall sharing percentage to be unacceptable. They may negotiate a contingent sharing schedule, however, that gives the first partner a very high share of profits above some level and the second partner most of the profits below that amount. The two partners may thereby make a mutually beneficial deal. This first class of situations, then, involves inherent uncertainty about the event itself in which the parties are interested. In this case, the parties may profitably use divergent probability estimates through contingent agreements.

De facto randomization may be employed in a second common class of situations where the parties believe that they can positively affect the chances for a favorable outcome of the randomizing event. Each side may assess the odds of an outcome favorable to itself as high conditional upon its future efforts to affect that outcome. An example of this might be the voluntary submission of a dispute to arbitration. Each side, firmly believing in the moral persuasiveness of its position and highly confident in the quality of its representation before the tribunal, may feel that the chances of obtaining its desired outcome are very good. These beliefs may be incompatible, and the two parties may thus be unable to negotiate their way to one or another of the distinct possible outcomes. They would likely reject the game theorist's suggestion to let the overt flip of a coin decide such a serious question. With both sides nonetheless believing in the value of a settlement, the parties might in effect agree to a randomized (contingent) settlement. From each disputant's standpoint, the uncertain event is the arbitrator's decision. Other third-party settlements as well may be thought of as randomizations with different probabilities.

In international negotiations, the participants often do not categorically resolve the difficult issues. Instead, the parties create a mechanism to handle the particular disputes that will inevitably arise. Each side expends a great deal of effort in bargaining for aspects of the constitution, powers, procedures, and voting methods of the dispute-resolution mechanism. Each party may thereby think itself capable of affecting the future resolution of these issues (and will certainly make this claim to watchful constituents). It may well be that, however grudgingly, any points in the currently contemplated bargaining range would now be acceptable to all sides. All parties may now want a settlement, but an agreed outcome that greatly favors one of them could be politically unthinkable. All may agree, however, to an outcome randomized by a future panel. Perhaps self-delusively, each side may feel that its chances are excellent, thereby facilitating an agreement.

Negotiations often leave much ambiguity in a treaty, with the tacit understanding that a definite resolution of the issue, perhaps strongly favoring one party, will later become necessary. Leaving the ambiguity for resolution by a future mechanism that may be subject to influence can be thought of as randomizing the outcome on an event with different probabilities. The zone of possible agreement is enhanced. One thinks of the French saying, "There could be no treaties without *conflicting* mental reservations."

If the uncertainty takes time to be resolved, moreover, other aspects of the agreed treaty regime may settle into place, making even a relatively adverse settlement of the formerly contentious issues at least tolerable to both sides. Forcing a resolution of one of these issues strongly in favor of one party during the initial negotiation may place unbearable strain on the overall settlement process, whereas leaving it for subsequent (randomized) solution in a more amenable future context may be a common and beneficial procedure.

Two oligopolists may be unable to agree on market shares for reasons of law or pride. However, they would still like the benefits of collusion. Since both are painfully aware of the ills of price competition, they may be able to agree on prices. Because advertising and research and development are hard to monitor, however, economic analysis and experience suggest that the oligopolists may effectively agree to compete along these nonprice lines. Consistent with such behavior would be an explanation that found each oligopolist supremely confident of his advertisers and his research and development staff. Each may well be willing to agree on a market share outcome that is effectively randomized on the success of marketing and of research and development, which is uncertain but subject to influence. Divergent success probabilities may enlarge a zone of possible agreement on prices, as with the analogous case of arbitration in treaty negotiations.

A third kind of situation in which randomization may profitably be used is that in which aspects of the actual negotiation or settlement process make resolution difficult. Then randomization on an uncertain event (preferably over which the parties have probability disagreements) may make a beneficial agreement possible. If the randomizing event is entirely separate from the negotiating issues, the participants may avoid otherwise problematic aspects of the negotiation process.

Consider a particularly difficult distributive negotiation over one of two possible outcomes. Each party prefers the *substance* of either of

NEGOTIATING THE LAW OF THE SEA

these outcomes to no agreement, but each outcome is seen to favor a different party. To agree to a particular outcome, say, A or B, might be extraordinarily hard. The party agreeing to a barely acceptable result that greatly favors the other party may be seen as "conceding," may "lose face," or may be perceived as having made a de facto admission of relative weakness. Figure 5.7 shows the utility of the outcome associated with A or B chosen by a painful negotiation; A' and B' are the utilities of the *substantive* outcomes independent of the choice process. (Other reasons that A' and B' could dominate A and B, respectively, would be, for example, that the parties cared about their relationship after the negotiation.) Recourse to an impartial, unrelated chance mechanism may allow resolution along the $A'B'$ segment without concession, loss of face, or admission of weakness. In effect, randomization can shear off these undesirable attributes of the process. (Notice that disagreement on the probabilities of an event, say E, may offer further joint gains, say, to $\langle A'/E; B'/E' \rangle$.) The acceptance of an admissible outcome that favors the other side may be rationalized as a bad, but tolerable, break.

An example from the Law of the Sea negotiations involves a number of these elements: (1) a subnegotiation that was at a political impasse over (2) an issue that in substance could probably have been resolved either way without major trauma to either side, where (3) the parties could have avoided further negative consequences of negotiation and

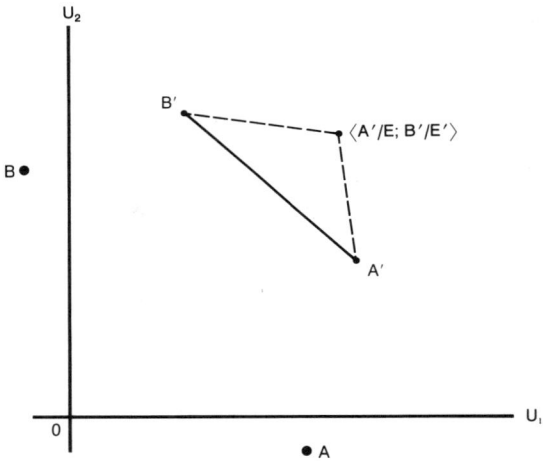

Figure 5.7   Randomization to avoid negative consequences of negotiation process

possible repercussions in other issue-areas by effectively randomizing the issue on the decision of a future body, and where (4) each side believed that its influence over the future mechanism's choice would be strong; that is, there were disagreements on probabilities.

As part of a major seabed compromise, delegates had earlier agreed to finance the initial operations of a new international seabed mining entity, the Enterprise. A designated body would specify the amount of money for this purpose. States ratifying the treaty would pay a percentage of the amount equal to their preset percentage share of funding of the United Nations' budget. The delegates appeared to be relatively unconcerned about the *amount* of money to be specified; they showed keen interest in their *percentage* shares of this sum.

At a subsequent negotiating session, an overlooked problem became evident: what if only a fraction of U.N. member states ratified the convention? Then there would be a monetary shortfall, and the Enterprise, as the centerpiece of the developing countries' aspirations and one of their principal negotiated victories, would not be certain of a secure start. The developed countries opposed mandatory supplemental contributions; they felt that the accepted "deal"—an overall seabed system in return for the Enterprise—implied the U.N. scale percentages and no more. National budgetary processes were said to demand certainty for international contributions. A supplement would be of uncertain size, however, and would be dependent on the ratification decisions of other states. For days a negotiating impasse prevailed. Developed countries had instructions against mandatory, uncertain supplements; developing states saw this stance as reneging on the Enterprise deal and feared a threat to the existence of this new entity.

Despite these intense political problems for both sides, and the virtual impossibility for either side to concede, there was an underlying realization that either solution—supplements or no supplements—would in substance be at least barely tolerable for the parties. For one thing, the participants generally thought that the ratifications of major contributing countries would only occur together: that few or none of the group consisting of the United States, the United Kingdom, the Federal Republic of Germany, France, and Japan would ratify unless they all did; similarly, their ratifications and that of the Eastern bloc were felt to be mutually conditional; and these ratifications by themselves would ensure about three-quarters of the funds for the Enterprise. Other major states would quickly bring the total to over 90 percent. (In fact, these expectations proved to be wrong.) Thus, by the logic of the commonly articulated predictions on ratification, the shortfall and its implied supplements would either be small or so large as to be unworkable if any of the larger states stayed out. Moreover, the actual money amount to be specified for Enterprise finance could be shaded upwards in anticipation of some nonratifications. Finally, if money in fact proved to be short, there were many less expensive alternatives to the particular Enterprise operation envisioned in the deal: this new entity could engage in joint ventures, "mining-only" operations instead of an integrated mining-transportation-processing system, or it could start with a smaller-scale project. In sum, the shortfall scenario posed an enormous political and negotiating problem of clashing principles — a threat to the integrity of the Enterprise versus mandatory, uncertain supplements beyond an agreed deal. In substance, delegates did not widely expect this to be a serious problem; the Enterprise was probably not threatened and any supplements were expected to be small.

Although neither side felt that it could give in politically, each could probably live with any ultimate outcome. A solution was proposed and finally accepted: once the treaty entered into force, the Seabed Authority would be given a mandate to deal with the shortfall problem. Thus, this future body *must* deal with the problem. This solution allowed delegates from the developing countries to reassure their constituents about the Enterprise; yet each of the sides felt that its influence over the Authority's future decision processes would probably be sufficient to make an acceptable solution likely. In effect, the delegates avoided the negative consequences of a current forced concession by randomizing the outcome on the actions of a future entity. Each side believed in its influence over these actions, and thus that the chances of a favorable settlement were in its favor. All sides, however grudgingly, could most likely accept any probable outcome. It is easy to imagine the compromise as a coin flip, where each side felt the coin to be biased in its favor. Conceptualizing the negotiating problem in these terms pointed the way toward opening up a zone of agreement.

At least three institutionally plausible classes of situations exist, therefore, in which de facto randomization allows joint gains. When the uncertain event itself is of interest, there are the familiar economic contingent contracts with "betting" based on probability differences. When there is an uncertain event that the parties feel capable of influencing, effective randomization on this event arises, as with voluntary arbitration, dispute settlement mechanisms, treaty ambiguities, and some forms of nonprice competition. Finally, randomization offers a device for shearing negative attributes from some difficult bargaining processes, thereby enabling substantive accords to be reached.

5.1.2.3 RANDOMIZATION WHERE PROBABILITIES DIFFER: EXTENSIONS

A mediator who is convinced that randomization with probability disagreements would be useful to his negotiating clients should have basic guidelines on how to set up the requisite contingent agreements. Section 5.2.1 demonstrates that the appropriate rule is the intuitive one: Give each side its preferred outcome contingent on the result of the randomizing event that it feels is more likely than does the other side. The greater the disagreement on probabilities, the higher and more equally balanced are the possible joint gains under this procedure. If the disagreements are small, the gains from the use of this method over those of a randomization with "objective" probabilities will be small and skewed toward one party.

Since the discussion so far includes randomizing events with only two possible outcomes, there are only two contending contingent agreements. If the potential gains from such a choice are skewed and the mediator wishes to balance the settlement, it is still possible to use the disagreement to dominate any objectively randomized solution. This procedure, which is discussed in Section 5.2.1, essentially consists of objectively randomizing between one of the discrete settlement points and the (subjectively) randomized outcome that results from using the differences according to the above guidelines.

Suppose that two bargainers differ on the chances of an event that has many, even a continuum, of possible outcomes, like the level of the Dow Jones average or the amount of rain to fall in a growing season. Section 5.2.2 shows that such disagreements may be the foundation of mutually advantageous contingent agreements that are analogous to bets. In effect, the agreement is to make "payoffs" to one or the other party depending on the outcome of the uncertain event. A number of considerations should be taken into account if one wishes to construct such a bet schedule in an optimal way, that is, in a manner that cannot be improved from the standpoint of one party except at the expense of the other. The optimal arrangement is defined point by point over the range of possible outcomes. The payoff increases to one party for those results he thinks are increasingly likely relative to his opponent's beliefs; the payoff increases for the other party over those results she believes more strongly to be increasingly probable. The risk aversion of both parties is a mitigating factor; any increase in the bet schedule is always reduced by their combined risk aversion. The shape of the overall betting schedule is determined by two factors: how the probabilities and the aversion toward the betting risks of one party are changing relative to those of the other. With these factors in mind, an optimal, if more complex, use of wide-ranging probability differences may be made.

5.1.3 Differences in Risk Aversion

Theories of risk bearing and the appropriate economic arrangements for efficiently allocating risks among agents are an important preoccupation of economic theory. A voluminous literature exists on insurance and risk spreading, as well as risk reduction through diversification. From the perspective of the differences approach, both types of transactions — risk spreading through purchases of insurance and risk reduction through portfolio diversification — can be viewed as arising from differences between individuals in attitudes toward risk and in endowments across various possible states of the world.

Agreements can be used to "smooth" endowments across states when some individuals will be well off in some states and others will be well off in others. This smoothing is precisely the effect of either insurance or diversification. It is made possible by the existence of enforceable agreements that will apply across various possible states of the world. It is made desirable by the fact that people generally prefer to avoid risk. It works because people's endowments are distributed differently across states of the world, and therefore they can each reduce the risk they face ex ante by agreeing to share their wealth ex post. Each party finds this ex ante agreement desirable because it smooths out the possible variations in his endowments — he is better off in some states and worse off in others, but faces less variation across states. This net reduction in variation for trading partners can only be achieved if their endowments are differently distributed across states. Once again, differences are at the root of the joint gains.

Even if people's endowments are similarly distributed across time, joint gains may arise if some dislike risk less than others. In this case, the reallocation across states will reduce the variation faced by the more risk-averse party. Thus, the trades need not result in an absolute decrease in variation faced by all parties together. As in the theory of pure exchange in the two-commodity case, people with similar endowments can trade as long as they have dissimilar tastes. But they must differ, or they have nothing to offer to each other that is of less value to the offerer than to the offeree.

If negotiators face risky prospects about whose probabilities they agree, a variety of risk-sharing mechanisms may be employed to the advantage of all parties. The analysis in Section 5.2.4 shows in general that such mechanisms optimally should shift more of the risk to the party who is *relatively* less risk-averse than the other.

One might legitimately ask whether there are many situations in which risk attitudes could be expected to be useful in fashioning negotiated settlements. A variety of such cases suggest themselves. Obviously, some individuals are simply more avid risk takers than others. This may also be true in negotiations between small, entrepreneurial companies and more established, conservative firms. If negotiators are at different levels of their respective organizations, they may exhibit different risk attitudes. Different expected job mobility or career paths may imply dissimilar risk preferences. (It is also true that people with higher-level positions may be able to diversify across several issues and may not be as concerned about the specific risk of one negotiated outcome as a person on a lower organizational rung with fewer subjects of responsibility.)

A group of individuals facing a large, risky project may be able to divide it up in such a way that each of the members takes on a manageable piece. The group may thereby act in a considerably more neutral way toward risk than do its individual members. Thus, in negotiations among different-sized groups, or between a single firm and a consortium, or between a company and a national government, considerable scope for the use of risk differences may exist. Arrow and Lind have shown that, under fairly general conditions, a large government should act in a risk-neutral manner when evaluating uncertain prospects.[12] Thus, public/private negotiations might be facilitated by the invention of risk-shifting mechanisms, especially where the private party has a greater aversion to risk. In all these situations, advantageous agreements may be constructed to reflect the differences.

To give an example, provisions of taxation systems or contractual arrangements — fixed fees, royalties, and profit shares — shift risk very differently. Suppose that the investment costs, operating costs, and revenues of a project are uncertain but that the parties undertaking it share beliefs about these uncertainties. If one party's share is a fixed fee, the other party bears the risk of lower than expected returns while enjoying the prospect that higher returns may result. Different combinations of fees, royalties, and profit shares may all be *expected* to yield the same payment, but the "upside potential" and the "downside risks" of each such combination may increase or decrease its attractiveness to a party depending on its risk attitudes. The optimal way to dovetail such differences into agreements between a risk-neutral party and a risk averter is worked out in Section 5.2.5 for these very common tax and contractual instruments.

If two very risk-averse parties are negotiating over an uncertain prospect, it may be possible to bring in a third, more risk-neutral actor to "buy" the risk from the original bargainers, and thereby facilitate their deliberations. For example, the output of a commodity with a volatile price could be sold under long-term contracts. Rather than bargaining over the shares of an uncertain revenue stream, the original commodity owners may then bargain more easily over the division of a known amount of revenue. Passively bringing in third parties with different risk attitudes to enable an advantageous agreement is discussed in Section 6.2.2.

It is quite possible that both probability estimates and risk attitudes will differ between negotiating parties. If this is the case and the parties are dealing with uncertainty over a continuum of possible outcomes, optimal contingent agreements may again be formulated, as discussed in Section 5.2.4. Such agreements or schedules should be constructed point by point over the uncertain range. At the margin, *separate* risk-sharing and betting effects govern the payoffs to each party. Analysis shows that these effects, even when present together, can be conceptually disentangled at the margin. Payoffs to the first side should be more certain where that side is relatively more risk-averse than the other side and should increase where the first side's probability beliefs are becoming relatively stronger. The increase in payoffs due to these changing probability differences, however, is reduced by the *combined* risk aversion of the two sides, as was the case when betting schedules were analyzed by themselves. The shape of the overall agreement is again determined by the relative rates of change of probabilities and risk aversion of the two sides.

5.1.4 Differences in Time Preference

Finally, consider differences in attitude toward the passage of time. People may value the same event quite differently depending on when it occurs. If one side is relatively less impatient than the other, mechanisms for optimally sharing the consequences over time may be devised, as discussed in Section 5.2.7.

A particularly simple form of time-preference difference may be reflected in discount rates. Suppose that party 1 has a 10 percent discount rate, that party 2's rate is 20 percent, and that each party cares about the present value of income. Party 1 will receive $100 next year; party 2 is slated to receive $100 the year afterward. Thus the present value of party 1's income is about $91, and party 2's is $69. The parties could engineer a variety of profitable trades to dovetail this difference.

Because party 2 values early income relatively more than does party 1, party 2 should get the first year's $100. If, in the second year, party 1 gets $100 plus $20 from party 2, the present value of party 1's income rises from $91 in the original division to $99. The present value of party 2's income stream (+ $100, − $20) remains at about $69. If party 2 gave $10 to party 1 in the second period, party 1 could have the same present value as in the original division ($91) while the present value of party 2's income would be $76 instead of the original $69. Any outcome in which party 2 gets the first $100 and party 1 gets between $110 and $120 in the second period is as good or better for both parties than the original division.

As this simple example suggests, analysis of trades between individuals over time involves only a simple extension of the usual static exchange model of the Edgeworth box. Economists often study separately exchanges involving two or more periods of time as "capital market transactions." In the language of the differences approach, one could simply observe that these transactions are driven by differences between traders in their tastes and endowments over time. Trade is a particularly important means for exploiting such differences, since it may be physically impossible to carry out reallocations involving time through any other mechanism. It is perhaps stretching the point only a little to observe that capital markets play a central role in economic exchange in part because there are dramatic differences among economic agents in tastes and endowments over time that cannot be used to mutual advantage other than through the avenue of trade.

The principle of a rearrangement of future consequences in a way that gives earlier amounts to the more impatient party may similarly be useful to negotiators whenever time-preference differences exist. As with the discussion of risk aversion, such characteristics are likely to find useful application in a variety of circumstances. Apart from ad hoc instances of the presence of such differences in individuals, they may be important in cross-cultural negotiations where time attitudes vary considerably. Where parties are of quite different ages or where opportunities for the use of, say, money are not the same, joint gains may be possible. People at different organizational levels may have very different time horizons for valuing the results of a negotiation. Time-preference differences may be particularly important in some public/private negotiations over projects with future ramifications; governments or public entities may weigh benefits or costs to future generations more heavily than do their private counterparts. This state of affairs may offer room for mutually advantageous temporal divisions that enhance the possibilities of agreement.

5.1.5 Difference Example from the LOS Negotiations

The negotiations over the financial terms of seabed mining contracts, discussed in Chapters 1 – 3, implicitly contained elements of these ideas. Within the context of the LOS conference, the negotiations in part concerned the system of fees, royalties, and profit shares to be paid by future seabed miners to the "international community" for the right to mine nodule resources that were universally agreed to be the "common heritage of mankind." Although the overall LOS negotiation foundered on other issues, the successful results of this apparently intractable financial aspect of the treaty involved an arrangement that effectively exploited differences among the participants in probability, risk aversion, and time preference.

A great deal of technical and economic uncertainty surrounded ocean mining. Even after lengthy negotiations and the introduction of much common information, a divergence of opinion persisted between developed and developing countries about the likely economic profile of mining. Developed countries saw mining as providing a new, lower-cost source of minerals and argued that this industry would show attractive but modest economic returns. Many delegates from developing countries, however, felt that profitability prospects were very good indeed. In short, expectations diverged.

Any eventual revenue from seabed exploitation would be divided up among the members of the world community and would not represent a major share of any country's national income. The international community can be thought of as a large syndicate that might wish to maximize expected income rather than trying to assure itself of a smaller, steady stream. Corporate investments in seabed mining operations, however, could represent significant portions of their assets. In particular, managers of the ocean mining divisions of these companies were quite concerned with the potential impact of relatively fixed charges such as fees or royalties on the economic success of troubled projects. They seemed willing to share profits at high rates for successful projects in return for "low-end" protection of economically marginal ventures. Attitudes toward risk thus were different.

Finally, there was the question of timing. The companies' private, after-tax discount rates appeared to be higher than those implicitly used by the negotiators from developing countries, who saw themselves as setting up an enduring system. The welfare of future generations figured heavily in their negotiating statements and in their evaluations of proposals. The two sides' attitudes toward time seemed to differ.

An agreement was reached only after two years of difficult bargaining. The outcome can be seen as dovetailing these three differences. Two sharing schedules were agreed upon, one with a low royalty and a low profit share, the other with much higher payment rates in each category. The low schedule is in effect until the overall cash flow of the operation, cumulated forward at an appropriate real interest rate, is sufficient to recover the preproduction investment (also cumulated forward with interest). Higher rates then take effect.

The two negotiated schedules use the differences in profitability estimates by effectively giving each side an advantageous tax schedule for the economic outcome it portrayed as likely. Negotiation of a single set of rates had proved extremely difficult, with any proposal either being opposed by the developed countries as too high or being opposed by the developing countries as too low. The use of two schedules represented an effectively randomized solution, where estimates differed on the chances of each outcome. Given the developing countries' expectations of high profits, negotiation of low rates for modestly successful projects was no great concession. Similarly, accepting high rates for bonanza projects was tenable for potential mining companies, given their lower profit forecasts. It was critical, however, that the low rates were neither so low nor the high rates so elevated that the ultimate result would be politically unsustainable. The parties knew that they would have to live with and defend the outcome, however the profit uncertainties resolved themselves.

Under the agreement, troubled or marginal projects are relatively well protected against overly high fixed charges. In return for such lower rates, however, the miners face much higher rates for successful projects than likely would have been negotiable otherwise. The signal for switching to the higher rates is based on the "accumulated" present value of a project's cash flows, that is, inflows and outflows cumulated forward with interest. Therefore, the higher rates apply only to projects whose risk — that the investment and its opportunity costs would be lost — has substantially diminished. Differences in risk attitudes are dovetailed: the international community has a higher expected take, while the companies enjoy "low-end" protection. In effect, contingent high-end premiums are paid for contingent low-end insurance.

Finally, since the economic success of a project can normally be expected to increase over time, the stream of payments should be low at first and then much higher later. Although this is hardly a claim for larger social optimality, this arrangement accords well with the apparent and expressed differences in time preference among the negotiators.

While it is not likely that any one of these differences by itself would have been sufficient to lead to a negotiated settlement, in combination they reinforced each other in indicating a possible solution. It is remarkable that the technical solution to this negotiation problem resulted in an essentially new form of mineral taxation agreement. Its invention implicitly in response to the participants' differences helped to avert the negotiating impasse on the financial issues that was widely predicted.

5.1.6 Asymmetric Information

Recourse to betting over probability differences may be fine in theory, one might assert, but what about the situation in which one party has "better" information, or access to data; is it still "fair," "optimal," or even "rational" to place bets? This troublesome question might be posed in terms of a negotiation between a Third World country and a transnational mining company. Should the country be willing to bet on differences in (perhaps weakly held) beliefs? What if it is suspected that the company knows more, or in some sense has a "better" probability distribution over the profitability of the venture? A full discussion of these extremely difficult questions would require much time, but a few of the issues they raise are worth touching on here.

To order thinking about these issues, first recall that a marginal payment schedule can be decomposed into a risk-sharing effect and a betting effect. The question of possibly different information enters only through the second effect: at the margin, risk sharing is unaffected by probability estimates. If the parties share the description of uncertainty, any betting vanishes. Suppose that after extensive consultation and negotiation, however, the parties hold to greatly divergent views about the likelihood of different values of the uncertain quantity, then the risk-sharing component of the agreement should remain unaffected at the margin.

Of course, learning of another's probability assessment may induce a change in one's probabilistic beliefs. The willingness to take a bet itself may reveal information about the basis of one's assessments. If the appraised value of some land Sally owns is $10,000, and Joe offers her $50,000 for it, she may suspect that there is oil below it, or that a development is planned nearby. In order not to alert Sally to this possibility, of course, Joe may make a $12,000 offer. However, the general point remains: actions taken on the basis of probabilistic beliefs communicates something about those beliefs. A stylized argument in

Section 5.2.6 illustrates a class of situations in which one of the parties ultimately turns down *any* proposed contingent arrangement that is based on different probability assessments of an uncertain event. In discussing the proposed agreement back and forth, the parties indirectly reveal enough about their own privately obtained information that the divergent views necessary for the contingent (or betting) aspects of the agreement are eliminated. If the parties' original information and means of processing new information are the same and both are "common knowledge," then this "no-betting" result holds.[13]

To carry the analysis further, it is useful to review the formal mechanism by which beliefs (probability distributions) are altered about uncertain quantities and events. One's initial beliefs (*prior* probabilities) are combined with new information (data, observations, opinions of others) by way of a model (*likelihood function* or means of processing information) to form updated beliefs (*posterior* probability distributions) about uncertain quantities or events. Each of these elements — priors, models, posteriors — can play a role in thinking about contingent arrangements based on differences in belief.

Suppose that party 1 feels woefully ignorant about an uncertain quantity and that party 2 exhibits fairly specific beliefs. One way to define "better" information from party 1's viewpoint might be to say that party 1 prefers to use party 2's distribution rather than his own in making decisions. This phenomenon may be fairly common when an agent is hired by a principal. Part of the reason for the contract may be that the principal feels the agent has "better" information, and, in any case, gives instructions for the agent to use his own assessment in decision making on the principal's behalf.[14] If one party to a contingent agreement feels that this substitution is appropriate, then any betting effect in the optimal sharing schedule vanishes. From a more Bayesian point of view, one might roughly say that party 1 had diffuse prior beliefs and that exposure to party 2's more peaked distribution resulted in posterior beliefs for party 1 that were virtually identical to those of party 2. This line of reasoning has promise but requires more precision in its application.

Imagine a case in which parties 1 and 2 share the same prior information, as well as the same likelihood function (model, method of processing information, or partition of the space of possible outcomes). Party 2 has "better" information in that she has gathered data, performed experiments, or taken samples and updated her prior distribution of beliefs accordingly. If this is known, party 1 would certainly not want to bet on the basis of his prior and her posterior distributions. He would immediately realize that his prior should be similarly updated, and the bet would vanish.

The parties may share a common informational endowment (prior distribution) but differ in their models (say that one is a Keynesian, the other a monetarist or Marxist). Thus receipt of the same subsequent data will not necessarily lead to convergent forecasts of the future. Or the parties may differ on prior distributions but agree on models. Say that, in this circumstance, party 2 is known to have gathered much information and to have updated accordingly. In such cases party 1 would often be able to infer something about this data and would also update. Less betting might then be expected than would have occurred if party 1's original prior and party 2's posterior distributions had been used to construct the contingent payment schedule. In either case, however, nonzero betting on the basis of different priors or models makes sense.

If party 1 were confronted with party 2's posterior distribution but were uncertain about both her prior and model, party 1 could infer probabilistic conclusions about party 2's observed information. This fuzzy information could then be used to update party 1's prior. Notice that if party 1's prior were diffuse, if party 1 thought that he probably shared a model with party 2, and if party 1 thought that party 2's announced posterior was primarily a function of her observations, then, loosely, party 1's posterior distribution would likely be similar to party 2's, and betting would be less important. (Of course, the foregoing discussion ignores the question of deliberate deception; some discussion of this issue can be found in Section 5.2.3.)

These arguments particularly apply where observable data would result in similar posterior distributions for both parties. If the uncertainty were about the amount or grade of ore in a particular deposit, for example, this sort of analysis would often apply. Where the uncertainty is about a quantity such as the price of gold in five years, one might expect to see strongly held beliefs result in bets.

This general discussion suggests that, as a practical matter, betting should take place only after the uncertain items have been fully considered in negotiation. In situations where one side, in effect, would prefer to make decisions using the other's distribution, there is no good way to use the original differences. If the uncertain quantity is differentially assessed on both sides as a result of asymmetric data collection or observation, betting should generally not be too significant. In situations where prior information, likelihoods (models), or simple interpretations are different, however, betting in accord with these criteria may be mutually advantageous.

5.1.7 Consideration Ex Post

Whatever the information characteristics of the situation, some people feel uneasy about the suggested use of contingent agreements, effective bets, or randomizations. One hears statements like the following: "That's all fine to do before the fact, but what about afterwards, when the uncertainty is resolved, and one of the parties is relatively worse off than the other?" Suppose, for example, that a third party has induced the warring factions in a divided country to agree to a cease-fire and to hold an election, and suppose that this was possible primarily because each side had an overoptimistic estimate of its chances to win. Once the election is held, high expected utility is replaced by a declared winner and an army of angry losers. Was thought given, for example, to the questions of mechanisms ex post to form a dominant coalition?

Contingent agreements in more prosaic situations are not likely to pose such problems if the participants understand and accept the uncertainty, and if they have managed to make a binding contract. Say that parties 1 and 2 have made a deal that is favorable to party 2 if heads come up on the toss of a coin. The coin is tossed — and comes up heads:

> How unfair to 1! If the coin comes up heads, why doesn't party 1 immediately change his mind and call for a different decision rule . . . ? The answer, of course, is that the individuals entered into a contract that favors 2 if heads and 1 if tails. Furthermore, the payoffs are so balanced that the overall procedure is acceptable to each individual *before* the coin is tossed. It is not fair for one individual to back out of his contract with the other *after* the coin is tossed.[15]

Often, however, the aftermath of a contingent agreement requires more than a ringing affirmation of rationally maximized expected utility. Such questions about the parties' relationship once uncertainties are resolved might be called "morning after" problems. The first thing to ask is *whether* there will be a morning after; that is, whether the agreement was explicitly one-shot, or whether the parties have already carried out their agreed actions and the question of "backing out" is moot since the consequences are all that remain to be suffered or enjoyed. Given, however, that many, if not most, negotiated arrangements require some continuing involvement of the parties, the ex post sustainability of such agreements deserves analysis.

The sustainability of a contingent agreement depends in part on its institutional context. In market or other economic transactions carried out under an accepted legal framework, there is relatively little question about the legitimacy of different outcomes. There is general agreement about the desirability of being able to make contingent contracts; the participants appreciate the character of the involved risks; and powerful sanctions exist against noncompliance.

It may be that any outcome of the bargain, if certain, would be refused by at least one of the negotiators who preferred the status quo. From this statement, it may seem a short step to the argument that if such an outcome is realized (after a contingent agreement has been made), the unhappy side will not accept the result. The two situations — refusal ex ante of an alternative for certain and reneging on the same outcome after a contingent agreement has been made — are not necessarily identical. In the latter instance, by entering into the agreement (legally or by the stake of one's reputation, for example) a party may incur additional costs in case of noncompliance. Therefore, despite the substantive unattractiveness of the outcome, it is not certain that the agreement will be violated.

In many instances of negotiated agreements, however, the legitimacy of particular *outcomes* may be an issue. Even though the parties agreed to contingent terms, some outcomes may not be viewed as "fair" after the fact. For example, suppose that a mining venture in a developing country was portrayed as incredibly risky, was subject to fairly light taxation as a result, and ended up as a bonanza. With the "sunk risks" forgotten or minimized and suspicions of original misrepresentation, the costs to the host government of leaving the contract intact — especially if there is vocal political opposition — may be higher than the costs of demanding new terms. If this situation could have been anticipated in the original negotiations, then there would not have been much sense in leaving it as a possible contractual outcome (unless, of course, there were ulterior motives involved).

Beyond such distributional grounds for regarding an outcome as illegitimate, other aspects of the process of reaching an agreement or resolving the associated uncertainty may taint the result. Surprises such as oil price shocks may leave the agreement workable but may radically change its effects on the parties from those originally contemplated. *Ceteris paribus* assumptions may have been implicit. The formation of and adherence to an agreement may be tacitly conditional on the observance of certain conventions or norms. One side may perceive the other as having possessed or concealed relevant, perhaps superior information in the negotiation, as having cheated in some way, or as having improperly influenced the resolution of the uncertain event that was the basis of the contingent agreement. The first side may thereby feel tricked and justified in repudiating the accord.

Bargaining power or the walk-away conditions may themselves change as a result of an initial agreement. Before a mining company has made a large, fixed investment in a country, it may have great leverage over contractual terms simply by virtue of its option not to build the mine. Afterwards, it cannot as convincingly threaten to leave, and the host's new power may be exercised. This situation may result in further contractual instability. For example, suppose the company recognizes the impending shift of power and tries frenzied short-term measures to recover its investment. The resulting bulge in profits paradoxically may increase the chances of a forced renegotiation, as the host perceives the situation as even less fair.

Despite the attractions of contingent agreements, then, negotiators should consider their sustainability. The sustainability of an agreement depends on how binding a commitment the parties have made to it and the advantages that may flow from adherence (even if these advantages do not derive from the same negotiation). Typically, the degree of commitment to an agreement is established by incurring costs that are conditional upon noncompliance with the terms. The more these costs are known, certain, and large relative to the cost of keeping the agreement, the more the other side will regard the commitment as binding. The costs of keeping the agreement in all contingencies include perceptions of unfairness—distributionally, in process, from surprises or treachery. If the parties can anticipate these factors, they should be considered for inclusion in the original agreement.

Of course, parties may wish to conclude some forms of contingent arrangements—say, on arms control—even though they could foresee circumstances that would render the agreement unworkable. The odds of this occurring may be seen as low, however, and the parties may assess the expected value of having an agreement as high enough to offset the chance of such happenings. Compliance need not be a certainty for an agreement to be better than no agreement.

When constructing a contingent agreement, then, the parties should anticipate the possible later problems. They should carefully analyze the chances of self-destruction from considerations of ex post unfairness or illegitimacy. If the parties see the agreement in a wider context, with ties to other negotiations (ongoing or future) or to other parties (parallel or future), then the value of compliance may be enhanced and may be seen as greater than a loss on the issues immediately at hand. If the contingent parts of the agreement form part of a larger relationship among the negotiating parties, moreover, the case for holding to the terms can be more compelling.

5.1.8 Other Differences

Important elements of negotiated agreements consist of creatively dovetailed differences. Thus far, this section has analyzed four such differences. Generally, however, negotiators can find ways to combine differences, regardless of whether these characteristics allow formal representation and analysis. Although it is obviously impossible to enumerate most such qualities — indeed, the art of a "differences orientation" lies in their creative identification and use — a few additional kinds of differences arise frequently enough to merit brief discussion.

Negotiators often differ in their access to production opportunities, technologies, or capabilities to convert resources physically. Farmer Jones, with arid land and a tractor, may combine with Farmer Smith, who has seeds and water rights. The more different the parties' original arrangements of stocks and production opportunities, the more different will be their joint production possibilities from those held by either individual. (Of course, scale economies may allow identical people to gain by joining forces.) Differences in the ability to produce commodities can take many forms. Individuals may have differing access to technology, to the rights to use it, or to the physical, financial, or human capital needed to implement it. They may face differing costs of investment — for example, large organizations often have lower transaction costs in financial markets, may face lower costs of borrowing, or may have access to investment opportunities that yield higher rates of return. At any given moment, some individuals and organizations will have their assets in a more liquid form than others and will therefore be in a better position to take advantage of transient opportunities. One party may have access to better diversification possibilities. From the perspective of individual negotiators, differences in corporate and personal income tax status can generate opportunities for arrangements that produce higher aggregate after-tax income. Any of these production opportunity differences can form the basis for mutually satisfying agreements.

Parties may regard attributes of proposed solutions very differently. Apart from straightforward risk aversion, they may experience dissimilar tolerance for unresolved uncertainties. Even after agreeing to a coin flip or another random event in a way that is consistent with its probabilities and risk aversion, one side may be consumed with anxiety until the outcome is known, while the other party might remain unruffled. In this case, the time until resolution may be critical. Some may anticipate substantial "postdecisional regret"; others may be immune. Certain people may be indifferent to or may enjoy the process of making decisions; others may loathe the prospect. A future agreement might be decided on a once-and-for-all basis, or it might commit the parties to a sequence of analyses and later decisions. The more such differences can be found, the more potential grist there is for fashioning solutions.

The attractiveness of an agreement may be evaluated by very different criteria. Some parties may look primarily to its absolute value compared with that of no agreement. Exogenous "aspiration levels" may be the measure, or the relative advantage to the parties of the settlement may be central. Some people may be extremely concerned with outcome "fairness" relative to their negotiating partners; others may evaluate the attractiveness of the result in comparison to outside reference groups such as fellow workers, or with respect to the outcomes of previous negotiations. One negotiator may judge on the net present value of an agreed contract while another's superior may care only about gross margin, return on total assets, or effect on earnings per share. Differences in such evaluation criteria may suggest mutually beneficial settlements.

If the parties are acting to further different mixtures of economic, social, legal, political, or other sorts of goals, agreements may sometimes be tailored to fit them. The LOS regime for deep seabed mining, for example, displays aspects that are nominally and visibly designed by the negotiators to encourage mining, to protect land-based producers, and to foster international cooperation and the rule of law, as well as to further some tenets of the New International Economic Order.

Varied attitudes toward the precedential features of an agreement may be central in its desirability. In some cases, one party will be primarily concerned with the immediate consequences of the issue at hand, while others will evaluate the agreement in terms of its substantive, procedural, or legal implications or precedents.

Great differences may be found in the relationship of a negotiating agent and the principal. It may be that the negotiator must satisfy only himself, or the results of bargaining may require the approval of superiors or the ratification of the Senate, Parliament, or union rank and file. If negotiators have different audiences or constituencies — domestic or international, local or regional, political groups or geographic coalitions — outcomes may be invented that are simultaneously attractive to more than one of them. The importance and type of public image implied by possible settlements — involving power, face, self-image, status, daring, or prudence, for example — may be differentially valued. These varied relationships with principals, audiences, or constituencies may be building blocks for agreement. An agreement for the government to distribute large amounts of food to poor people may be variously framed as a compassionate welfare policy or a stabilizing farm program.

It is also clear that differences in personal and organizational situations may have implications for the desirability of negotiated outcomes. Earlier sections discussed possible time-preference or risk-aversion consequences of being in a particular organizational position. For example, a person wishing to become known early in a career as a crusading government official may have quite different goals from those of a more senior, stodgy bureaucrat. A private company in negotiation with either of these types might look to quite distinct resolutions, especially if the firm expected to deal with the same government agency for a long time.

Many other dimensions of difference may be relevant. Variations in ideology, moral sense, religious leanings, conceptions of fairness or equity, as well as altruism, nationalism, or internationalism, need not imply divisive conflict. Often these elements will conflict in complementary ways and thus will become candidates for dovetailing into advantageous arrangements. The intent of this analysis, however, is not exhaustive enumeration but to suggest the possibilities of a differences orientation. All of these differences among negotiating parties—in what they have and under what conditions they have it, in what they want and when they want it, in what they think is likely and unlikely, in what they can produce, and so forth—can be used, separately or in concert, to fashion mutually satisfying agreements.

5.2 More Formal Difference Analysis

5.2.1 Randomization Where Probabilities Differ

Suppose that an analytically inclined mediator is convinced that randomization with probability disagreements offers possible joint gains to his negotiating clients. How should he set up such randomized agreements in practice? Imagine that he faces the simple situation described earlier in this chapter.

Two individuals—call them parties 1 and 2—are trying to agree on one of two possible outcomes, A or B. Party 1 evaluates these outcomes by a von Neumann–Morgenstern utility function $U_1(\cdot)$ and prefers A to B. Party 2's utility function is $U_2(\cdot)$, and she prefers B to A. Figure 5.8 displays this situation. If parties 1 and 2 cannot agree on A or B, their resulting no-agreement utility is represented by the origin. Any point

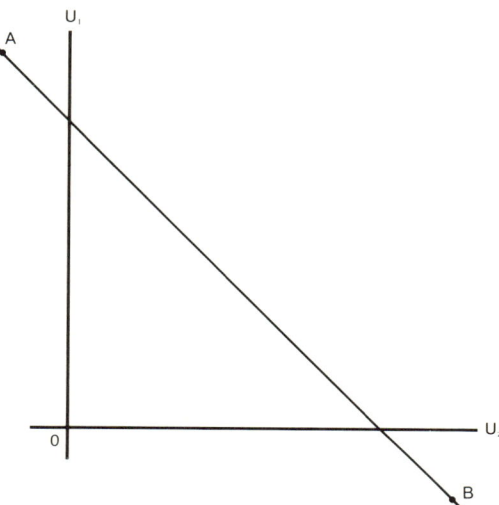

Figure 5.8 Basic negotiating situation with randomization

on the segment joining A and B can be achieved by a contingent agreement based on a randomizing device, such as a weighted coin, where the parties agree on the probabilities of a head (H) or tail (T).

Say that the agreed probability of heads is r, where $0 \leq r \leq 1$. If $r = 1$, then the contingent agreement $\langle A/H; B/T \rangle$ yields point A (in Figure 5.9) since both sides are sure that heads will come up. If $r = 0$, parties 1 and 2 expect B to be the certain result. Point C, which is midway between A and B, is achieved by $\langle A/H; B/T \rangle$ when $r = \frac{1}{2}$. Point D results from $r = \frac{3}{4}$; point E comes about if $r = \frac{1}{4}$.

Suppose that the parties are contemplating point C ($r = \frac{1}{2}$), when for some reason party 1 revises his opinion about the weighted coin: he now believes the chances of its coming up heads are $\frac{3}{4}$. Party 2 holds fast to her beliefs that $r = \frac{1}{2}$. Should the mediator stick with the contingent agreement $\langle A/H; B/T \rangle$, or should he pick the other possibility, $\langle A/T; B/H \rangle$? Agreement $\langle A/H; B/T \rangle$ is clearly the best choice, since it gives party 1 an increased chance of achieving his preferred outcome, A, while leaving party 2's prospects unchanged. As far as party 1 is concerned, the agreement is really represented by D. The joint utility evaluation of this situation is represented by F. Had $\langle A/T; B/H \rangle$ been chosen, party 1 would have felt that there was a $\frac{3}{4}$ chance of outcome B. He would have evaluated the agreement at point E on the chord; the joint evaluation of the contingent agreement would have been at point

NEGOTIATING THE LAW OF THE SEA

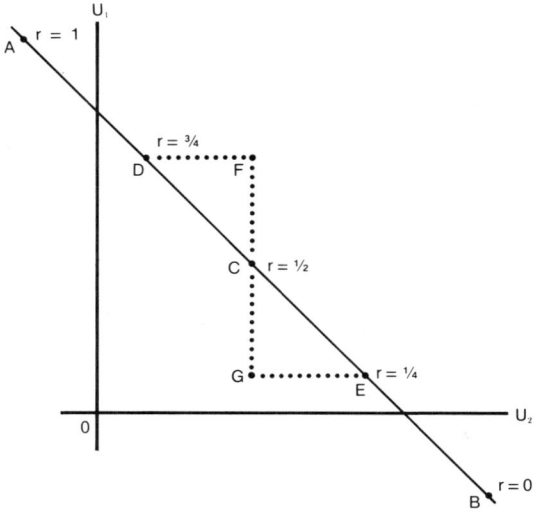

Figure 5.9 Randomization with disagreed probabilities

G (which is dominated by the points on the AB segment that are achievable by standard randomization with agreed probabilities).

Suppose the mediator has a more general problem. Party 1 assesses the chances of heads at r_1 and party 2 believes heads will come up with probability r_2, where $r_1 \neq r_2$. What should be the contingent agreement? It is easy to show that the appropriate rule is to pick $\langle A/H; B/T \rangle$ if $r_1 \geq r_2$, and $\langle A/T; B/H \rangle$ if $r_2 \geq r_1$. That is, if party 1 believes that the chances of a particular outcome of the randomizing event are higher than party 2 does, then the agreement should make party 1's preferred consequence contingent upon that outcome, and vice versa.

Figure 5.10 displays the joint utility evaluations of contingent agreements constructed according to this rule for all values of r_1 and r_2 between zero and unity. Point H is achievable when disagreement on r_1 and r_2 is total. If $r_1 = 1$ and $r_2 = 0$, the mediator should choose $\langle A/H; B/T \rangle$; if $r_1 = 0$ and $r_2 = 1$, $\langle A/T; B/H \rangle$ should be chosen. Both situations yield point H. Points in region (2), where the maximum joint gains are possible, are achievable only when one of r_1 and r_2 is greater than $\frac{1}{2}$ and the other is less than $\frac{1}{2}$. The more divergent the probabilities, the greater are the joint gains in this region. Points in regions (1) and (3) come about when there is relatively greater agreement on the values of r_1 and r_2.

Of course, a contingent agreement such as $\langle A/H; B/T \rangle$ only yields a

DIFFERENCES AND JOINT GAINS

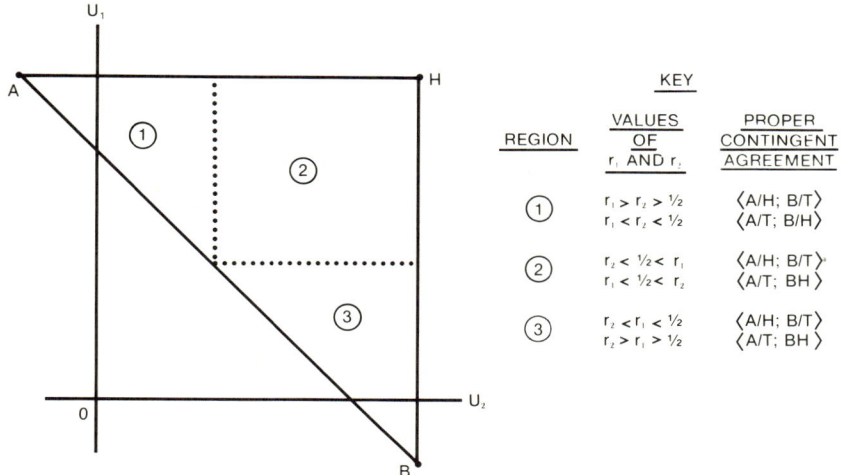

Figure 5.10 Regions of achievable utility with various probability disagreements

single point in the expected utility plane, and this point may greatly favor one or the other party. The mediator may prefer to suggest a point that is more equal in desirability to both parties. Suppose, as in Figure 5.11, that randomization with agreed probability (r) of heads would yield point C. The mediator discovers another event about whose probabilities the parties disagree. This event has possible realizations E and E'. Party 1 thinks that the probability of E is r_1; party 2 thinks that E will occur with probability r_2. Suppose that $r_1 > r_2$. Application of the preceding rule yields contingent agreement $\langle A/E; B/E' \rangle$, represented by point D in Figure 5.11. This agreement favors party 2 relative to the agreement represented by C. Of course, the disagreement about the probabilities of E is still useful. The mediator can find feasible points that are above and to the right of C by randomizing between points A and D. The desired points are indicated on the hatched portion of the AD segment.

It is not difficult to calculate the probabilities necessary for this additional randomization between points A and D. The randomization will give a chance p at outcome A, and a $(1 - p)$ chance at outcome D, $0 \leq p \leq 1$. (There is no reason that the parties need to use a randomizing device with *agreed* probabilities, but there is no point in overdoing it!) To be better for both parties than the agreed-probability randomization represented by C, the value of p must satisfy the inequalities

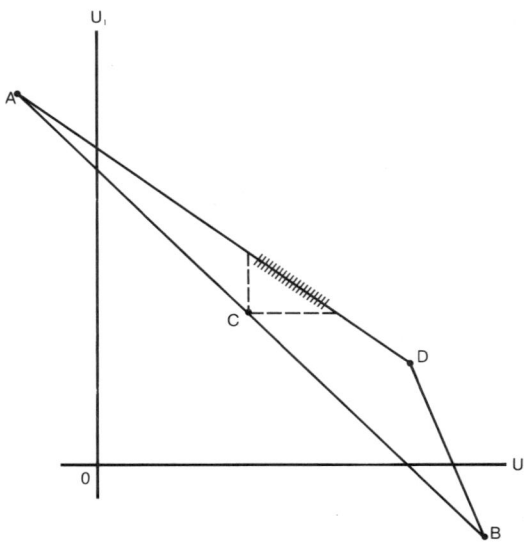

Figure 5.11 Generating Pareto-superior points using probability disagreement

$$pU_1(A) + (1-p)U_1(D) > rU_1(A) + (1-r)U_1(B)$$

and

$$pU_2(A) + (1-p)U_2(D) > rU_2(A) + (1-r)U_2(B).$$

Equivalently, p must satisfy

$$pU_1(A) + (1-p)[r_1U_1(A) + (1-r_1)U_1(B)] > rU_1(A) + (1-r)U_1(B)$$

and

$$pU_2(A) + (1-p)[r_2U_2(A) + (1-r_2)U_2(B)] > rU_2(A) + (1-r)U_2(B).$$

Any positive value of p in the interval $[(r-r_1)/(1-r_1), (r-r_2)/(1-r_2)]$ can be shown to do the trick. The interval is of positive length and is relevant where $r > r_2$.

If D were located such that points both on segments AD and DB dominated C, as in Figure 5.12, another randomizing mechanism could be defined that would offer a q chance at B and a $(1-q)$ chance at D. Any positive value of q in the interval $[(r_2-r)/r_2, (r_1-r)/r_1]$ has the desired property. Such values of q are relevant where $r_1 > r$. It is obvious from the figures and the algebra that *the mediator can dominate any point achievable through randomization with agreed probabilities (like C)*

DIFFERENCES AND JOINT GAINS

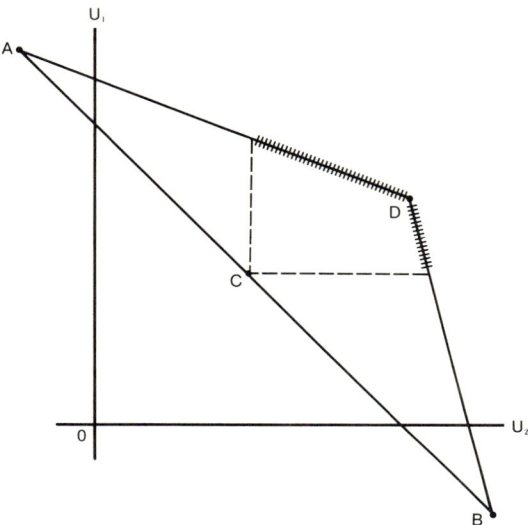

Figure 5.12 Generating more Pareto-superior points using probability disagreements

by points generated from randomization with disagreement on probabilities (like the hatched parts of AD and DB). Disagreements are always useful in this sense.

These rules for setting up contingent agreements are relatively simple to apply. For example, to choose between $\langle A/H; B/T \rangle$ and $\langle A/T; B/H \rangle$, the mediator only needs to know the parties' *rankings* of A and B and their relative ranking of the probabilities of one outcome of a binary randomizing event. Even subsequent randomizations (between A or B and the contingent event) do not require additional utility information. The values of p and q are independent of utilities. Of course, the more pronounced the disagreement about the probabilities of the randomizing event, r_1 and r_2, the greater is the potential value of the contingent solution.

This section has developed principles for the use of probability disagreements in a simple class of problems. A more general setting will now be investigated, where disagreements on probability are over a continuum of possible outcomes of a random variable.

5.2.2 Optimal Betting

Two individuals, parties 1 and 2, argue over an uncertain event. Their different opinions have not been reconciled by discussion or outside consultation. Party i's beliefs about the value of the uncertain quantity $\tilde{\xi}$ can be described by the differentiable probability density function,[16] $f_i(\xi)$, for $i = 1,2$. Party i also has a von Neumann–Morgenstern utility function, $U_i(\cdot)$, which is assumed to be well-behaved (it is strictly monotone, twice continuously differentiable, and concave) for $i = 1,2$. Assume that each of the disputants makes decisions by an expected utility criterion, and that each is honest about beliefs and preferences.

Different odds suggest a betting situation. The parties engage an analytically inclined mediator to suggest ways to make their bets in an "efficient" manner. They decide to define a betting function or schedule $B(\xi)$. Let $B(\xi)$ denote the payment by party 2 to party 1 when ξ is observed, with the understanding that if $B(\xi) < 0$, then party 1 pays the amount $-B(\xi)$ to party 2. Any betting function will give each party some level of expected utility. Parties 1 and 2 decide to rule out any proposed betting function if there exists another such function that is at least as acceptable to each party, and that is definitely preferred by one or both of them. All the bets that cannot be so ruled out meet this minimum agreed criterion of Pareto optimality.[17]

Efficient betting functions are those that maximize party 1's expected utility when party 2's expected utility is held at an arbitrarily constant level. By varying that constant, the full range of efficient schedules may be characterized. From among this set of betting functions, parties 1 and 2 may choose an attractive one. Perhaps the choice would derive from shared concepts of fairness, or it might be determined by hard bargaining.

The formal problem is to maximize party 1's expected utility by a choice of the function $B(\cdot)$ to maximize

$$\int U_1[B(s)]f_1(s)ds \tag{5.1}$$

subject to

$$\int U_2[-B(s)]f_2(s)ds = k, \tag{5.2}$$

where k is constant. (It would be more accurate, but for present purposes no more insightful, to include a term in the argument of $U_i(\cdot)$ reflecting the expected wealth of party i exclusive of the bet, given the occurrence of ξ, for $i = 1,2$. For simplicity, here and subsequently, this wealth effect will be neglected.)

If $\tilde{\xi}$ itself were the variable of interest to the parties—say it were profit instead of an arbitrary random event as is assumed here—and if

DIFFERENCES AND JOINT GAINS

ξ occurred, party 2 would receive $\xi - B(\xi)$ and party 1 would get $B(\xi)$. Then the problem would become one of risk sharing and betting, which is discussed in Section 5.2.4.

Before stating the main result, it is useful to define two functions that will play major roles in the analysis. First, let the function $h(\xi)$ be the logarithm of the ratio of the density functions. That is,

$$h(\xi) \equiv \ln \frac{f_1(\xi)}{f_2(\xi)} \tag{5.3}$$

for all ξ. Notice that $h(\xi)$ is positive, zero, or negative as $f_1(\xi)$ is greater than, equal to, or less than $f_2(\xi)$, respectively. Second, define absolute risk aversion, $r_i(x)$, at x, to be

$$r_i(x) = \frac{-U_i''(x)}{U_i'(x)} \tag{5.4}$$

for $i = 1,2$.

PROPOSITION 1. *The optimal betting function, $B(\xi)$, has the property that*

$$B'(\xi) = \frac{h'(\xi)}{r_1[B(\xi)] + r_2[-B(\xi)]} \tag{5.5}$$

for all ξ.[18]

Proof. Standard variational techniques can be used to show that the solution to the constrained maximization problem of expressions (5.1) and (5.2) satisfies the Euler equation

$$\frac{U_1'[B(\xi)]f_1(\xi)}{U_2'[-B(\xi)]f_2(\xi)} = \lambda \tag{5.6}$$

for all ξ, and where λ is a constant.[19] That is, the ratio of the probability-weighted marginal utilities in each state of nature (ξ) should be equated to a constant. Rearranging (5.6), differentiating with respect to ξ, and omitting the arguments of functions, obtain

$$U_1'' B' f_1 + U_1' f_1' = -\lambda U_2'' B' f_2 + \lambda U_2' f_2'. \tag{5.7}$$

Substituting (5.6) into (5.7), and rearranging terms, obtain

$$B' = \frac{f_1'/f_1 - f_2'/f_2}{-U_1''/U_1' - U_2''/U_2'}. \tag{5.8}$$

Noting that (5.3) implies

$$h' = \frac{f_1'}{f_1} - \frac{f_2'}{f_2} \tag{5.9}$$

and substituting expression (5.4) into the denominator of (5.8), the desired result (5.5) is proved.

If the parties are risk-averse, Proposition 1 implies that $B(\xi)$ is increasing wherever f_1/f_2 is increasing (as well, of course, as is the logarithm of this ratio, $h(\xi)$). It is interesting to note that the function $h(\xi)$ plays a central role in information theory. Kullback and Liebler argue that if H_i is the hypothesis that ξ was selected from the population with density function $f_i(\xi)$, for $i = 1,2$, then $\ln[f_1(\xi)/f_2(\xi)]$ is a natural measure of the information in ξ for discrimination between H_1 and H_2.[20] To put it another way, if one believed that the likelihood of ξ was a priori described by $f_1(\xi)$, and then one were informed that the "actual" likelihood of this realization was $f_2(\xi)$, then $f_1(\xi)/f_2(\xi)$, or some function thereof, would be an indication of one's "surprise." Albert Renyi showed that if this indication is required to satisfy some reasonable properties, primarily additivity for independent events, then the logarithmic function of the ratio is the only possible measure.[21] It is interesting that if one moves beyond an information-theoretic or inferential orientation to a subjective probability-expected utility context, then the action that one should optimally take at the margin—bet on the basis of divergent beliefs—is guided by the change in this "surprise" function, $h(\xi)$.

Proposition 1 characterizes the change in the optimal betting schedule in terms of $h'(\xi)$, an intuitively meaningful quantity. In general, of course, one should not expect $h(\xi)$ to characterize the bet schedule itself. However, some of Proposition 1's implications can usefully be explored in the case of the negative exponential class of utility functions, where $h(\xi)$ plays a central role.

Special case: Negative exponential utilities. Let $U_i(\cdot)$ be a negative exponential utility function with constant absolute risk aversion parameter r_i, where $i = 1,2$. Expression (5.5) is then readily integrated to obtain

$$B(\xi) = \frac{h(\xi)}{r_1 + r_2} + c, \tag{5.10}$$

where c, the constant of integration, is a function of the parametric level at which party 2's expected utility was held constant in the Paretian problem.

Expression (5.10) has an appealing interpretation. For values of ξ such that $f_1(\xi) = f_2(\xi)$, there is no bet that depends on the densities; there is only c, which is best thought of as a side payment. The bet can thus be conceptually disentangled from the side payment. The two parties' bargained level of k (their point on the Pareto frontier) does *not* affect the optimal wager.

In situations where party 1 believes a particular outcome ξ is more likely than does party 2, $h(\xi) = \ln[f_1(\xi)/f_2(\xi)]$ is positive; for such ξ, party 1 receives something positive from the bet. Where party 2 believes more strongly than party 1 that a particular ξ will occur, $h(\xi)$ is negative; that is, the betting payoff is positive for party 2. The optimal bet is directly proportional to $h(\xi)$ and is defined pointwise.

Risk aversion affects only the first term of expression (5.10). The more risk-averse the parties are, the smaller is the optimal bet at any point. The *sum* of the risk aversion parameters is the important quantity; how relatively risk-averse party 1 is compared with party 2 is irrelevant.

As long as utility functions are exponential, expression (5.10) holds for *any* nonzero, differentiable density functions (and can readily be extended to the case of discrete densities). It may be useful, however, to offer a few specific, simple density functions to go with the negative exponential utility functions assumed in this example.

If $f_i(\xi)$ is normally distributed with mean μ_i and standard deviation σ_i, for $i = 1, 2$, then

$$h'(\xi) = \frac{\sigma_1^2 - \sigma_2^2}{\sigma_1^2 \sigma_2^2} \xi + \frac{\mu_1 \sigma_2^2 - \mu_2 \sigma_1^2}{\sigma_1^2 \sigma_2^2}, \tag{5.11}$$

which, when integrated, would indicate a quadratic bet schedule. The sign of its squared term would be the same as the sign of $(\sigma_1^2 - \sigma_2^2)$. If $\sigma_1 = \sigma_2$, the bet schedule would be linear.

If $f_i(\xi)$ is exponentially distributed with mean μ_i, for $i = 1, 2$, then

$$h'(\xi) = \frac{\mu_1 - \mu_2}{\mu_1 \mu_2}. \tag{5.12}$$

If (5.12) is integrated, a linear bet schedule results. Its slope is positive or negative depending on the sign of $(\mu_1 - \mu_2)$.

Special case: HARA utilities. Closed-form expressions for the optimal betting schedule can also be obtained for other common utility functions. For example, betting schedules for the HARA (hyperbolic absolute risk aversion – linear risk tolerance) class can easily be derived. Let $r_i(\cdot) = c/(x + b_i)$ be the absolute risk aversion function for utility functions in this class, for $i = 1,2$. Substituting this into (5.5) and integrating, obtain a simple equation for B,

$$\frac{b_2 - B}{b_1 + B} = (e^{\gamma+h})^{1/c}, \qquad (5.13)$$

where γ is a constant of integration that depends on k. (Incidentally, the negative exponential utility function is a member of this class (b_i, $c \to \infty$; $r_i = c/b_i$), as are the logarithmic ($c = 1$) and power functions.) While these chosen cases are readily integrable, expression (5.5), as a first-order differential operation with an initial condition, is numerically tractable.

Certain factors behind the change in $B(\xi)$ have now been discussed. It is useful to examine the determinants of the shape of the optimal betting function.

PROPOSITION 2. $B(\xi)$ is convex, linear, or concave depending on whether

$$\frac{h''(\xi)}{[h'(\xi)]^2} - \frac{r_1'[B(\xi)] - r_2'[-B(\xi)]}{\{r_1[B(\xi)] + r_2[-B(\xi)]\}^2} \qquad (5.14)$$

is positive, zero, or negative.

Proof. Differentiating (5.5) with respect to ξ, obtain

$$\frac{h''(\xi)}{r_1[B(\xi)] + r_2[-B(\xi)]} - \frac{[h'(\xi)]^2 \{r_1'[B(\xi)] - r_2'[-B(\xi)]\}}{\{r_1[B(\xi)] + r_2[-B(\xi)]\}^3}, \qquad (5.15)$$

which can readily be shown to have the same sign as expression (5.14).

The shape of $B(\xi)$ at any point is thus dependent on two quantities. The first is the shape of $h(\xi)$, the logarithm of the ratio of the density functions. Second, the shape of $B(\xi)$ depends on whose risk aversion is changing more rapidly. Notice that the levels of risk aversion are not sufficient to define the concavity or convexity of $B(\xi)$.

Inspection of (5.14) immediately yields the following result.

COROLLARY. If the $r_i(\cdot)$ are constant (implying that the $U_i(\cdot)$ are negative exponential) or if $r_1'[B(\xi)] = r_2'[-B(\xi)]$ for all ξ, then $B(\xi)$ is convex, linear, or concave as $h(\xi)$ is convex, linear, or concave.

5.2.3 Honest, Worthwhile Betting

The last section showed that, in general, the Pareto-optimal betting function changes in direct proportion to $h'(x)$, the change in the logarithm of the ratio of the density functions. The actual optimal betting function, of course, is not in general logarithmic. But $h(x)$ is a particularly easy function to think about, as, for example, is a constant exponential discount rate in evaluating a future income stream. The conditions under which a constant discount rate is strictly correct are stringent, however, but the assumption is frequently very useful for intuition. Logarithmic betting schedules are likewise easy to conceptualize and implement. The purpose of this section is to demonstrate two useful properties of these particular betting schedules: (1) they are frequently preferable (even if not optimal) to the no-betting alternative; and (2) they engender truthful revelation of probabilities in a variety of important situations.

Suppose that party 1 makes decisions by an expected value criterion and that his *true* beliefs about an uncertain $\tilde{x}$ can be described by the density function $f_1(\cdot)$. A mediator has suggested the bet schedule [$a \ln(g_1(x)/g_2(x)) + b$], for all x, where $g_i(\cdot)$ is the *announced* probability belief of party i, for $i = 1,2$. Party 2 has already announced her probabilities as $g_2(\cdot)$. What should be party 1's announcement of $g_1(\cdot)$? The betting function, rewritten as [$a \ln(g_1(x)) - a \ln(g_2(x)) + b$], can be interpreted as a reward function that is linear in the logarithm of party 1's announced probabilities. It is well known that truth telling is the dominant strategy for such functions.[22] Party 1 should thus announce $g_1(x) = f_1(x)$, for all x. (The constants a and b are inessential to the argument, and the assumption that $a = 1$ and $b = 0$ will be in effect for most of the remaining exposition.)

Even when a truth-telling strategy is dominant, there may be no obvious reason for party 1 to find the bet attractive when compared with a no-bet alternative. If party 1 were risk-neutral, however, it is easy to see that choosing $g_1(x) = g_2(x)$ for all x would yield an expected value of zero (abstracting from wealth effects). In general, then, his dominant strategy ($g_1(x) = f_1(x)$) should thus yield positive expected utility, and the logarithmic bet would be worthwhile.

More generally, Proposition 3 shows that, unless an individual is "very" risk-averse, it is worthwhile to accept a logarithmic betting schedule *and* to announce true probabilities when faced with an arbitrary probability announcement by an opponent.

PROPOSITION 3. *Accepting a logarithmic bet schedule and announcing one's true probabilities regardless of the opponent's announced probabilities is preferable to not betting if one's absolute risk aversion function is less than unity.*

Proof. Denote the von Neumann–Morgenstern utility function by $U_1(\cdot)$, the expected utility of taking the logarithmic bet by EU_1B, the absolute risk aversion function by $r_1(\cdot)$, and recall that the betting function is $h(x) = \ln[g_1(x)/g_2(x)]$ to be received by party 1 if x is the realization of $\tilde{x}$.

It is necessary to show that

$$EU_1B = \int U_1[h(s)]f_1(s)ds \geq U_1(0), \tag{5.16}$$

where $g_1(x) = f_1(x)$, for all x, and where the absolute risk aversion coefficient of $U_1(\cdot)$ is less than unity over the appropriate range.[23] Define $g(x) = f_1(x)/g_2(x)$, for all x, and note that

$$\int g(x)g_2(x)dx = 1. \tag{5.17}$$

Define $\phi(t) = tU_1(\ln t)$, and note that since $0 < g(x) < \infty$, for all x,

$$\phi[g(x)] = \phi(1) + [g(x) - 1]\phi'(1) + \tfrac{1}{2}[g(x) - 1]^2\phi''[s(x)], \tag{5.18}$$

where $s(x)$ is between $g(x)$ and 1 for all x, and thus, $0 < s(x) < \infty$, for all x. Now

$$\phi(1) = U_1(0), \tag{5.19}$$

and

$$\phi'(1) = U_1'(0) + U_1(0), \tag{5.20}$$

and

$$\phi''[s(x)] = \frac{U_1''[\ln(s(x))]}{s(x)} + \frac{U_1'[\ln(s(x))]}{s(x)}, \tag{5.21}$$

assuming that these quantities always exist. Then

$$EU_1B = \int U_1[\ln(g(t))]f_1(t)dt \tag{5.22}$$

$$= \int g(t)U_1[\ln(g(t))]g_2(t)dt \tag{5.23}$$

$$= \int \phi[g(t)]g_2(t)dt \tag{5.24}$$

$$= U_1(0) + \int [g(t) - 1]\phi'(1)g_2(t)dt$$

$$+ \frac{1}{2}\int [g(t) - 1]^2\phi[s(t)]g_2(t)dt \tag{5.25}$$

$$= U_1(0) + \frac{1}{2}\int [g(t) - 1]^2\left\{\frac{U_1''[\ln(s(t))]}{s(t)} + \frac{U_1'[\ln(s(t))]}{s(t)}\right\}g_2(t)dt \tag{5.26}$$

$$= U_1(0) + \frac{1}{2}\int [g(t) - 1]^2 \{U_1'[\ln(s(t))]s(t)\}^{-1}\{1 - r_1[\ln(s(t))]\}g_2(t)dt$$

$$\geq U_1(0), \tag{5.27}$$

if $r_1[\ln(s(x))] \leq 1$, for all values of x.

Some intuition may be helpful into the condition that the absolute risk aversion function $r_1(\cdot)$ be less than unity. Linear utility functions, negative exponential utility functions of the form $a - be^{-\lambda x}$ where $\lambda < 1$, and logarithmic utility functions of the form $\ln(x - b)$ with $(x - 1) > b > 0$, all have this property. The certainty equivalent for a 50-50 lottery with prizes of zero and one hundred dollars to an individual with a negative exponential utility function where $\lambda = 1$ would be about 69 cents. Most people would probably regard this as extremely risk-averse behavior. In general, a risk aversion function less than unity implies very roughly that one's risk premium for a proposed lottery is less than one-half its variance.[24]

A corollary to Proposition 3 proves the previous assertion that the dominant strategy for a risk-neutral party 1 is truthful revelation. (The proof is offered in part because of the elegance of its inequality argument relative to the constrained maximization method of proving the underlying result on honest reward functions.)

COROLLARY. *A risk-neutral individual should accept a logarithmic betting schedule and should announce his true probabilities regardless of what are the announced probabilities of his opponent.*

Proof. Let $f_i(\cdot)$ and $g_i(\cdot)$ be the true and announced probabilities of party i, respectively, for $i = 1,2$. That the bet is worthwhile,

$$\int f_1(t) \ln \frac{f_1(t)}{g_2(t)} dt \geq 0, \tag{5.28}$$

follows immediately from Proposition 3. It is also true for any $g_1(\cdot)$ that

$$\int f_1(t) \ln \frac{f_1(t)}{g_1(t)} dt \geq 0. \tag{5.29}$$

Expression (5.29) equals

$$\int f_1(t) \ln \frac{f_1(t)}{g_2(t)} dt + \int f_1(t) \ln \frac{g_2(t)}{g_1(t)} dt, \tag{5.30}$$

which equals

$$\int f_1(t) \ln \frac{f_1(t)}{g_2(t)} dt - \int f_1(t) \ln \frac{g_1(t)}{g_2(t)} dt. \tag{5.31}$$

By (5.29),

$$\int f_1(t) \ln \frac{f_1(t)}{g_2(t)} dt \geq \int f_1(t) \ln \frac{g_1(t)}{g_2(t)} dt, \tag{5.32}$$

or that individual 1 should choose $g_1(x) = f_1(x)$, for all x.

So far the analysis has assumed that the betting probability announcements of one party did not depend on those of the other. This might be the case if negotiations had proceeded without the expectation of betting, and if existing, divergent probability assessments were suddenly proposed as the basis for a bet. Or an arbitrator might inform each side separately that he had the other side's probabilities in hand, and that he now wanted the remaining probabilities for a logarithmic bet. Suppose, however, that a mediator proposes the logarithmic bet schedule and the parties then discuss their probabilities until they reach some equilibrium. How will this affect the announcements? This question can be investigated in two steps. First, let party 1 be risk-neutral, and consider his announcement problem where he takes into account the reactions of party 2. Then let party 1 be risk-averse, and again let him take party 2's reactions into account. (So far, the analysis abstracts from the difficult problem of information transfer that may take place during the interchange. This problem is discussed in Section 5.2.6.)

Case 1. Party 1 is risk-neutral and anticipates the reactions of party 2. Let x be a discrete random variable that takes the values x_i, $i = 1, \ldots, n$. Party 1's true and announced probabilities for x_i are f_{1i} and g_{1i}, respectively. Party 1 will choose the g_{1i} to maximize

$$\sum_{i=1}^{n} \left[a \ln \left(\frac{g_{1i}}{g_{2i}} \right) + b \right] f_{1i} \tag{5.33}$$

subject to

$$\sum_{i=1}^{n} g_{1i} = 1, \tag{5.34}$$

where g_{2i} is party 2's announcement of the probability of x_i, $i = 1, \ldots, n$. The first-order conditions of this constrained maximization problem are

$$f_{1i} - \frac{\partial g_{2i}}{\partial g_{1i}} \frac{g_{1i}}{g_{2i}} f_{1i} = -\frac{\lambda}{a} g_{1i}, \qquad (5.35)$$

for $i = 1, \ldots, n$, and where λ is the constant multiplier that adjoined the constraint (5.34). By summing (5.35) over all i, obtain

$$-\frac{\lambda}{a} = 1 - \sum_{i=1}^{n} \frac{\partial g_{2i}}{\partial g_{1i}} \frac{g_{1i}}{g_{2i}} f_{1i}, \qquad (5.36)$$

implying that

$$g_{1i} = \left[\frac{(1 - \epsilon_{12i})}{\left(1 - \sum_{i=1}^{n} \epsilon_{12i} f_{1i}\right)} \right] f_{1i}, \qquad (5.37)$$

for $i = 1, \ldots, n$, and where $\epsilon_{12i} = (\partial g_{2i}/\partial g_{1i})(g_{1i}/g_{2i})$ is the elasticity of party 2's announcement (g_{2i}) with respect to party 1's announcement (g_{1i}) of the probability of x_i. The bracketed term in (5.37) implicitly represents party 1's distortions of his true probabilities. Notice that in the Nash equilibrium of announcements (that is, where $\partial g_{2i}/\partial g_{2i} = 0$, for all i), the bracketed term in (5.37) is unity, and party 1 will announce his true probabilities.

Case 2. Party 1 is risk-averse and considers the reactions of party 2. Intuition suggests that party 1 will announce higher probabilities where the bet may result in losses for him and lower probabilities where gains are possible. Risk aversion should make such a shifting of announced probabilities desirable, effectively as insurance against losses. To investigate this case, let $U_1(\cdot)$ be party 1's utility function, and let $f_i(\cdot)$ and $g_i(\cdot)$ be the true and announced (this time, continuous) density functions of party i, respectively, for $i = 1,2$. Then, suppressing arguments of functions, party 1's problem is to choose g_1 to maximize

$$\int U_1\left(a \ln \frac{g_1}{g_2} + b\right) f_1 \, dx \qquad (5.38)$$

subject to

$$\int g_1 dx = 1. \qquad (5.39)$$

The solution to this satisfies

$$aU_1'\left[\frac{g_2 - g_1(\partial g_2/\partial g_1)}{g_2^2} \frac{g_2}{g_1}\right] f_1 + \lambda = 0, \qquad (5.40)$$

where λ is constant. Under the equilibrium assumption that $\partial g_2/\partial g_1 = 0$, this becomes

$$\frac{aU'_1 f_1}{g_1} = -\lambda. \tag{5.41}$$

The value of λ is readily shown to be

$$\lambda = -a \int U'_1 f_1 \, dx, \tag{5.42}$$

implying that

$$g_1 = \left[\frac{U'_1}{\int U'_1 f_1 \, dx}\right] f_1, \tag{5.43}$$

for all x.

This expression implicitly represents the distortion in the probability announcements that party 1 will make when confronted with a logarithmic bet schedule. At any point, if the ratio of the marginal utility to the *expected* marginal utility (the bracketed term in expression 5.43) is greater than unity, party 1 will exaggerate his true probability value. This will happen where the argument (B) of U'_1 is small, and hence U'_1 is large. That is, to avoid extreme losses, party 1 will shade his probability announcements of low values of B upward, profitably counterbalancing them by downward shading for higher possible values of B in equilibrium.

As before, assume that U_1 is linear. Then the bracketed term in (5.43) is unity and the true probabilities will be revealed. Conversely, note that the only way $g_1 = f_1$ for all x is for U'_1 to be constant (since, for the equilibrium values of g_i, $\int U'_1 f_1 dx$ is constant). This implies the following proposition.

PROPOSITION 4. *The Nash equilibrium announcements of probabilities under a betting schedule of the form $[a \ln(g_1/g_2) + b]$ will be the true probabilities if and only if the parties' utility functions are linear.*

5.2.4 Risk Sharing and Betting Optimally

Two individuals — the familiar parties 1 and 2 — hold different beliefs about an uncertain event $\tilde{x}$. Party i's opinion can be described by the differentiable density function $f_i(\cdot)$, for $i = 1,2$. Both parties are open, honest, and expected utility maximizers. In contrast to the preceding analysis, however, let $\tilde{x}$ itself be the payoff of interest. For example, one

DIFFERENCES AND JOINT GAINS

could think of $\tilde{x}$ as the profit from an uncertain venture. (It is easy to generalize the analysis to an arbitrary payoff x and information ξ.) If x occurs, party 2 will keep $x - S(x)$ and pay $S(x)$ to party 1. Parties 1 and 2 wish to endow the sharing function $S(\cdot)$ with desirable properties; they agree as before that it should be Pareto-optimal. Formally, the problem is to choose $S(\cdot)$ to maximize

$$\int U_1[S(w)] f_1(w) dw \qquad (5.44)$$

subject to

$$\int U_2[w - S(w)] f_2(w) dw = k, \qquad (5.45)$$

where k is constant.

A variational argument yields the Euler equation

$$\frac{U_1'[S(x)] f_1(x)}{U_2'[x - S(x)] f_2(x)} = \lambda, \qquad (5.46)$$

for all x, and where λ is constant. By multiplying through, differentiating with respect to x, substituting for λ from (5.46), defining the risk-aversion function, $r_1(\cdot)$, in the usual way, and omitting arguments of functions, the following proposition can be obtained.

PROPOSITION 5. *The optimal risk-sharing and betting function, $S(x)$, satisfies the condition that*

$$S'(x) = \left\{ 1 + \frac{r_1[S(x)]}{r_2[x - S(x)]} \right\}^{-1} + \frac{h'(x)}{r_1[S(x)] + r_2[x - S(x)]}, \qquad (5.47)$$

for all x.

Expression (5.47) separates into two terms. The second term, which uniquely contains density functions, is familiar from the discussion of optimal betting (Section 5.2.2); it characterizes the optimal marginal side bet.

If $f_1(x) = f_2(x)$ for all x, then the betting term vanishes and expression (5.47) reduces to a case of pure risk sharing discovered by Wilson and treated by Leland.[25] The latter found it useful to regard $S' = dS/dx$ as a local measure of risk sharing. If party 1 is quite risk-averse relative to party 2, then r_1/r_2 is large, $(1 + r_1/r_2)^{-1}$ is small, and S' tends to zero. With S' small, as the outcome (x) changes, payments to party 1 do not change very much. The payments are relatively fixed, and party 2 can be said to bear most of the risk; that is, party 2 absorbs most of the fluctuations of the outcome at that point. If party 2 is quite risk-averse relative to party 1, a similar argument suggests that S' tends to unity. As the outcome changes, so do the payments, and party 1 can be said to bear most of the risk.

Special case: Exponential utilities. If r_i is constant, implying that $U_i(\cdot)$ is a negative exponential utility function, for $i = 1,2$, expression (5.47) is easily integrated to obtain

$$S = \left(1 + \frac{r_1}{r_2}\right)^{-1} x + \frac{\ln\frac{f_1}{f_2}}{r_1 + r_2} + c, \qquad (5.48)$$

where c is a constant of integration that can be readily evaluated from the constraint in the problem posed in (5.44) and (5.45). The first term of (5.48) indicates the proportion of x that party 1 will receive in all states of nature. It is independent of probabilities, agreed or not. Proportional risk sharing depends on how *relatively* risk-averse party 1 is compared with party 2. The second term in (5.48) is the familiar side bet, depending on the logarithm of the ratio of the densities at each point. Unlike proportional risk sharing, side bets are deflated by the *sum* of the parties' absolute risk aversion coefficients. A side payment is represented by the constant of integration. It is only in this term that the choice of k, the arbitrary expected utility level for party 2 in the Paretian problem, makes an appearance. The side bet and the proportional sharing rule are independent of k.

Special case: HARA utilities. Let $r_i(x) = c/(x + b_i)$, for $i = 1,2$. Then it is easy to verify from (5.46) that

$$S = \frac{x + b_2 - b_1(\lambda f_2/f_1)^{1/c}}{[1 + (\lambda f_2/f_1)^{1/c}]}, \qquad (5.49)$$

where λ is constant.

It is interesting to investigate the factors determining the shape of $S(\cdot)$. If S' is differentiated with respect to x, algebraic manipulation of the result yields a characterization.

PROPOSITION 6. *The optimal risk sharing and betting function, $S(\cdot)$, is convex, linear, or concave, depending on whether*

$$h'' + \frac{r_2'(r_1 - h')^2 - r_1'(r_2 + h')^2}{(r_1 + r_2)^2} \qquad (5.50)$$

is positive, zero, or negative.

DIFFERENCES AND JOINT GAINS

The shape of $S(\cdot)$ is thus dependent on the shape of $h(\cdot)$ and on the levels and relative rates of change of the absolute risk aversion functions. If the utility functions are negative exponential, then $r_1' = r_2' = 0$, and the shape of $h(\cdot)$ fully determines that of $S(\cdot)$, as indicated in (5.48).

In the special case with agreement on probabilities, the shape of $S(\cdot)$ depends on which party's risk tolerance (denoted t_i, where $t_i(\cdot) = r_i(\cdot)^{-1}$, for $i = 1,2$) is changing faster. To see this, let $h(x) = 0$ for all x in (5.50). Algebraic manipulation then yields the following corollary, noted by Leland.

COROLLARY. *With agreement on probabilities, the optimal sharing function $S(\cdot)$ is convex, linear, or concave depending on whether $(t_1' - t_2')$ is positive, zero, or negative.*

The corollary immediately implies that the sharing schedule should be linear for the HARA class of utility functions (including the exponential, logarithmic, and power) when the parties agree on probabilities. This implication also follows directly from inspection of (5.49).

5.2.5 Risk-Spreading Properties of Common Tax and Contract Instruments

This section analyzes the relative risk-spreading properties of lump-sum taxes, royalties, and profit shares. For equal expected payments, conventional wisdom generally ranks profit sharing as the most effective means of risk spreading, followed in turn by royalties and lump-sum taxes. The results in this section demonstrate that although this ranking is often valid, it need not hold in nonpathological instances when both costs and revenues are stochastic.

It should be noted immediately that the analysis focuses only on how these three contractual instruments spread purely exogenous risks and does not examine many of the diverse aspects of contractual relations that have interested economists. Specifically not discussed are incentive questions that might arise from differences in risk attitudes, differential information and ability to take actions, or imperfect monitoring ability. Likewise, problems arising from imperfect auditing of revenues and costs are ignored, as are the issues raised by the effects of a levy on production and investment decisions.

Even after the analysis has been restricted along these lines, however, the risk-spreading aspects of many policy-relevant contracts remain within its purview. For instance, not only have various combinations of fixed fees, royalties, and profit taxes been the primary forms of levy in past Third World mineral contracts, but LOS conference negotiators turned to these instruments when working out financial arrangements for future deep seabed mining of manganese nodules. Similarly, oil leases on the U.S. outer continental shelf have predominantly consisted of a fixed-fee bonus bid with a prescribed royalty. Other examples include fixed advances combined with subsequent royalty payments in book publishing; management compensation schemes made up of bonuses, salaries, and profit shares; and fixed wages, rents, or share contracts under sharecropping.

If markets for contingent claims were complete and perfect, of course, there would be no need to examine the risk-sharing properties of tax instruments whose levels depend on the variation of revenues and costs across states of nature. In actuality, however, there is little question about the importance of risk-spreading properties of contractual provisions. There is also little question about which instruments are held to be most risky, even when expected payments are constant. For example, in justifying their "resource rent tax" proposal, Garnaut and Ross explain that from the standpoint of "risk of loss for any given tax yield . . . a fixed annual or once-for-all license fee is the least satisfactory and a profits tax the most satisfactory of [the fixed license fee, the specific or *ad valorem* royalty, and the profits tax]."[26] Commenting on oil leasing arrangements, Leland similarly notes that "profit sharing payments share risk more effectively [than royalties],"[27] while Reece goes on to say that "bonus bidding schemes, of course, do not share risk at all."[28] In an agricultural context, fixed rent and wage contracts are said to place all the risk on tenant and landowner, respectively, while Cheung indicates that share tenancy (akin to royalty payments) "may then be regarded as a device for risk sharing."[29]

To examine the validity of this intuitive risk ranking, consider the case of a risk-averse party (the "firm") opposite a risk-neutral party (the "government"). Because the government will be indifferent among all uncertain prospects with the same expected value, the firm's expected utility across alternative contractual instruments can be compared to determine which is "riskiest." (Clearly, the optimal mode of risk sharing in such instances is for the firm to receive the mean value of the contract in all states, while the government bears all the risk. In light of the obvious incentive difficulties with such arrangements and exclusion of such issues in the present context, questions of contractual optimality are ignored.) Nevertheless, a number of important problems, such as the effects of tax policies of a risk-neutral government on private risk taking,[30] fall directly within the framework of this section, while others have the same formal structure.

For the firm assume an increasing, concave, twice continuously differentiable utility function U over a single monetary attribute. Revenues (r) and costs (c) are random variables with a joint density that defines profit ($\pi \equiv r - c$). Assume agreement between the firm and government on probabilities. The means of r, c, and π are denoted by $\bar{r}$, $\bar{c}$, and $\bar{\pi}$, and their (finite) variances by σ_r^2, σ_c^2, and σ^2. The covariance of r and c is given by σ_{rc}. Profits are shared at a constant rate $p \in (0,1)$, with expected payments thus equal to $p(\bar{r} - \bar{c})$. Royalties are levied on r at a constant rate $\beta \in (0,1)$ and are set to yield the same expected payments as profit sharing. Thus, $\beta r = p(\bar{r} - \bar{c})$, or $\beta = p(1 - \bar{c}/\bar{r}) \equiv pm$, where m is the expected profit margin, which is assumed to be positive. Finally, fixed fees are set at the expected level of the other charges: $p(\bar{r} - \bar{c}) = pm\bar{r} = \beta\bar{r}$.

5.2.5.1 COMPARISON OF PROFIT-SHARING RULES AND FIXED FEES
In this comparison the firm pays either a random share of profits $p\pi$ or a sure fee $p\bar{\pi}$, with the government receiving the same expected payment in either case. Since the risk-averse firm would prefer to *receive* a sure payment rather than an uncertain one (Jensen's inequality), intuition suggests that the firm would rather *pay* the uncertain income tax. Mean variance analysis shows the same mean, $(1 - p)\bar{\pi}$, for both alternatives, but a variance for the profit-sharing alternative, $(1 - p)^2\sigma^2$, which is less than the variance of the post-fee residual σ^2. In fact, this fee/profit-share comparison is the only case considered in which conventional wisdom is unconditionally vindicated. It is interesting to note that $EU[(1 - p)\pi] \geq EU(\pi - p\bar{\pi})$ does not immediately follow from Jensen's inequality or a first-order stochastic dominance argument.

This general result does obtain, however, if one notes that if x and h lie in the domain of the firm's concave utility function U, then $U(x) \leq U(h) + U'(h)(x - h)$. Letting $x = \pi - p\bar{\pi}$ and $h = \pi - p\pi$, monotonicity of integration over π gives

$$EU(\pi - p\bar{\pi}) \leq EU(\pi - p\pi) + pE[U'(\pi - p\pi)(\pi - \bar{\pi})]$$
$$\leq EU(\pi - p\pi) + p \operatorname{cov}[\pi, U'(\pi - p\pi)]. \quad (5.51)$$

Since $\operatorname{cov}[\pi, U'(\pi - p\pi)] < 0$, the desired result follows. Recall that Rothschild and Stiglitz prove that every risk averter will prefer a random payoff X to a random payoff Y if and only if Y is a mean-preserving spread of X.[31] Intuitively, this means that Y can be obtained from X by taking some of the probability mass from the center of the probability density of X and moving it to the density's tails in a way that leaves its mean unchanged. Prospect Y is then "riskier" than prospect X. Thus, Eq. (5.51) says that the probability density of the post-fee

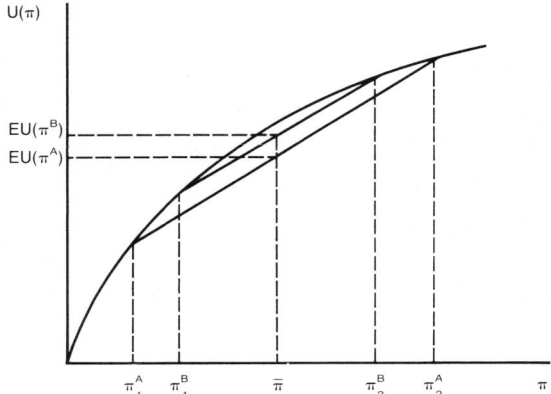

Figure 5.13 Preference of risk-averse firm for instrument B over instrument A

residual is a mean-preserving spread of the density of the post-profit-sharing residual.

As a simple but illuminating special case of this result, let the firm's pre-levy profits take on just two values, π_1 and π_2, with equal probability, where $0 < \pi_1 < \pi_2$. The firm then receives either $\pi_1^P = \pi_1 - \rho\pi_1$ or $\pi_2^P = \pi_2 - \rho\pi_2$ with equal probability under profit sharing. Under the fee the firm receives $\pi_1^F = \pi_1 - \frac{1}{2}\rho(\pi_1 + \pi_2)$ or $\pi_2^F = \pi_2 - \frac{1}{2}\rho(\pi_1 + \pi_2)$ with equal probability. An easy computation shows that the firm receives the same expected profits $\bar{\pi}$ in each case. Furthermore, $\pi_1^F < \pi_1^P$ and $\pi_2^F > \pi_2^P$, since $\pi_1 < \pi_2$. This situation is shown in Figure 5.13, which illustrates the preference of a risk-averse firm for a profit-sharing over a fee contract. Here π_i^A and π_i^B refer to profits in state i under the fee and profit share, respectively.

Figure 5.13 suggests that the effect of a fee is to move probability mass from the center of the profit-share density toward its tail while preserving its mean, and thus that the random post-fee residual is a mean-preserving spread of the random post-profit-sharing residual. Equation (5.51), in conjunction with the Rothschild-Stiglitz result, shows this result to be generally valid. The following sections use this figure to illustrate nonpathological cases that reverse the intuitive risk rankings of fees relative to royalties and royalties relative to profit shares.

5.2.5.2 COMPARISON OF FIXED FEES AND ROYALTIES

Consider first the choice between royalty and fee contracts in a mean-variance framework. Under the fee contract the firm keeps $r - c - \beta\bar{r}$,

DIFFERENCES AND JOINT GAINS

with mean $(1-\beta)\bar{r}-\bar{c}$ and variance $\sigma_r^2+\sigma_c^2-2\sigma_{rc}$. Likewise, under a royalty scheme it keeps $(1-\beta)r-c$, with the same mean but with variance $(1-\beta)^2\sigma_r^2+\sigma_c^2-2(1-\beta)\sigma_{rc}$. A royalty will be preferred to a fee if and only if the variance of the post-royalty residual is less than the variance of the post-fee residual, or

$$\sigma_{rc} < \frac{(2-\beta)\sigma_r^2}{2}. \qquad (5.52)$$

Note that this condition always holds when $\sigma_{rc} < 0$: in this case cost and revenue can be regarded as negatively correlated securities, the variance of whose combination is less than the sum of their individual variances. Moreover, Eq. (5.52) suggests that a royalty will also be preferred to a fee when σ_{rc} is positive but small relative to σ_r^2, but that for sufficiently large σ_{rc} a seemingly counterintuitive preference for fees might arise.

This insight can be used to construct a simple von Neumann–Morgenstern example of such a preference. Suppose that there are two equiprobable revenue-cost realizations, (r_1,c_1) and (r_2,c_2). Under a fee contract in state i, the firm receives $\pi_i^F \equiv r_i - c_i - \beta\bar{r}$ and achieves expected utility $\frac{1}{2}U(\pi_1^F) + \frac{1}{2}U(\pi_2^F)$. Assume that $r_2 < \bar{r} < r_1$, $c_2 < \bar{c} < c_1$, and $r_1 - c_1 < \bar{r} - \bar{c} < r_2 - c_2$, or, equivalently, that the covariance of revenues and costs is sufficiently positive. An easy computation then gives $\pi_1^F < \bar{\pi} < \pi_2^F$. Under a royalty contract, on the other hand, the firm receives $\pi_i^R \equiv r_i - c_i - \beta r_i$ in state i and achieves expected utility $\frac{1}{2}U(\pi_1^R) + \frac{1}{2}U(\pi_2^R)$. Since $r_1 > \bar{r}$ and $r_2 < \bar{r}$, however, it follows immediately that $\pi_1^R < \pi_1^F$ and $\pi_2^R > \pi_2^F$, respectively. If A is interpreted as a royalty and B as a fee in Figure 5.13, then the constructed relationships among the various post-levy residuals illustrate that a fee can produce higher expected utility than a royalty for concave U. Since the reverse can also be true, depending on the covariance structure of revenues and costs, it follows that an unambiguous royalty/fee risk ranking is impossible without prior knowledge of this structure.

To understand the intuition underlying this example, note that state 1 is characterized by high revenues and costs but low pre-levy profits. In state 2, on the other hand, revenues and costs are both low but pre-levy profits are high. Hence, in state 1 a royalty payment, which falls on revenue alone, makes the low-profit situation under a fee payment even worse by decreasing the revenues that the firm has available to meet its relatively high costs. This implies that $\pi_1^R < \pi_1^F$. In state 2, by contrast, a royalty scheme further improves the high profit situation resulting under fee payment: in effect, the government absorbs part of the firm's revenue decline through decreased royalty collection relative to the level of fee collection. Hence, the government aids the firm in meeting its already low costs, implying that $\pi_2^R > \pi_2^F$. Since the fee shields the post-levy residual in the low-residual state, while leaving the mean of the residual unchanged, a risk averter would choose a fee over a royalty.

Finally, conditions can be derived under which the density of π^F is a mean-preserving spread of the density of π^R. Note that $\pi^F \equiv \pi^R + \beta(r - \bar{r})$ and, since U is concave, that

$$U(\pi^F) \leq U(\pi^R) + \beta(r - \bar{r})U'(\pi^R). \tag{5.53}$$

Taking the expectation of Eq. (5.53) over r and c then gives

$$\begin{aligned} EU(\pi^F) &\leq EU(\pi^R) + \beta\, E[(r - \bar{r})U'(\pi^R)] \\ &\leq EU(\pi^R) + \beta\, \mathrm{cov}\,[r, E_{dr}U'(\pi^R)], \end{aligned} \tag{5.54}$$

where E_{dr} denotes the expectation operator over c conditioned on r. (If E_x is the expectation operator over X, then $E_{rc}[(r - \bar{r})U'(\pi^R)] = E_{rc}[rU'(\pi^R)] - \bar{r}\, E_{rc}U'(\pi^R) = E_r[r\, E_{dr}U'(\pi^R)] - \bar{r}\, E_r[E_{dr}U'(\pi^R)] = \mathrm{cov}\,[r, E_{dr}U'(\pi^R)]$.)

Two remarks about Eq. (5.54) are in order. First, whether the density of π^F is a mean-preserving spread of the density of π^R turns on the sign and magnitude of the covariance term. The intuition behind this result is analogous to that behind the two-state example described earlier. If the covariance of revenue and conditional expected marginal utility is negative, then Eq. (5.54) indicates that a royalty is preferred to a fee. This situation will hold when a rise in revenue causes a rise in the conditional expected post-royalty residual, and hence a fall in conditional expected marginal utility. Likewise, a fee can be preferred in the reverse instance, or when a surge in revenue entails a decline in the post-royalty residual because of increased costs.

Second, note that Eq. (5.54) and its associated interpretation can also be used to rank instruments involving mixtures of fees and royalties relative to each pure instrument. Suppose that the residual of a mixed instrument π^M is given by $\alpha\pi^F + (1 - \alpha)\pi^R$, $\alpha \in (0,1)$. Since $\pi^F \equiv \pi^R + \beta(r - \bar{r})$, it follows that $\pi^M = \pi^R + \alpha\beta(r - \bar{r})$, which can be used to derive analogues to Eqs. (5.53) and (5.54) and to rank π^M relative to π^R. Substitution for π^R in the expression for π^M can be used in the same way to rank π^M relative to π^F.

5.2.5.3 COMPARISON OF PROFIT-SHARING RULES AND ROYALTIES

Finally, consider the choice between profit-sharing and royalty contracts. In the mean-variance framework, a risk-averse firm will prefer paying a share of profits $\rho(r-c)$ to a royalty $\rho mr \equiv \rho(1-\bar{c}/\bar{r})r$ if and only if var $[(1-\rho)(r-c)] <$ var $[(1-\rho m)r - c]$, or

$$\sigma_{rc} < F\sigma_r^2 + G\sigma_c^2, \qquad (5.55)$$

where F and G are positive constants independent of the covariance structure of r and c. Equation (5.55) thus suggests that a sufficiently positive covariance of revenue and cost can lead a risk-averse firm to prefer a royalty contract.

In the von Neumann–Morgenstern context an example can, in fact, be constructed in which revenue and cost covary positively, and the post-profit-sharing residual is a mean-preserving spread of the post-royalty residual. Under profit sharing in the two-state example of Section 5.2.5.2, the firm receives $\pi_i^P \equiv (1-\rho)(r_i - c_i)$ in state i and expected utility $\tfrac{1}{2}U(\pi_1^P) + \tfrac{1}{2}U(\pi_2^P)$. Similarly, a royalty with the same mean yields a residual $\pi_i^R \equiv (1-\rho m)r_i - c_i$ in state i and expected utility $\tfrac{1}{2}U(\pi_1^R) + \tfrac{1}{2}U(\pi_2^R)$. In state 1 suppose that revenue and cost are both low relative to their respective means, but that revenue is high relative to cost. In state 2 the reverse holds. Specifically, let (i) $r_1/c_1 > \bar{r}/\bar{c}$; (ii) $r_2/c_2 < \bar{r}/\bar{c}$; and (iii) $(1-\rho m)(r_1 - r_2) < c_1 - c_2$. These conditions yield in succession (i) $\pi_1^P < \pi_1^R$; (ii) $\pi_2^P > \pi_2^R$; and (iii) $\pi_1^R < \pi_2^R$. This configuration of residuals is illustrated in Figure 5.13, if instrument B is interpreted as a royalty and A as a profit share. In this example, then, the post-profit-share residual is a mean-preserving spread of the post-royalty residual, leading a risk-averse firm to prefer the royalty.

The intuition underlying this example is similar to that described in the preceding royalty-fee comparison. Note first that revenue under a royalty exceeds revenue under a profit share if both are required to have the same mean payment, since $(1-\rho m)r > (1-\rho)r$. Likewise, costs under a royalty exceed those under a profit share, since $c > (1-\rho)c$. Hence, when the realization of revenues sufficiently exceeds the realization of costs, as in state 1, the first effect can dominate, with the royalty leading to a higher residual. Similarly, since the profit share discounts costs in arriving at its levy, while the royalty does not, the profit share can become the preferred instrument when costs are relatively high, as in state 2. Finally, since the royalty here shields profits in the low-profit state, and the profit share does not, firm risk aversion suggests preference for the royalty.

To derive general conditions under which the density of the post-royalty residual is a mean-preserving spread of the post-profit-sharing residual, note that $\pi^R \equiv \pi^P + \rho[(\bar{c}/\bar{r})r - c]$. Concavity of U then yields

$$U(\pi^R) \le U(\pi^P) + \rho U'(\pi^P)[(\bar{c}/\bar{r})r - c], \tag{5.56}$$

which, upon taking the expectation over r and c, becomes

$$EU(\pi^R) \le EU(\pi^P) + \rho EU'(\pi^P)[(\bar{c}/\bar{r})r - c]$$
$$\le EU(\pi^P) + \rho\{(\bar{c}/\bar{r}) \operatorname{cov}[r, U'(\pi^P)] - \operatorname{cov}[c, U'(\pi^P)]\}. \tag{5.57}$$

Like Eq. (5.54) in the case of the royalty-fee comparison, Eq. (5.57) allows determination of when a royalty is "more risky" than a profit share in light of the covariance structure of revenue and cost. Interpretation of Eq. (5.57) generalizes the discussion of this section's two-state example. If a cost increase signals a decrease in the after-levy residual (an increase in marginal utility) and a revenue increase an increase in after-levy residual (a decrease in marginal utility), then cov $(c, U') > 0$ and cov$(r, U') < 0$. In this case cost and revenue are negatively correlated, Eq. (5.57) holds, and a risk averter always prefers the profit share to the royalty. When cost and revenue are independent or negatively correlated, the situation becomes somewhat more complex. If costs rise in the latter case, the increase in revenue may exceed the cost increase, thus decreasing marginal revenue and yielding cov$(c, U) < 0$. The net effect, however, is determined by cov$(r, U') < 0$. If the absolute value of this term is small relative to cov(c, U'), then it is possible for a risk averter to prefer the royalty, implying a reversal of the usual risk ranking.

Finally, it is worth noting briefly that the preceding analysis and its interpretation can be used to rank a mixed profit-share/royalty instrument $\pi^M \equiv \alpha\pi^P + (1 - \alpha)\pi^R$ relative to each of the pure instruments. The details are entirely analogous to the ranking of a fee/royalty mixed instrument described in Section 5.2.5.2.

This section began with a conventional risk ranking that placed profit sharing as least risky, followed in turn by royalties and fees. It was shown that profit sharing unambiguously dominates fee payment, but that comparisons among the other instruments depend on the underlying covariance structure of revenues and costs. Reversals of the usual risk ranking can occur for sufficiently positive covariance between revenue and cost, which seemingly cannot be excluded in a variety of contexts. Intermediate goods industries in a competitive economy, especially those with constant returns, are likely to display strong positive correlation between input and output prices. For example, a firm that processes oil into plastics or that buys logs and sells wood chips may show parallel trends in revenues and costs that could result in preferences for fees over royalties or royalties over profit shares.

Hence, when costs and revenues are independent or move in oppo-

DIFFERENCES AND JOINT GAINS

site directions, the conventional ranking of these instruments holds well. When they move together, a closer examination is necessary to evaluate the risk-spreading properties of the system and make the appropriate adjustments for joint gain.

5.2.6 *Don't Bet on It: Contingent Agreements with Asymmetric Information*

If two people have different probability assessments about the realization of an uncertain event, they can design a bet that offers positive expected value to each person. Yet in the process of tentatively agreeing to the bet, each may reveal information about the basis for his or her probabilities. The very willingness to accept a proposed bet conveys information. This section models a process by which private, asymmetrically held information is progressively unveiled. If the parties share priors and their information partitions are common knowledge, simple discussion of the acceptability of any proposed bet reveals enough about their differential information to ultimately render the bet unacceptable. This finding bears on numerous situations in which differing probability assessments are the basis for apparent joint gains, including contingent agreements in negotiations, side bets proposed as part of sharing rules in syndicates,[32] and incentives for decentralized decision making.[33] Bets or contingent agreements are often proposed as the means to joint gains. Yet, quite apart from risk aversion, people often exhibit reluctance to bet. Say that Joe proposes a wager with Sally, who reasons: "If Joe wants to bet, he must know something that I don't." Of course, Sally may have her own information. Echoing Groucho Marx, Joe might muse: "If Sally seems willing to accept my proposed bet, then perhaps I should reconsider." And so on. The purpose of this section is to make clearer the circumstances under which would-be parties to contingent agreements based on probability differences *should* reconsider.

The process of information transfer modeled here is loosely related to the inferences one may draw when confronted with an unexpected proposal. If a landowner, for example, put his holdings on the market for $10,000 and was immediately offered $100,000, he might suspect that oil was on the property or that a new development was planned nearby. In another instance, the off-season vacationer considering an exotic trip at one-third the "normal" price might guess that the weather would be miserable. Closer to the betting theme of this section would be the example of a novice racing enthusiast who goes to the track optimistic about a particular horse, but who finds 100-to-1 odds against his favorite. A bet that seemed attractive on the way to the track might be refused after exposure to the quoted odds.

Studies by Aumann and by Geanakoplos and Polemarchakis have investigated the reconciliation of subjective probabilities under different circumstances.[34] Aumann gives an elegant equilibrium result: if two people have the same priors, and if their posteriors for an event are "common knowledge," then their posteriors must be equal. The concept of common knowledge is central to Aumann's analysis. Intuitively, an event is common knowledge for parties 1 and 2 if 1 and 2 know it; if 1 knows that 2 knows it, and conversely; if 1 knows that 2 knows that 1 knows it, and conversely; and so forth. It is not sufficient that each party knows it; Aumann's result fails if the parties merely know each other's posteriors. Geanakoplos and Polemarchakis supplement this equilibrium analysis by exhibiting a *process* for agents to revise their posteriors about an arbitrary event, which is not restricted to be common knowledge. Under the assumption of common priors, if both agents' information partitions are finite, they show that simple communication of posteriors back and forth will lead the agents to make revisions that converge to a common, equilibrium posterior.

Although it may be difficult to imagine parties repeatedly announcing posterior distributions to each other, it is not hard to imagine parties discussing possible actions that are based on their probabilistic beliefs. Bets and gambles are examples of such actions. A bet is an agreement that party 2 will pay one unit to party 1 if an event A happens, and party 1 will pay one unit to party 2 if A does not happen. A gamble is a more general agreement: a random variable G is specified, and it is agreed that party 2 will pay party 1 G units if G is positive and party 1 will pay party 2 G units if G is negative. Suppose such a gamble is proposed and party 1 is tentatively willing to take it. Knowing this, party 2 may tentatively accept or decline. Party 1 then has the same option if party 2 has accepted, and the dialogue continues until both are finally satisfied or a rejection is encountered. These assumptions correspond to a situation in which the parties discuss the gamble before making it and not to a situation in which a firm offer is made and simply accepted or refused.

The main result of the analysis of this section is that, if the parties have the same prior and if they have finite information partitions, one party will ultimately refuse *any* such gamble even though each side may have based its posterior assessment on very different, private information. Knowing this, the parties should refuse to gamble at the outset. A simple example is given in Section 5.2.6.1, and the general result is proved in Section 5.2.6.2.

DIFFERENCES AND JOINT GAINS

5.2.6.1 DON'T BET ON IT: EXAMPLE

Suppose that Ω, the set of possible states of the world, is represented by the large rectangle in Figure 5.14. Parties 1 and 2 both adopt a uniform prior distribution over the rectangle. Party 1 partitions the rectangle into (p^1, p^2, p^3) by the horizontal lines and receives the private information that the true state of the world ω is in p^2. Party 2, whose information partition (q^1, q^2, q^3) is indicated by vertical lines, finds out privately that $\omega \in q^2$. Each side knows the other's partition, and that information has been received, but does not know what the information is.

Suppose that event A, known to both parties and represented by the shaded subset of the large rectangle, is of interest. The following bet is proposed: if $\omega \in A$, party 2 pays one unit to party 1, and if $\omega \notin A$, party 1 pays one unit to party 2. This implies that the bet is attractive to party 1 if the probability of A is greater than one-half and that the bet is attractive to party 2 if the probability of A is less than one-half. Both parties are assumed to be risk-neutral. The parties successively announce their willingness or unwillingness to take the bet. Denote by c_i the knowledge of parties 1 and 2 about each other's information. Each party can deduce c_i. Before discussion (0th iteration), both parties know only that $c_0 = (p^1, p^2, p^3; q^1, q^2, q^3)$.

The bet is offered to party 1, who says yes (denoted Y) since the conditional probability of $\omega \in A$ (given knowledge that $\omega \in p^2$) exceeds one-half. Party 2 thereby knows that party 1's information could not have been that $\omega \in p^3$, or party 1 would have said no (N). However, the

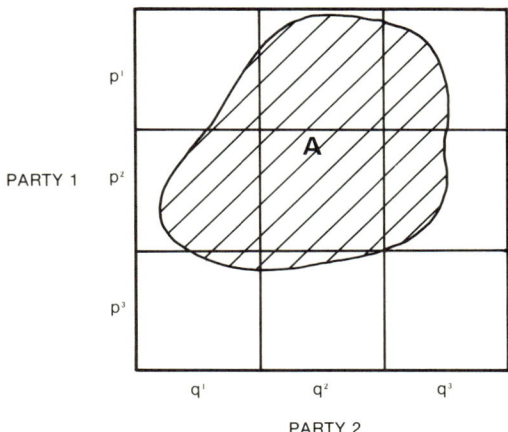

Figure 5.14 Vulnerable bets where parties have private information

possibility that $\omega \in p^1$ or $\omega \in p^2$ cannot be ruled out. Thus $c_1 = (p^1, p^2; q^1, q^2, q^3)$, a fact now known to each potential bettor. Party 2 then calculates the conditional probability that $\omega \in A$ given that $\omega \in q^3$ and that either $\omega \in p^1$ or $\omega \in p^2$, finds it to be less than one-half, and also tentatively says Y. Party 1 deduces that party 2's information could not have been that $\omega \in q^2$, but must have been that $\omega \in q^1$ or $\omega \in q^3$. Thus, $c_2 = (p^1, p^2; q^1, q^3)$. Since the conditional probability that $\omega \in p^2$ and that $\omega \in q^1$ or $\omega \in q^3$ exceeds one-half, party 1 again says Y, and both sides realize that $c_3 = (p^2; q^1, q^3)$. Party 2 now says Y, implying that $c_3 = (p^2; q^3)$. Since the conditional probability of A given that $\omega \in p^2$ and $\omega \in q^3$ is less than one-half, party 1 now refuses the bet. The sequence of responses to the proposed bet is YYYYN.

5.2.6.2 DON'T BET ON IT: GENERAL RESULT

Now consider a general probability space (Ω, S, π) where Ω is the space of states of the world, S is the collection of all possible events (sets) that are made up of elements of Ω, and π is the common prior of parties 1 and 2. Party 1's partition of the space is P with elements p^i ($i \in I_0$, a set of m integers). Party 2's partition is Q with elements q^j ($j \in J_0$, a set of n integers). Assume that the coarsest common refinement of P and Q consists of events whose probability does not vanish. If the true state of the world is ω, then party 1 is privately informed of that element of P which contains ω (denoted $p^i(\omega)$). Similarly, party 2 privately learns which element of Q contains ω (denoted $q^j(\omega)$). Each side knows the other's partition. Suppose a gamble G is proposed. The two parties take turns saying Y or N to G, beginning with party 1. Assume that a party says Y if and only if his or her current expectation from the gamble is strictly positive.

PROPOSITION 7. *The gamble G will be refused by one of the parties after a finite number of repetitions of this process. The number of Y's before an N is at most min $(2m - 2, 2n - 1)$.*

To prove this proposition, set
$$P_1 = \{p^i | i \in I_0, E(G|p^i) > 0\}$$
and
$$Q_1 = \{q^j | j \in J_0, E[G|q^j \cap (\cup P_1)] < 0\},$$
and define P_k and Q_k for $k > 1$ by

DIFFERENCES AND JOINT GAINS

$$P_k = \{p^i | i \in I_0, E[G|p^i \cap (\cup(Q_1 \cap \ldots \cap Q_{k-1}))] > 0\}$$

and

$$Q_k = \{q^j | j \in J_0, E[G|q^j \cap (\cup(P_1 \cap \ldots \cap P_k))] < 0\}.$$

Notice that P_k and Q_k, for $k \geq 1$, do not depend on the true state of nature and hence are known to both parties at the outset.

LEMMA 1. *Suppose all the announcements preceding party 1's (party 2's) turn in round k are Y's. Then party 1's (party 2's) announcement in round k will also be Y if and only if $\omega \in \cup P_k$ ($\omega \in \cup Q_k$). (Notice that $\omega \in \cup P_k$ is equivalent to $p^i(\omega) \in P_k$ and $\omega \in \cup Q_k$ is equivalent to $q^j(\omega) \in Q_k$.)*

To prove Lemma 1, consider the first round of announcements. Party 1, who makes the first announcement, will announce Y if and only if

$$E[G|p^i(\omega)] > 0,$$

that is, if and only if $p^i(\omega) \in P_1$. Party 2 knows this, and so after party 1's Y, party 2's expectation for G is

$$E[G|q^j(\omega) \cap (\cup P_1)].$$

Party 2 will now say Y if and only if this expectation is less than zero, that is, if and only if $q^j(\omega) \in Q_1$. The proof of Lemma 1 can be completed by induction.

LEMMA 2. *(a) Suppose party 1's announcement in the first round is Y. If party 2's announcement in the first round is also Y, then $P_1 \cap P_2$ is a proper subset of P_1. (b) Suppose all the announcements preceding party 1's (party 2's) in round k are Y's, where $k > 1$. If party 1's (party 2's) announcement in round k is also Y, then $Q_1 \cap \ldots \cap Q_k$ is a proper subset of $Q_1 \cap \ldots \cap Q_{k-1}$ ($P_1 \cap \ldots \cap P_{k+1}$ is a proper subset of $P_1 \cap \ldots \cap P_k$).*

To prove (a), suppose that both parties say Y in round 1. Then $p^i(\omega) \in P_1$ and $q^j(\omega) \in Q_1$, or $\omega \in (\cup P_1) \cap (\cup Q_1)$. Hence $(\cup P_1) \cap (\cup Q_1) \neq \emptyset$. Now if $P_1 \cap P_2$ is not a proper subset of P_1, then every element p^i of P_1 is in P_2 and thus satisfies

$$E[G|p^i \cap (\cup Q_1)] > 0. \tag{5.58}$$

Now every element q^j of Q_1 satisfies

$$E[G|q^j \cap (\cup P_1)] < 0. \tag{5.59}$$

Equations (5.58) and (5.59) are contradictory. To see this, note that the sets $p^i \cap (\cup Q_1)$ for $p^i \in P_1$ and the sets $q^j \cap (\cup P_1)$ for $q^j \in Q_1$ are simply two different partitions for the nonempty set $(\cup P_1) \cap (\cup Q_1)$, and that it is impossible for all the conditional expectations in one partition to be negative while all the conditional expectations in another partition are positive. Hence $P_1 \cap P_2$ is a proper subset of P_1. The proof of (b) is similar.

If the first $2k$ announcements are Y's, then Lemma 1 implies that $p^i(\omega) \in P_1 \cap \ldots \cap P_k$ and $q^j(\omega) \in Q_1 \cap \ldots \cap Q_k$. Similarly, if the first $2k+1$ announcements are Y's, then $q^j(\omega) \in Q_1 \cap \ldots \cap Q_{k+1}$. But Lemma 2 implies that $P_1 \cap \ldots \cap P_{k+1}$ is always a proper subset of $P_1 \cap \ldots \cap P_k$, and similarly for the Q's. The stated limit on the number of consecutive Y's follows directly from these observations.

The foregoing analysis suggests a straightforward generalization of Aumann's proposition. Given two partitions $P \equiv \{p^i | i = I_0\}$ and $Q \equiv \{q^j | j \in J_0\}$, define their meet $R \equiv P \wedge Q \equiv \{r^k | k \in K_0\}$ to be the finest partition of Ω that is refined by both P and Q. In the example, R consists of the single set Ω itself. Given any $\omega \in \Omega$, note that $p^i(\omega)$ and $q^j(\omega)$ are both contained in $r^k(\omega)$. Say that an event A is common knowledge at ω if $r^k(\omega) \subset A$. (For an exposition, see Milgrom.)[35]

Let G be an arbitrary real-valued random variable defined on (Ω, S, π). Define the random variables $e_P(\omega) = E[G|p^i(\omega)]$ and $e_Q(\omega) = E[G|q^j(\omega)]$. Let a be a real number. It is then possible to state the following proposition.

PROPOSITION 8. *If it is common knowledge at ω that $e_P \leq a$ and $e_Q \geq a$, then it is common knowledge at ω that $e_P = e_Q = a$.*

The proof is similar to that of Lemma 2. Aumann established Proposition 8 in the case where G takes on the values 0 and 1 and where it is common knowledge at ω that $e_P = b$ and $e_Q = c$ by showing then that $b = c$. (A related result is given in Milgrom and Stokey.)[36]

Proposition 8 implies that for any "bet" or "gamble" as described earlier, it cannot be common knowledge that both sides wish to take it. More precisely, if it is common knowledge that the expectation of each side given its information is nonnegative, then it is common knowledge that this expectation is zero. It is not necessary to go through the stylized process of offers and acceptances that underlies the explicit convergence result of Proposition 7. Instead, at the moment when it becomes common knowledge that both sides wish to gamble — as they extend their hands, so to speak, to shake on the deal — there is a contradiction and at least one side will withdraw. In effect, if there is nothing to prevent the time interval required for each response and counterresponse from being arbitrarily short, then, before the outstretched hands can meet, one of the parties will refuse the bet.

The assumption of common priors used here bears some discussion. The information partitions (or, equivalently, the manner of information processing, the likelihood function, or the model) must themselves be common knowledge in the sense of Aumann. The way in which information is learned by each person is part of the required complete description of the state of the world. If an experiment were to be the source of the information, the parties would have to share opinions on its possible outcomes. The set of all possible such experiments and the number of their possible repetitions must likewise be the subject of common priors. If each party were to observe a vector of information corresponding to some element of the partition, the parties would have to have common priors on the set of all such vectors. Clearly the information requirements for all but the simplest problems would be monumental. But when the stringent conditions of common knowledge are met, rational analysis bears out the childhood admonition: Don't bet on it. All bets need not be off, however, when priors or models genuinely differ.

5.2.7 Optimal Sharing over Time

In situations where economic actors are different, gains from trading on the basis of these differences may improve the welfare of all concerned. Previous sections have examined optimal arrangements involving differences in preferences, beliefs, and attitudes toward risk. Another important dimension of difference involves time preferences. In this section, explicit and intuitively appealing conditions are derived for optimally sharing an income stream that accrues to two actors who have divergent attitudes toward the passage of time.

Rearranging future monetary consequences may be a welfare-improving action whenever time preferences differ. Apart from ad hoc instances of the presence of such differences in individuals, time attitudes may vary systematically in cross-cultural dealings. In situations where parties are of significantly different ages, where one party cares significantly more about bequests, or where opportunities for the use of money are not at all the same, joint gains may be possible. People at different organizational levels may have very different time horizons for evaluating the results of long-term transactions. Time-preference differences may be especially important in negotiations between public and private organizations jointly to undertake projects with future ramifications. Governments or public entities may value benefits or costs to future generations in a manner that is distinct from the way that private collaborators might regard the same consequences. There are, therefore, many possible reasons for discount rates to be unequal across entities, especially between public and private ones.[37]

Taking the possibility of time-preference differences as given, Section 5.2.7.1 briefly characterizes the obviously optimal sharing role in the simplest possible context: two parties, two periods, and constant but different discount rates. In Section 5.2.7.2, the optimal sharing rule is derived for the continuous case in which discount rates vary over time. Throughout the discussion, it is assumed that there is no uncertainty, that enforcement of agreements over time is assured, and that both parties are honest about their preferences.

5.2.7.1 TIME-PREFERENCE DIFFERENCES: TWO-PERIOD MODEL

Two individuals will jointly receive one dollar today and another in a second period. To the first individual, party 1, a dollar received in the second period is worth $(1 + \alpha)^{-1}$ dollars today. Party 2 is less impatient; to her, a second-period dollar is worth $(1 + \beta)^{-1}$. Both α and β are taken to be positive.

Assume that parties 1 and 2 wish to divide the income stream in a Pareto-optimal way; that is, they wish to give a present value of k dollars to party 1 in a way that leaves party 2 with the maximum possible value. Algebraically, party 1 will get c dollars today and d dollars in the second period, where c and d are chosen so that

$$c + \frac{d}{1 + \alpha} = k. \tag{5.60}$$

Party 2's value is then

$$\left[1 - \left(k - \frac{d}{1 + \alpha}\right)\right] + \frac{(1 - d)}{(1 + \beta)}, \tag{5.61}$$

which readily reduces to

$$\left[\left(\frac{2 + \beta}{1 + \beta}\right) - k\right] + \frac{(\beta - \alpha) d}{(1 + \alpha)(1 + \beta)}. \tag{5.62}$$

The first term of (5.62) is a constant; the second is maximized by setting $d = 1$ if $\beta > \alpha$, or setting $d = 0$ if $\beta < \alpha$; that is, if party 2 has a higher discount rate than party 1 ($\beta > \alpha$), party 1 should receive as much as possible of his share later, and conversely. (Notice that when d is restricted to the unit interval, borrowing and lending are implicitly

DIFFERENCES AND JOINT GAINS

ruled out, and with them the mathematical result that the low discounter early on should lend an infinite amount to the high discounter. This assumption is maintained throughout the analysis.) This simple result accords with immediate intuition and underscores the general principle that optimal rearrangement of future consequences gives earlier amounts to the more impatient party.

5.2.7.2 TIME-PREFERENCE DIFFERENCES: MORE GENERAL MODEL

Parties 1 and 2 will receive a stream of income in the amount $x(t)$ at time t. Party i's generalized discount function for money received at time t is $f_i(t)$, for $i = 1,2$. Typically $f_i(t)$ will be positive and declining in t. Assume further that party i's value function for money is $U_i(\cdot)$, where $U_i' > 0$ and $U_i'' < 0$. Under these assumptions, which are equivalent to multiplicative separability of intertemporal utility functions, a sum $x(t)$ received by party i at time t would now be worth $U_i(x(t))f_i(t)$.

Parties 1 and 2 wish to disallow any proposed sharing rule if another such rule exists that is at least as acceptable to each party and that is definitely preferred by one or both of them. Such Pareto-efficient sharing rules or functions are those that maximize party 1's utility when party 2's utility is held at an arbitrarily constant level, say k. By varying k, the full range of efficient rules may be characterized. From among this set of rules, the parties could choose an attractive one. This distributional choice could derive from shared concepts of fairness; it might result from bargaining; or an analytically inclined arbitrator might even dictate the division.

The formal problem is to choose a sharing function, $T(x(t))$, to maximize

$$\int U_1[T(x(t))] f_1(t) \, dt \qquad (5.63)$$

subject to

$$\int U_2[x(t) - T(x(t))] f_2(t) \, dt = k, \qquad (5.64)$$

where all integrals are taken over the appropriate time period and where k is constant.

Standard variational techniques can be used to show that the solution to the constrained maximization problem of expressions (5.63) and 5.64) satisfies the Euler equation

$$\frac{U_1'[T(x(t))] f_1(t)}{U_2'[x(t) - T(x(t))] f_2(t)} = \lambda, \qquad (5.65)$$

NEGOTIATING THE LAW OF THE SEA

for all t and where λ is constant. Expression (5.65) represents the intuitive condition that, at optimality, the ratio of the discounted marginal utilities should be a constant. Differentiating (5.65) with respect to t, substituting for the value of λ from (5.65), suppressing the arguments of functions, and denoting differentiation with respect to t by a raised dot ($\cdot$), obtain

$$\dot{T} = \left[\frac{(-U_2''/U_2')}{(-U_2''/U_2') + (-U_1''/U_1')}\right]\dot{x} + \frac{\frac{d}{dt}[\ln(f_1/f_2)]}{(-U_2''/U_2') + (-U_1''/U_1')}. \quad (5.66)$$

Define

$$\rho_i(\cdot) \equiv \frac{-U_i''(\cdot)}{U_i'(\cdot)}, \quad (5.67)$$

for $i = 1, 2$. (While $\rho_i(\cdot)$ is formally equivalent to the usual absolute risk aversion function, it should be recalled that the present problem contains no uncertainties. The expression $\rho_i(\cdot)$, always positive, is a measure related to varying marginal valuations of the monetary outcomes of the sharing.) The following proposition results from substituting expression (5.67) into expression (5.66).

PROPOSITION 9. *The optional dynamic sharing rule, T, decomposes at the margin into a valuation effect and a time-preference effect. Formally, T satisfies the condition that*

$$\dot{T} = \left(\frac{\rho_1}{\rho_1 + \rho_2}\right)\dot{x} + \frac{\frac{d}{dt}[\ln(f_1/f_2)]}{\rho_1 + \rho_2} \quad (5.68)$$

for all t and where arguments of functions are as implied in expression (5.65).

Expression (5.68) is a characterization of the optimal dynamic sharing role. A number of its properties merit brief discussion. First, at the margin the optimal sharing rule is independent of k, the (parametric) level of party 1's utility in the Paretian problem of expressions (5.63) and (5.64). Second, the rule for how sharing increases is determined pointwise for all t. Third, the increase (or decrease) in sharing can be decomposed into two terms. The first term of expression (5.68), the "valuation effect," proportionately allocates the instantaneous rise or fall in the payment stream, $x(t)$, between the parties according to $\rho_2/(\rho_1 + \rho_2)$, which is always between zero and one. The influence of different discount functions, the "time-preference effect," is entirely reflected in the second term of expression (5.68).

If $f_1(t) > f_2(t)$ for all t, then party 1 has a higher discount factor and everywhere values the future relatively less than does party 2, and conversely. Note that as $f_1(t)$ is greater than, equal to, or less than $f_2(t)$, the logarithm of their ratio is positive, zero, or negative. The sign of the time derivative of this ratio's logarithm is the factor that determines the effect of the two discount rates on the change in optimal sharing at any point.

Consider the effect of the second term of expression (5.68) under the conventional assumption of constant discount rates. That is,

$$f_1(t) = e^{-\alpha t}, \qquad (5.69)$$

and

$$f_2(t) = e^{-\beta t}. \qquad (5.70)$$

Then the numerator of the second term of expression (5.68) becomes

$$\frac{d}{dt}\left[\ln\left(\frac{f_1(t)}{f_2(t)}\right)\right] = \alpha - \beta. \qquad (5.71)$$

Since $\rho_1 + \rho_2$ is positive, expression (5.71) implies that, if $\alpha > \beta$, the second term of expression (5.68) is positive, and thus that optimal payment should correspondingly increase over time. To put it another way, if party 1 has a higher discount rate than party 2, party 1 should receive more money earlier in the optimal arrangement. The later increase in payments to party 2 is an efficient means of compensation. This corresponds to the analysis in the two-period case. If $\alpha < \beta$, of course, the reverse result obtains.

If two parties have different discount rates, rearrangement of a future stream of income may be to their mutual benefit. In the general case, the optimal dynamic sharing rule separates at the margin into a valuation effect and another effect due solely to time-preference differences. Expression (5.68) offers a guide to the efficient formulation of such rules. The general principle for the continuous case is the same as for the simple two-period model: give more to the most impatient party early on and compensate the other party later.

6 Negotiation Arithmetic: Adding and Subtracting Issues and Parties

6.0 A Common Point of Departure

A common approach to the analysis of negotiation commences with a given set of parties, a given set of issues, and the parties' fixed value or preference orderings for different possible settlements of the issues. Within this framework, theorists have investigated a wide class of negotiation phenomena: cooperative moves in reaching jointly beneficial settlements, situations of pure conflict, commitments, threats, promises, and so forth.

This chapter seeks to complement such work with an investigation of the proposition that the issues and parties themselves are often important choice variables in negotiation. For example, agendas must be tacitly or explicitly adopted by a process of adding and subtracting issues. The original issues may change during the course of negotiation, often as the result of conscious moves. Similarly, the parties may change. For example, two children may noisily argue over a single ice cream cone found in the freezer. Their choice to involve a parent, whose interest they hope lies in a silent settlement, may produce funds for a second cone (but does risk angry confiscation of the first one). These cases represent only a few simple examples of the class of strategic moves to select or alter the parties and issues in a negotiation. Consideration of the purposes, methods, and results of such moves can offer a common framework for analysis of diverse aspects of the negotiation process, such as issue linkage and the setting of "bottom lines." Under the rubric of adding and subtracting parties and issues, a number of general propositions emerge.

Five views on issue linkage provide some background for the discussion. William Wallace sounds a dominant theme in writings on the subject when he notes that "linkage between unrelated or only loosely-related issues in order to gain increased leverage in negotiation is an ancient and accepted aspect of diplomacy."[1] Roger Fisher, however, counsels caution. "The joining of issues as leverage or bargaining currency even when constructively looking toward a negotiated agreement," he writes, "tends to shift the focus away from the merits of a problem and to put relative bargaining power in issue."[2]

Robert Tollison and Thomas Willett have recently suggested an alternative rationale for linkage that offers a challenge to which this chapter seeks to respond: "Our theory stresses issue linkage as a means of overcoming distributional obstacles to international agreement where direct side payments among countries are not a politically feasible alternative. The mutual benefit theory contrasts with and supplements the traditional rationale for linkage in terms of extending one's leverage in one area to other areas. Integration of these two approaches . . . is an important task for future research."[3] Kenneth Oye provides a complementary challenge when he observes that "aside from observing what linkages have been constructed in the past, no clear criteria have emerged for predicting patterns of issue linkage."[4]

Although linkage has attracted attention from analysts over the last two decades, its consideration is by no means a modern phenomenon. The approach developed in this chapter was presaged in the wise words of François de Callières, writing in 1716.

> An ancient philosopher once said that friendship between men is nothing but a commerce in which each seeks his own interest. The same is even truer of the liaisons and treaties which bind one sovereign to another, for there is no durable treaty which is not founded on reciprocal advantage, and indeed a treaty which does not satisfy this condition is no treaty at all, and is apt to contain the seeds of its own dissolution. Thus, the great secret of negotiation is to bring out prominently the common advantage to both sides and to link these advantages that they may appear equally balanced to both parties. For this purpose when negotiations are on foot between two sovereigns, one the greater and the other the less, the more powerful of those two should make the first advance, and even undertake a large outlay of money to bring about the union of interests with his lesser neighbors . . . The secret of negotiation is to harmonize the interests of the parties concerned.[5]

These several views confirm that issue linkage is a prominent and venerable practice, but they differ on its rationale and usefulness. They certainly do not suggest the existence of a unified theory. Analogous observations apply to the inclusion and exclusion of parties to negotiations. This chapter attempts to incorporate certain occasionally contradictory insights from qualitative studies of negotiation into a more systematic framework. Success in this endeavor depends on two contentions: first, that issue and party manipulation can usefully be conceived of as common classes of negotiation moves; and second, that these moves can be related to each other by straightforward analytic devices.

Most of the propositions developed here are known in at least some version from other diverse contexts. Several are implicit in writings on negotiation; many are second nature to bargainers. But the applicability of these ideas may be enhanced by isolating them, making them explicit, and showing their connections under a set of broader principles. At a minimum, the analysis can be regarded as an extended checklist of considerations relevant to structural aspects of negotiation that analysts often assume as a point of departure. Section 6.1 treats the issues of negotiation as variable; Section 6.2 considers the parties in a similar way; and Section 6.3 summarizes the main conclusions.

6.1 Adding and Subtracting Issues

De Callières' analogy suggests a useful orientation: one can think of issues as different types of commodities and of negotiators as traders in a market. Depending on preferences, endowments, institutional and legal arrangements, and relative market power, certain items will enter the market and possibly be traded while others will be kept out. A suitably modified economic theory of exchange could be useful to describe the interactions and results.

For the exposition, assume that the negotiator-traders have defined preference functions over the attributes of the possible issues. Think of the trade-offs among several issues that these functions capture as being implied by a set of negotiating instructions. Analysts often represent this framework as in Figure 6.1. The parties' value functions, V_1 and V_2, have the attributes of the issues under consideration as arguments and are measured along the different axes. The curve in the northeast quadrant—the Pareto frontier—represents the evaluations of the set of those possible agreements on the issues that could not be improved upon from the standpoint of either party without harming the other. The origin (point O) represents the values of failing to reach agreement on the set of issues that are actively being negotiated.

The evaluations of possible resolutions of single issues can be displayed as in Figure 6.2. Say that issue A is a discrete or discontinuous issue with only two possible resolutions, A' and A'', and that each such

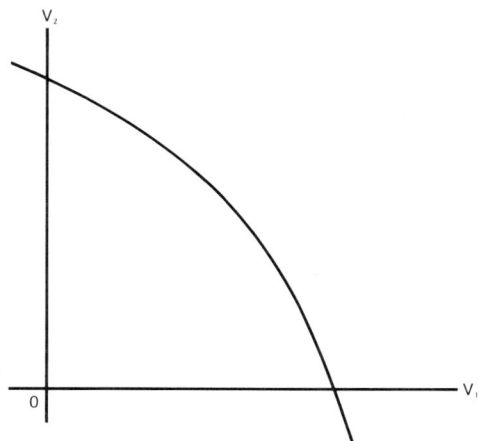

Figure 6.1 Common representation of the bargaining problem

resolution greatly favors one side at the other's expense. As shown, A' is worse for party 1 than no agreement, A'' is similarly undesirable for party 2, and the outcome would be no resolution. (Notice that no interpersonal value comparison is required, only each side's rankings of

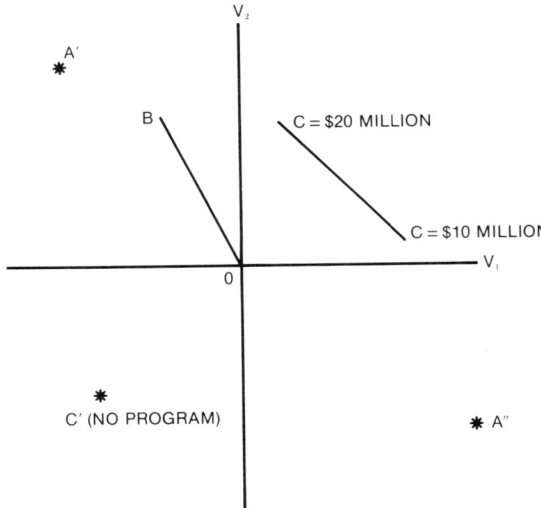

Figure 6.2 Basic graphic apparatus for considering value of individual issues

the possible issue resolutions *relative* to its own no-agreement level.) A second issue, B, is continuous and can be settled at any value between two extremes (represented by the origin and point B). Say that B is the level of military aid that party 1 gives party 2. The joint preference levels of B's various outcomes are represented by the line in the northwest quadrant of Figure 6.2. But settlement is preferable to no agreement only for points in the northeast quadrant; thus, issue B by itself would remain unresolved. Issue C has a discrete outcome point C' in the southwest quadrant (say a decision against undertaking a proposed program) and a continuous series of outcomes (line segment C) that both parties prefer to the status quo (say an affirmative program decision with the chosen level of expenditure ranging from $10 to $20 million). The parties could profitably settle this issue at any bargained point on the segment C in the northeast quadrant.[6]

This representation of the values of single issues assumes that the other arguments of the preference functions are held at status quo levels. Such arguments include both the attributes of the other issues specifically involved in the negotiation (such as issues A, B, and C in Figure 6.2) and those of the rest of the potential issues between the two parties. These latter issues, which are explicitly or tacitly held constant in many negotiation analyses, constitute the elements of a larger interaction or "supergame" among the parties. The analysis of issue addition centers around the attempt by one or another negotiator to vary the values of these other issues.

There are, however, several caveats for the use of this type of graphic analysis and the value functions that underlie it. First, one should exercise some care in the analysis when defining the appropriate attributes of the issues. Two examples make the point. Roger Fisher and William Ury discuss the possible resolution of the Egyptian-Israeli Sinai dispute, which could be viewed as a classic zero-sum case of bitter haggling over the location of a frontier. One might consider the amount of land assigned to each side as the relevant attribute. If Egypt were primarily interested in sovereignty and Israel were concerned with security, however, these differentially valued attributes could be unbundled by creating a demilitarized zone under the Egyptian flag.[7] More prosaic would be the case of two people arguing over the division of one orange, each feeling an absolute need for three-fourths of it. If, however, their discussion reveals that one is hungry and the other wants the orange peel for a recipe, the negotiation could shift from the apparent issue of where to cut the fruit. The real question is how to separate its different relevant "attributes." For analytic purposes, the more fundamental attributes are the appropriate arguments of negotiators' value functions.

It is also of practical importance that the chosen value functions not be defined too narrowly. Analysis may go awry if consideration is limited to the immediate, substantive issue at hand when, for example, precedent is a key question.[8] Certain tactics, as well, may effectively expand the relevant set of attributes. "Take-it-or-leave it" offers, forced linkages, commitment moves, threats, and preemptive actions contain the potential for eliciting strong negative reactions that may overwhelm the original issues at stake. A trade union's motivation for strikes, for instance, may shift over time from a strictly economic reason to a desire for revenge. Likewise, wars can escalate out of all proportion to the possible substantive gains for either side. The sudden Argentinian occupation of the Falkland Islands in 1982 and the British response quickly involved the dispute in weighty, irreconcilable attributes such as national "honor" and the "right" response to aggression. In many circumstances, threats, commitments, and deterrent moves are effective and can be analyzed in terms of values for the immediate issues involved;[9] in other cases such tactics can induce anger, loss of face, and aggression.[10] Thus, when using the value functions, analysts should recognize the possibility that certain bargaining tactics can cause the addition of other attributes and issues beyond the more utilitarian concerns ostensibly involved.[11]

Reliance on the use of value functions merits a few additional comments. Ideally, one might think of such functions as true "welfare" functions; in practice, one must take them to be a negotiator's idea of the relationship of the various issues to his or her own interests, or to the client's, the group's, or the national interest. It is frequently useful to consider the negotiator's personal "payoffs" from particular results. Of course, the different parts of a compartmentalized bureaucracy will try to weight heavily the issues in their respective purviews. Domestic pressure groups and others will act in ways that tend to frustrate trade-offs.[12]

Yet multi-issue negotiation depends on formal and informal judgments: in real negotiations some person or group does decide whether a proposed trade is worth taking, whether a contemplated concession should be made, and, ultimately, whether a final package is better than no agreement (in terms of Figure 6.2, whether it falls in the northeast quadrant). For present purposes, consider such decisions as being made from the point of view of the negotiator or of those to whom he or she may be accountable. A separate problem, of course, may involve inducing the negotiator to use a different set of values in making decisions.

A negotiator's ultimate judgment may well be subject to explicit external validation: the U.S. Senate either ratifies a signed treaty or does not; a union rank and file votes up or down a contract that its leadership has negotiated. During the bargaining prior to such validation, the negotiator must constantly assess the probability that the deal brought back will be formally affirmed. It is subject to this series of understandings about the negotiation context that value functions as an analytic means for representing trade-offs from the negotiator's point of view can be used — even given compartmentalized bureaucracies, pressure groups, internal divisions, and external constraints.

6.1.1 Definitions of Issue Addition and Subtraction

Issues are said to be *added,* combined, or linked when they are simultaneously discussed for joint settlement. One example is the consideration of deep seabed mining together with traditional maritime issues in the Law of the Sea conference. When issues are explicitly brought together for bargaining purposes, devices such as the package deal or the single negotiating text procedure (used at Camp David as well as the Law of the Sea) may be used.[13] When issues are joined at summit conferences, rather than being treated and evaluated separately at lower bureaucratic echelons, issue addition can be said to occur.

An issue is said to be *subtracted,* separated, or unlinked from a negotiation when it is removed from consideration in that forum, perhaps to be ignored or considered in an effectively independent arena. The acceptability of possible settlements on each separate issue may be evaluated on its merits, without respect to the outcomes of other issues. This may occur if acceptable solutions for each issue are determined independently, perhaps by different people or organizational entities; examples are tacit or overt agreement not to take up a question or to drop another question entirely. To illustrate the point, several marine negotiations were divided among the International Marine Consultative Organization, the International Whaling Commission, and the Law of the Sea conference. At one time NATO and the Organization for Economic Cooperation and Development (OECD) effectively separated most issues that the industrialized countries faced. Furthermore, within a particular negotiation, issues may be decoupled by considering them at different times, by distinct subgroups of negotiators, or one at a time without the possibility of logrolling.

One or more parties to a negotiation may seek to add or subtract an issue. The process may be formal or informal, express or implied. In some cases, when participants enter or leave a negotiation, the issues change correspondingly.

The following sections develop several propositions that involve issue addition and subtraction. First, analytic distinctions are suggested for issue linkage in its most familiar form, the traditional linkage for leverage noted earlier by Wallace. Then, in sharp contrast to this use of leverage for achieving one-sided gains, an investigation follows of the ways that issue addition can *create* a zone of possible agreement in the northeast quadrant. (Tollison and Willett's work represents a special case of such agreements.) The next set of propositions provides a counterweight to this optimistic analysis, delineating circumstances in which issue addition can *destroy* zones of possible agreement. A variety of miscellaneous purposes are then discussed.

The propositions are stated descriptively and, as such, imply common knowledge of parties' interests. The interests of nations in a set of negotiations are often fairly obvious to all, as a number of the following examples indicate. Nevertheless, if bargaining team A consulted any of the following propositions for advice, its subjective evaluation of team B's values would be required.[14] Predictive application of the propositions, in principle at least, is similarly straightforward. (For easy reference the propositions are listed in Section 6.3 at the end of the chapter.)

6.1.2 Proposition: Adding Issues Can Yield One-sided Gains to the Exercise of Power

Analysts frequently discuss the linkage of issues through the use of leverage. One side may force a new issue onto the negotiating agenda by the exercise of otherwise unexploited power. (Of course, rather than being used to force linkage, the same power might compel a particular settlement of an existing issue.) It is useful to distinguish between linkage induced by the threatened exercise of power in an area unrelated to the existing negotiation and linkage brought about by the use of power intrinsic to a given negotiation.

Case 1. Unrelated, unexploited power. Suppose that there is an ongoing negotiation between developed and developing countries over two potentially acceptable proposals for the transfer of technology (points A' and A'' in Figure 6.3). Suppose that the developing countries also want to discuss fixing a set of agricultural commodity prices at various levels, displayed in value terms along segment OB in the northwest quadrant; developed countries find the terms progressively more ob-

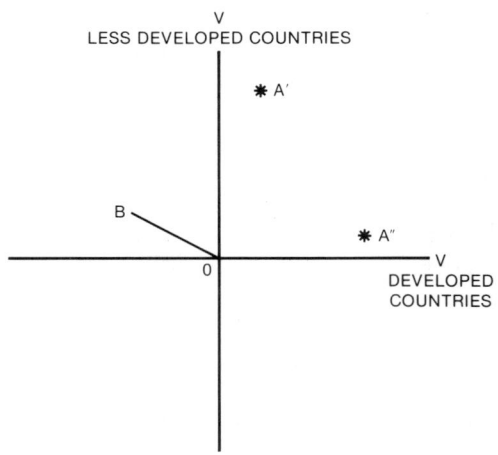

Figure 6.3 Unlinked negotiations between issues A and B

jectionable toward point B. The developed countries therefore refuse the linkage. But suppose further that another common argument in the representatives' value functions is the price of oil, which has been implicitly held constant in the negotiations so far. Suppose that the developing countries threaten the developed countries with a rise in the price of oil unless negotiations over agricultural prices are added to the original discussion.

Figure 6.4 displays the new situation, with the letter C representing the situation under current oil prices and C' representing the case with an oil price rise. Linkage of agricultural prices is graphically accomplished by attaching segment O(C)B(C) to points A'(C) and A"(C). Now the developed countries face the choice of unlinked negotiations with an oil price rise (points O(C'), A'(C'), and A"(C') in the northwest quadrant) or linked negotiations over segments A'(C)B(C) or A"(C)B(C) without a price hike. The linkage is forced by the threat of unilateral manipulation of an unrelated argument of the value functions.[15] This is an example of what is meant by the use of unrelated, unexploited power. (Beyond forcing the link, of course, the same power could influence the outcome of the linked negotiation.)

One could argue that coastal states' threats of accelerated territorial claims and restrictions on navigation and scientific research helped to enforce the continued linkage of a new regime for deep seabed nodule mining in the Law of the Sea conference even though many industrialized countries preferred a seabed mini-treaty. The same mechanism,

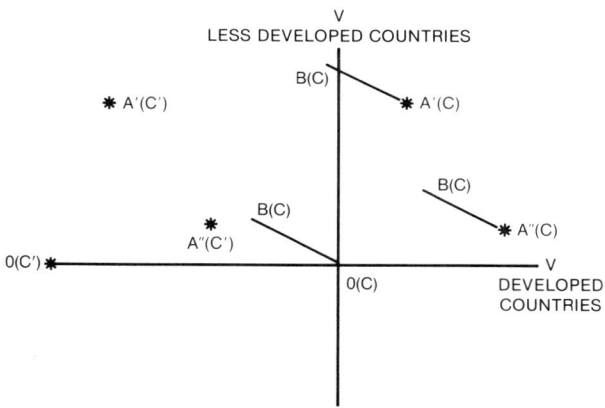

Figure 6.4 Use of unexploited power in issue C to force linkage of issues A and B

unrelated issue leverage to force linkage, would be present if a transnational mining company felt compelled to enter negotiations on building hospitals and schools in a host country lest the financial terms of its contract be unfavorably revised. In all such cases the threat of unilateral manipulation of a different issue in the "supergame" among the parties could be used as the lever to force the linkage.

Case 2. Intrinsic power from commitments. The power to force a linkage need not come from a threat whose source lies outside the negotiating issues at hand; it can come from within a pure bargaining situation in which a commitment can be successfully made. Imagine (as in Figure 6.5) that the bargaining range has narrowed to a single point, A, which both parties prefer to the status quo. Party 1 would now like to discuss the issue whose outcomes are evaluated along OB, but party 2 will not hear of it. Suppose that party 1 is able to make a binding, visible, and irreversible commitment to no agreement (the origin) unless party 2 agrees to the linkage (graphically made by attaching segment OB to point A to get the dashed segment $A(B)$). If party 2 has not committed itself similarly (in which case both sides would lose, ending up at the origin unless one commitment can be undone), its choice is to bargain over segment $A(B)$ or to get nothing. Party 1 will have forced the addition of another issue.[16]

If a traveler has carefully planned a tight itinerary and is confronted at the airport with an unexpected ticket surcharge (even without which the airline may be able to make a profit), there is a good chance that the fee will be paid. In the European negotiations to move to the mutually

NEGOTIATING THE LAW OF THE SEA

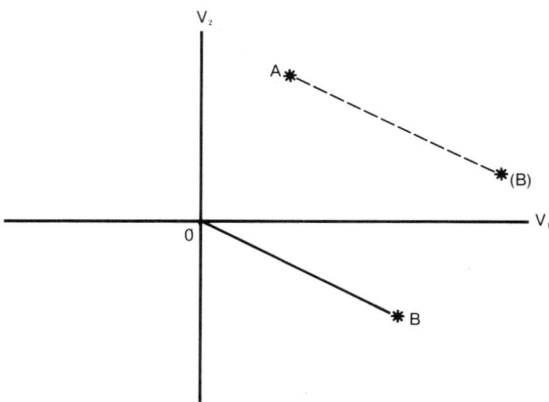

Figure 6.5 Linkage of issue *B* forced by intrinsic power of commitment

beneficial second stage of the Common Market, the French were able to force the linkage of an agricultural policy that the Germans, in particular, did not want but preferred to no agreement. Further examples of linkage forced by conditional commitments to no agreement fall in the categories of "tie-ins" and "last-minute" demands, as discussed by Fred Iklé.[17]

In each of these familiar cases of forced linkage — by unexploited, unrelated, or commitment power — it is worth noting that the party desiring the linkage need not actually be able to carry out the threat or abide by the commitment. The effectivenesss of such an action is a function of the threatened party's evaluation of the magnitude of the consequences, its assessment of the probability that the threat will be carried out, and its attitude toward taking risks. A very risk-averse party might respond to a large threat that had only a small chance of actual occurrence.[18]

This simple graphic apparatus for adding issues in a negotiation can, of course, be made to show the working of mechanisms to keep items *off* the negotiating agenda. This negative "second face of power" is often important.[19] These same tools are employed in the following analysis to demonstrate other propositions concerning issue choice.

6.1.3 *Proposition: Adding Issues Can Yield Joint Gains That Create or Enhance a Zone of Possible Agreement*

The analysis of this section demonstrates that separating certain issues from each other can preclude any chance of agreement while adding them together can create the possibility of a beneficial bargain for each side. It is useful to distinguish among three such cases: adding apparently unrelated issues together, overcoming distributional impediments to efficient agreements by adding issues, and exploiting actual dependencies among separate issues.

Case 1. Creating or enhancing a zone of agreement by adding differentially valued, unrelated issues. A particular subnegotiation within the seabed portion of the Law of the Sea conference illustrates this proposition.[20] As discussed earlier, approximately 90 percent of the issues in the conference were settled by 1978; still remaining were seven "hardcore" sets of articles whose resolution was critical to the fate of the treaty. One of these—the so-called financial arrangements—essentially involved two issues.

The first of these issues concerned the system of financial payments (fees, royalties, profit shares) that future seabed miners would pay to the international community in consideration of the "common heritage" principle. For the most part, the prospective mining countries—acutely aware of the uncertainties and risks of seabed mining—were amenable to paying low levels of profit based on flexible charges. Representatives of developing countries by and large felt that there should be high, fixed, rigid payments. An agreement on this issue by itself appeared to be impossible.

The second financial issue concerned the funding for the initial mining operation of a new International Seabed Authority, which, it was estimated, would cost on the order of one billion dollars. In question were the level of funds to be contributed and whether these would be in the form of grants, loans, or guarantees by states ratifying the ultimate treaty. The developing countries, many of whom regarded the successful launching of this project as crucial, wanted a high proportion of long-term, interest-free loans (for brevity, such loans are subsequently referred to as cash grants). The developed countries greatly preferred a system of loans that would supplement whatever funds the new entity could raise commercially. The financial negotiators felt at a complete impasse on this issue.

A highly stylized version of this situation is displayed in Figure 6.6. Possible outcomes of the negotiations on financial terms of contracts correspond to points on segment *OA*. Notice that the developed countries find higher, more rigid schemes increasingly objectionable. The developing countries, however, would not agree to any of the settlement points for financial terms displayed on *OA*. The reverse is true for various mixtures of funding for the first international mining operation: the developing countries prefer more direct cash grants, but any

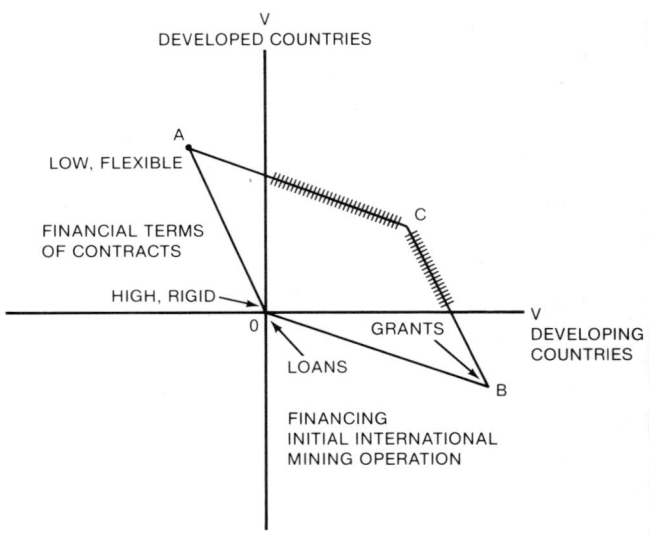

Figure 6.6 Combining individually unresolvable issues to generate a zone of agreement

proposed settlement of this issue would be blocked by the developed countries. No settlement points of either question appear in the feasible (northeast) quadrant.

Negotiators generally treated these two issues separately until 1979, when a bargaining linkage was forged between them. Adding them together is analytically equivalent to taking their vector sum. Segment *ACB* represents the evaluation of the combined issues; a zone of possible agreement (in the northeast quadrant) is created along the hatched segment. (Point *C*, for example, is a flexible system with full cash grants.) When the issues were considered separately, however, there was no possible agreement on them.

The analytic point is easily stated: adding differentially valued issues together can create or enhance zones of agreement where none would be possible if separate negotiations took place and the outcome of each such negotiation were separately evaluated for acceptability.

Case 2. Overcoming distributional impediments to jointly beneficial agreements by adding issues as side payments. Economists often concern themselves primarily with "efficient" policies (which, for example, maximize aggregate production) while giving short shrift to distributional aspects. The usual rationale is that the distributional "winners" from a truly efficient policy could more than amply compensate the "losers" by side payments; the winners would be better off than under the *status quo ante* even after paying the losers. Observing that direct side payments are often institutionally implausible in international negotiations, Tollison and Willett suggest that issues functioning as side payments may effectively be added to negotiations.[21] They present an involved example of negotiations to form an alliance that would yield some general benefits. There are also specific benefits to the parties that depend on where alliance production is located. Scale returns are involved in the production. Skewed benefits and costs interact in such a way that no proposed division of production leaves both parties better off than under the status quo; considerable total benefits thus stand to be lost for distributional reasons.

Figure 6.7 displays a version of this situation. At point A, country 2 produces the whole alliance output and enjoys great benefit while country 1, after paying the costs and getting no domestic production, is worse off than under the status quo. Point C reverses the situation, with country 1 producing all the alliance output. Point B represents a split in production, but a loss in scale economies makes the alliance too costly for either party. Suppose, however, that the parties find another issue (represented by segment OD) that has the character of a side payment from, say, country 1 to country 2. Adding this issue to the previously inconclusive negotiation affords numerous possible points (along curve

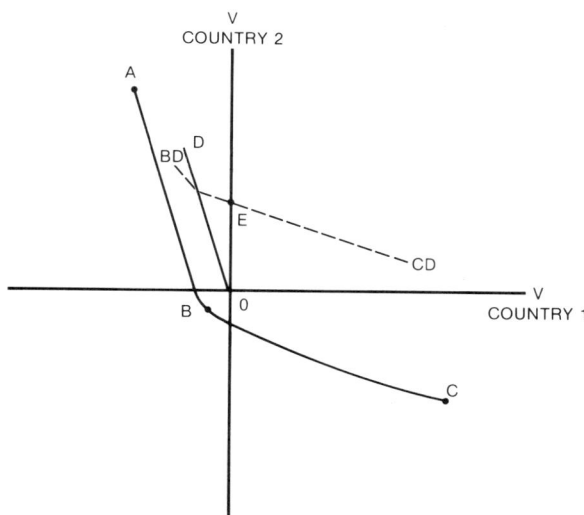

Figure 6.7   Adding an issue as a side payment

BDCD) that dominate the status quo. (For example, point *CD* results geographically from attaching segment *OD* to point *C*. Point *CD* corresponds to a settlement in which country 1 produces all the alliance output, but the new issue is added and settled at point D.)

The general principle is again easy to state: adding issues as side payments may allow the realization of efficient agreements that might otherwise be blocked for distributional reasons.

Case 3. Adding issues to exploit their dependencies. The analysis so far has proceeded under the implicit assumption that each party evaluated each issue in question the same whether the issue was taken by itself or combined with another. This has facilitated the graphic analysis, which has shown the potential for reaching the northeast quadrant (possible, mutually beneficial agreement) by the combination of issues. Yet sometimes there are positive dependencies among the valuations of issues when the issues are taken together. The effect may be described as one of synergy. A simple case is that of economic complements: pencils and paper are worth more in combination than singly, and the same may be true of coffee and sugar. If such positive interactions exist among negotiating issues, they may be exploited to the advantage of all the parties.

Imagine a very difficult political-military negotiation within a strained NATO, one that appears to have at best a grudgingly possible zone of agreement. Simultaneously, divided OECD members are seeking an economic agreement with the same painful prognosis. Adding the issues to each other may make resolution more valuable: the perceived value of the alliance members' hammering out successful agreement on both issues may make the whole greater than the sum of the parts and may thereby make joint resolution easier. Simultaneous resolution contributes to the additional attribute of alliance unity.

Two potential adversaries may be engaged in separate talks over reductions in conventional and nuclear arms. Each party holds a position of great relative strength in one of the two areas. In each separate area, equal force reductions are contemplated and there is no possible agreement in either forum — since equal cuts in, say, nuclear weapons would be only slightly harmful for the side with an initial nuclear edge while much more significantly detrimental to the power of the country that was relatively weaker in nuclear strength. The case with conventional arms could be similar. Figure 6.8 displays this situation. Notice that the combination (by simple vector addition) of these two issues would fall in the southwest quadrant, which is worse for each side than no agreement. Yet evaluation of the joint effect of mutual reductions in

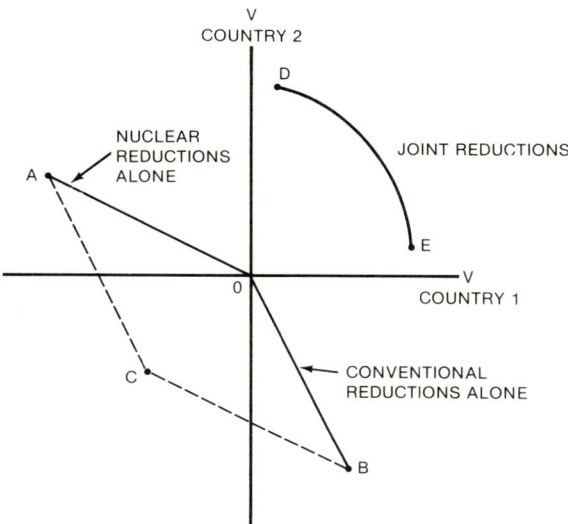

Figure 6.8 Combination of issues with positive dependence

both military categories may well be in the northeast quadrant. Each country would be reducing both its stronger and its weaker types of forces; each country would be spending less on arms; and the relative security levels would not change. The interaction between the issues lies in their effects on security and budget. (Of course, reductions by each side in its stronger forces alone might produce a zone of agreement as well.)

Another kind of dependence can be exploited by adding issues, in the same way that portfolio diversification can reduce investment risk. A standard economic example makes this point. Suppose that an entrepreneur owns two businesses on a tourist island, one with the concession for rain umbrellas, the other with the rights to sell suntan oil. He is negotiating the sale of each business to a different party. Neither is willing to pay the entrepreneur's price, partially because each business by itself is quite risky. When the sun shines, the suntan oil concession flourishes while the umbrella business languishes; when it rains, the reverse happens. A potential buyer in each negotiation has lowered her offer to compensate for this specific risk. Yet if the negotiations could be combined, the two potential buyers could form a partnership to buy both concessions, which together would have a much less variable cash flow than either single business. The price offered for both together may well exceed the sum of the offers for the separate components. Thus combining the issues enhances the possibilities of agreement.

The second overall proposition — that adding issues can yield joint gains that create or enhance a zone of possible agreement — is thus true for at least three types of situations: first, where unrelated but differentially valued issues can be combined; second, where distributional impediments to otherwise efficient agreements can be overcome by adding issues as side payments; and third, where actual dependencies (complementarities or synergies) among issues can be exploited by their combination.

One can take the analysis of this section as an argument for simultaneous rather than separate or sequential consideration of negotiating issues. If, for example, formulating a government's "bottom line" in negotiating instructions is done on an issue-by-issue basis, with only the contested items referred to a high bureaucratic level, certain beneficial agreements may be ruled out of consideration. What appears incontestably to be a bare minimum on one issue by itself may in fact be flexible when this issue is considered together with favorable settlements on other questions.

The use of a single negotiating text can facilitate the simultaneous consideration of several issues. Package deals can result in similar advantages. The social-psychological literature lends some experimental support to the proposition that juggling multiple issues together can lead to settlements that are Pareto-superior to those obtained by bargaining on an issue-by-issue basis.[22]

Issue-by-issue consideration may, of course, be necessary to avoid the sheer complexity of combination, and partial agreements may provide impetus to overall ones. In fact, Iklé considers a policy of "honoring partial agreements" as a virtual "rule of accommodation" that is followed by most international negotiators.[23] Such a practice, however, may lead to settlements that could easily be improved upon from the standpoints of all parties. Consider a related implication of the order of settling issues. Figure 6.9 displays a situation that is similar in structure to Figure 6.6. No agreement appears possible on the issues if they are considered separately, but their combination affords the possibility of settlement along the hatched segments in the northeast quadrant. Suppose, however, that agreement on the issue represented by segment OA is reached *first,* at point D. Combining this settlement with issue OB only allows points along segment DE to be reached. Many of these points are dominated by (that is, are less desirable than) the hatched segment FGE that could result from simultaneous consideration. (Of

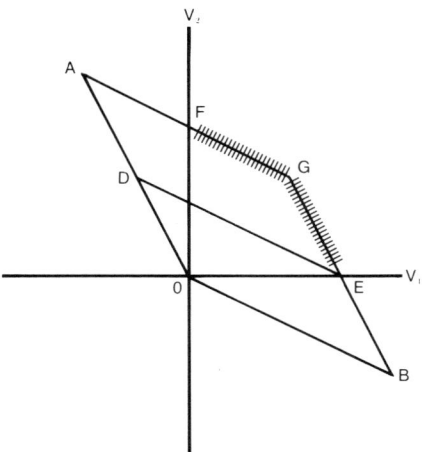

Figure 6.9 Combining issues but settling them on an issue-by-issue basis

course, for tactical reasons one side may well wish to settle one issue at a particular point to limit the effects of settlements on other questions.)

It is only a short step from stressing the value of simultaneous consideration of issues to the argument that as many issues as possible should be added together so that the best possible settlement may occur after "trading." In the case of the Law of the Sea conference, Evan Luard argued that

> Every country, and every group of countries, had a different and sometimes conflicting range of interest within ocean space: either on the surface of the sea, on the bottom, or both. Agreement was likely to be reached only if all these varying interests could be accommodated through a vast, comprehensive package. The outcome was thus bound to be a compromise; in which something was given, say in preferential fishing rights, to those countries which were mainly interested in fishing; something to the landlocked and shelf-locked countries without any waters or shelf of their own; something to the archipelago countries with special economic and security problems to protect; something to the highly developed which already had the capacity to exploit; and something for the developing as a whole, which reasonably felt that, if the resources at hand belonged to the whole world equally, the essential point was to assume that all obtained a return from them. Only if these varying interests were balanced would a solution be possible. And only if the manifold issues were considered together in a single, mammoth negotiation, so that a concession on one point could be

balanced by a concession on another, were the conflicting interests likely to be reconciled.[24]

Using the term "contract curve" for the Pareto frontier or the boundary of the zone of possible agreement, Tollison and Willett make the same point in general terms: "When the contract curve is clear and well understood by all parties, the aggregation of issues is quite helpful to the process of reaching international agreement. A multiplicity of issues creates more possibilities for indirect trades leading to productive agreements."[25]

The foregoing analysis supports these claims by laying out cases in which adding issues may be mutually beneficial. But the advice implicit in the last two quotations cannot be generalized to all situations. Adding issues together is *not* always desirable, even when they are well understood, as the next set of propositions seeks to demonstrate.

6.1.4 Proposition: Adding Issues Can Reduce or Destroy a Zone of Possible Agreement

Adding issues together, with the requirement of simultaneous explicit agreement on all of them, may reduce the chances for a successfully negotiated outcome. It is useful to distinguish between cases in which some of the included issues may have no separate solutions and those in which all the issues are resolvable individually until combined. There are several additional, miscellaneous reasons that may militate against the addition of issues.

Case 1. Adding issues that have no zone of agreement by themselves may destroy the overall chances of a settlement on other issues. In some cases the combination of issues that are individually impossible to resolve may facilitate agreement, but it is possible to go too far. If one adds a sufficiently divisive issue to other less contentious questions *and* one requires joint resolution of them all, then agreement may be rendered impossible. Figure 6.10 displays two discontinuous issues. Issue A has two possible resolutions (A' and A'') in the northeast quadrant. The parties would prefer either bargained outcome to no agreement. Issue B also has two possible settlements (B' and B''). Each outcome of issue B is mildly desired by one party and detested by the other. Adding the issues together (so that the parties must agree on $A'B'$, $A'B''$, $A''B'$, or $A''B''$; see Figure 6.11) takes all possible settlements out of the northeast quadrant. For example, requiring that the status of Jerusalem be resolved at the first stage of a possible Middle East accord might overburden a set of other issues that potentially could be settled. If the

201
NEGOTIATION ARITHMETIC

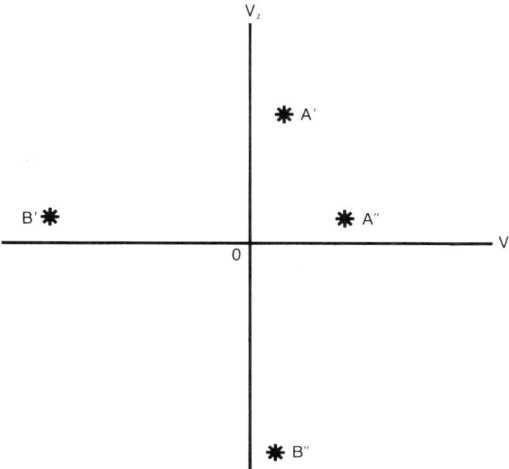

Figure 6.10 Separate discontinuous issues

negotiation agenda included Jerusalem, the parties might profitably agree to subtract it (and perhaps to take it up later if, say, benefits from agreement on the other issues sufficiently strengthened the parties' relationship).

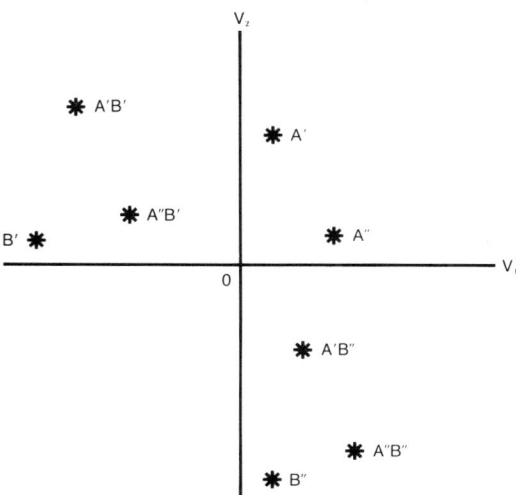

Figure 6.11 Adding issues to destroy possible zones of agreement

An instinctive response to a situation like this is to drop the requirement of simultaneous settlement, especially if both sides prefer a resolution of the remaining topics to no agreement. Of course, agreement to drop or postpone the settlement of a particular issue may not be neutral to the outcome on the other questions in the negotiation. Iklé cites an arms-control example: "Excluding underground tests from the nuclear test ban treaty surely facilitated agreement. But until the summer of 1963, Khrushchev vigorously opposed this separation of issues. He must have realized that once a partial treaty had been signed, the western powers would feel under much less pressure to accept his minimal detection arrangements for banning underground tests."[26]

Despite its obvious appeal, the separation of extremely divisive issues from other questions that do have mutually beneficial settlements by themselves is sometimes difficult or impossible. Appropriations bills in the U.S. Congress must sometimes be signed or vetoed in their entirety. Executive-legislative budget negotiations may produce bills that result in impasse because of a single divisive item. An entire, otherwise mutually acceptable, set of compromises thereby may be lost.

Case 2. Adding issues with individual zones of possible agreement may destroy or reduce a combined zone of agreement. A somewhat more interesting case involves issues that may be resolved individually to the benefit of all parties but cannot be settled when considered together. Usually this happens when a "smaller" issue takes on some of the attributes of a "larger," difficult, but potentially solvable question. Consider a proposed trade deal between two countries who are engaged in drawn-out, inconclusive, expensive hostilities that may be considered the status quo. Both the hostilities and the economic action may have outcomes preferable to the current situation, but it may be impossible to consummate the trade deal unless the hostilities are settled. Even a jointly desired agreement by two countries not to mistreat the other's prisoners or not to use particular tactics or weapons may be impossible to reach because of its symbolic overtones. Fisher offers an example: "In August, 1961, a civil aviation agreement between the United States and the Soviet Union was negotiated. The United States might have signed the agreement, treating it as a separate matter. We chose, however, to decline to sign it, and considered the matter related to Berlin."[27]

To avoid adding such issues together, they may be considered at a lower bureaucratic level. For example, sharing of the fur seals on the Alaska-Siberia border in the 1950s, at the height of the Cold War, was easily handled by relegating the questions to low-level officials. In another case, meteorologists in the Weather Bureau were able to maintain the common interest in exchanging weather data with Cuban stations even during the Cuban missile crisis.

Several other reasons for not adding issues together merit brief consideration. First, instead of positive dependence (synergy or complementarity), negative dependence may result from combination. Two issues may be worth less together than apart (substitutes) or may be riskier when joined (if the businesses in a previous example were, say, suntan oil and sun umbrellas rather than rain umbrellas). Part of a negotiation may involve such extreme uncertainty as to its effect (say, flexible versus fixed exchange rates) that when added to other, more certain issues (say, particular tariff levels) it may interact with them to make the whole package too uncertain.

It is possible to imagine adding some issues that are of interest only to a subset of the negotiators in a multilateral conference. The possible settlements on these issues could be quite contentious but necessary for an overall bargain. Other negotiators may have to make so many concessions to induce the smaller group to settle its dispute that overall resolution would be rendered impossible.

Finally, negotiations may reach some critical mass that stimulates third-party opposition. Mandatory transfer of seabed technology might have been possible as a part of a Law of the Sea package; but if it were combined with other technology transfer issues as a separate negotiation, even unrelated national industrial organizations might have mobilized against the more visible policy.

This discussion has considered numerous ways, quite apart from the traditional conception of linkage forced by leverage, in which adding or subtracting issues at various stages of a negotiation can create, enhance, reduce, or destroy a zone of possible agreement in negotiations. These can be related by a common analytic device that allows graphic combination or separation of issues. But there are other reasons to add and subtract issues.

6.1.5 *Further Reasons for Adding or Subtracting Issues*

1. *Adding issues can solidify coalitions.* Adding issues to a negotiation may be a way to strengthen a coalition by in effect offering an inducement for preserving solidarity. A national labor union may bargain primarily over issues such as wages that concern all of its members. Adding several issues that particularly concern different local unions, however, may earn their more enthusiastic support in a contest with management. There may be considerable uncertainty as to the resolution of these issues, the actual effects of a settlement, and the ultimate

distribution of any benefits generated. Including a number of such issues in a negotiation may be a way to hold coalition members together.

The developing countries' organization (the Group of 77) has displayed a remarkable solidarity across many international conferences even when internal divisions of interest were present. Part of the reason for this solidarity may consist of the large number of issues—terms of trade, technology transfer, debt relief, sovereignty over natural resources, and the like—that promise widely distributed but uncertain benefits if the group succeeds. The issues may have very poorly understood cause-and-effect connections. The likelihood of achieving success on any of these items, however, appears lower if overall solidarity is not maintained. Ernst Haas calls this phenomenon "fragmented linkage," in which "uncertainty about outcomes is part of the glue that holds the coalition together."[28]

2. *Issues may be added to strengthen bargaining commitments.* Issues may be "added" to a negotiation in a slightly different sense without being subject to settlement one way or the other. Commitment tactics often aim to link the resolution of the issue at hand to an arguably similar parallel or future set of issues. Suppose a negotiator persuades others that he will incur real costs elsewhere if they reach certain settlements on the current negotiating question. By this means he may be able to narrow the zone of possible agreement in his favor. If wage levels settled upon in one negotiation will be the focal point for other, parallel negotiations; if the terms of a mining company's latest Third World mineral contract will be applied to its other operations; or if these consequences can be presented as likely enough, their negotiators may credibly make a commitment not to accept terms less favorable than some specific amount. Developing countries in the Law of the Sea negotiations proposed seabed mineral production controls, mining technology transfer, and a special governing structure of a new International Seabed Authority. These proposals may have a small initial effect on a tiny new industry, but their potential as precedents for the moon, outer space, the airwaves, or the Antarctic may be invoked by developed countries to argue against them. These proposals, in turn, may not have been made with seabed benefits primarily in mind but rather with a vision of an overall New International Economic Order (perhaps embracing the other named resources).

If attributes of the issues in one negotiation are linked to those of another, one may, in effect, favorably "squeeze" the zone of agreement. Claims of adverse procedural precedents may be such an attribute: a negotiator may link her conduct or concession-making behavior to her "bargaining reputation" and claim grave future harm for taking an action now that appears in substance quite acceptable.

3. *Adding issues may alter the parties to a negotiation.* The addition of issues may, along with changing the substantive focus of a negotiation, have the effect of adding new parties whose primary concern is with the new issue. Indeed, changing the parties may be part of the reason for adding the issue. For example, the entry of a different, supposedly more reasonable group of bureaucrats may be triggered. (This "new party effect" could have accompanied many of the instances of issue addition discussed earlier.) It is also true that a particularly obnoxious set of negotiators may leave the bargaining if their issue is subtracted (dropped or postponed).

The legal officers of two corporations, working out a primarily legal agreement, may add the financial staffs to the negotiations by adding financial aspects to the original bargain. One way the Merchant Marine Committee could ensure that the House Ways and Means Committee members would leave their specific imprint on a bill to authorize U.S. companies to mine the seabed would be to add a minor tax provision to the bill. It is easy to imagine cases in which a party brought in with an issue might have still another useful relationship or connection with one of the original negotiators. (Section 6.2 deals with this question in more detail.)

6.1.6 Complicating Considerations in the Addition and Subtraction of Issues

There are several qualifications to this discussion of adding and subtracting issues. First, there is the question of complexity. As issues are aggregated, the amount of information required by a negotiator increases and the negotiation itself becomes more cumbersome. Trade-offs among more diverse areas may need to be made at ever-higher levels of the organizational structure. The issues themselves may be technically complex, while rationality and attention spans may be severely bounded.

Relationships among diverse issues may be complicated, and putting questions together in order to make bargaining trade-offs may be unintentionally harmful. Fisher and Ury argue for the separation of issues and individual settlement "on the merits." They use an example in which "a contractor in a negotiation with the owner of a building in the works said 'Go along with me on putting less cement in the foundations because I went along with you on stronger girders in the roof.' No owner in his right mind would yield. Nor would he yield if the contractor threatened to make the owner's brother-in-law lose his job or offered the owner a special favor."[29]

Adding issues together in a bargaining sense while ignoring their real interdependence (in Fisher and Ury's example it is physical) would be a bad idea. But all interdependencies are not so obvious. As Wallace suggested of the trade-off metaphor that Richard Nixon apparently favored ("It's all one ball of wax"), the international system in fact is better characterized as an intricate honeycomb.[30] To add issues is thus to run the risk of increasing complexity, causing information or analytic overload or fear of unintended consequences, and thereby burdening the negotiation itself with possibly significant costs. To subtract or separate issues, of course, can have opposite influences.

An attempt to force linkage, whether through unrelated, unexploited power or through intrinsic commitment leverage, may poison the negotiating atmosphere and, as discussed before, add new, undesirable attributes. The victim may regard the move as illegitimate and unethical, and thus it may backfire. As de Callières noted, "Menaces always do harm to negotiation, and they frequently push one party to extremities to which they would not have resorted without provocation. It is well known that injured vanity frequently drives men to courses which a sober estimate of their own interests would lead them to avoid."[31] Such a reaction seems more likely the more significant is the forced addition and the more unrelated it is intellectually to the original issue. As a practical matter, it is probably easier to sustain a linkage that has a substantive connection either with the other (voluntary) subjects of negotiation or, at least, with the recognized goals of one party.

Even proposing issues for addition that may enhance a zone of possible agreement may lead to problems. Such issues can transform a simple, tractable bargain into a complex, uncertain one. Proposing possibly beneficial trades among unrelated issues may engender more such suggestions, escalating the negotiation to include all possible aspects of a common relationship. This may not be objectionable a priori, but it may make small, desirable deals unlikely.

This tendency may also lead to the creation of a stingy trading ethos, which becomes "I won't do anything for you unless I get something in return." During the formation of the European Coal and Steel Community, Jean Monnet actively encouraged an *esprit communautaire;* common interests were to be the focus rather than logrolling, package deals, or trades based on conflicting interests in separate areas. He used many techniques to induce joint problem solving and to build long-term relationships rather than to foster the habitual use of bartered deals for immediate advantage.[32] Of course, apparent "concessions" now may be accompanied by the understanding and expectation that equity will be fostered in subsequent dealings. Recognizing that the relative importance each side attaches to different issues will vary over time can provide the basis for building longer-term relationships.

Addition or subtraction of issues can significantly affect the zone of possible agreement in a negotiation. Other considerations, however, will also be relevant: increased information or organizational burdens, unintended interrelationships among the joined issues, a clouded atmosphere for negotiation, or possible negative effects on the long-term relationship of the bargaining parties. Each of these situations may alter conclusions based on analysis limited to the substantive issues at hand.

6.2 Adding and Subtracting Parties

The central purpose of this chapter is to investigate the proposition that one should not regard a negotiation's issues and parties as fixed for analysis but rather as variable. Thus far the parties have generally been held constant in order to examine some of the reasons for, and methods and results of, expanding or contracting the set of issues under negotiation. In the marketplace analogy, the same traders acted to force or entice each other into considering fewer or more types of commodities. The analysis in the remainder of this section will keep the commodities the same in order to look at some of the means and ends of adding or subtracting traders.

Parties may be brought in or ejected by unilateral action of one side, by unanimous agreement, or by suitable votes of the original negotiators. New parties also may be able to force their way into the dialogue by means of their leverage over the existing players or their stake in the issues under negotiation. Their participation may be explicit or tacit. Their assent may or may not be required for a settlement, but their influence during the deliberations may be significant. Sometimes such parties will be the natural concomitant of added or subtracted issues. A change in organizational level may bring in or exclude players with different motivations, orientations, preferences, attitudes toward risk, or collateral relationships with other participants.

Of course, the number of participants in a negotiation may vary for other reasons. The size of a delegation may change; it may acquire or discharge advisers; or the negotiators may create or draw on outside bodies — secretariats, technical commissions, consultants, and the like. Bargaining agents, mediators, or arbitrators, as well as deceptive actors such as shills or false bidders, may be engaged. Although these situations are of independent interest, the following analysis concerns only the addition or subtraction of parties who themselves can be considered direct or indirect principals in the bargaining.

6.2.1 Common Reasons for Adding or Subtracting Parties

Several fairly straightforward reasons for changing the parties in a negotiation merit brief mention. If one is seeking a nonproliferation agreement or a division of market shares, those players with a tangible influence on and interest in any ultimate deal will normally enter the game at some stage.

It is common for one side to bring in a third-party ally with some (possibly) unrelated influence on a current bargaining opponent. For example, the Japanese automaker Nissan was negotiating unsuccessfully with the Mexican government for permission to manufacture in Mexico. Bringing in the Japanese government as an ally was a useful ploy: since Mexico's largest foreign-exchange earner at that time was cotton, and Japan absorbed 70 percent of Mexican cotton exports, the implied threat to cut imports was sufficient to assure Nissan the necessary license.[33] It is not necessary, of course, that an additional party have unrelated, unexploited power; one side can bring in new allies who simply add to existing power. Before the 1963 newspaper strike in New York, the publishers of nine newspapers formed a Publishers' Association to bargain with the newly forged "blood-brotherhood" of several unions in the Newspaper Guild.[34]

Third parties who have a variety of other relationships with the negotiators may be used to strengthen commitments arising from the negotiation. If either negotiating party were to renege on the bargaining agreement, the third-party agreement would be affected as well, possibly with consequences in several other areas. A commitment within a negotiation not to accept less than some settlement amount may be buttressed by a link to future or parallel negotiating parties (as was the case with issues). It is also possible to bring in parties to solidify an agreement or to add legitimacy to a bargain or aid in its implementation.

It is almost axiomatic that the more parties (and issues) there are, the higher are the costs, the longer the time, and the greater the informational requirements for a negotiated settlement. Manipulation of the parties can alter these characteristics. One of the most frequent comments about the long-running Law of the Sea conference was the "impossible" number of significant items to be negotiated among more than 150 countries. Especially complicating was the fact that many of these countries had no "tangible" national interest in many of the questions. As a practical matter, the conference's organization and procedures for reaching agreements eased this problem. Although all participants nominally had a say on all agreements, the principally interested parties frequently made deals in small groups. For example, negotiations to soften the impact of seabed mineral production on land-based producers were primarily carried out by a small group with the United States and Canada (the largest land-based producer of nickel) as the main figures. The final accommodation on the financial terms of contracts was reached in a four-country group. Separating issues and effectively subtracting parties served to reduce information requirements and strategic complexity, and, it was hoped, to create strong focal points for wider agreement. (This practice, of course, also greatly reduced the scope for cross-issue or cross-area trading as certain key negotiators came to work primarily on small subsets of the conference's questions.) In other cases, of course, the number of parties is radically reduced to allow agreement among a smaller group. The Soviet-U.S.-U.K. test ban treaty came about only after the eighteen-nation disarmament conference gave way to trilateral negotiations.

To summarize this discussion of the reasons for manipulating the parties in a negotiation, addition of parties is likely when they (1) have a tangible interest in or influence on the substance of the negotiation; (2) may strengthen an existing coalition directly or by leverage from unrelated issues; or (3) enable more binding commitments to be made. Subtraction of parties may take place for opposite reasons, as well as to reduce complexity and information costs and to provide focal points for larger settlements. The remainder of this section is devoted to an analysis of two general propositions on the addition and subtraction of parties to a negotiation: first, party addition or subtraction can significantly alter the zone of possible agreement among the original parties; second, changing the parties may alter the strategic complexion of a negotiation by improving or worsening the consequences of failing to reach agreement.

6.2.2 Proposition: Adding and Subtracting Parties Can Alter the Zone of Possible Agreement among the Original Parties

This section adopts the point of view of the original participants. In three general situations, negotiators might wish to bring in new parties or form coalitions to eject current or proposed participants. The first case involves the more or less active involvement of another party, while the second and third cases might be considered passive alteration of the parties.

Case 1. Adding or subtracting parties who have an interest in a settlement may alter the original zone of agreement. Generally, if the settlement of a dispute has value to outside parties, the original negotiators may try to appropriate some of that value. Involvement of the other parties is one method. The added value may be a windfall to the original parties (if they would have agreed anyway), or it may significantly increase the inducement for them to come to terms. In either case, addition of parties is likely.

Recall the earlier example of two siblings loudly arguing over a single ice cream cone and deciding to risk its summary confiscation by appealing to a parent. Their hope is that the parent will oblige by getting them a second cone, buying peace in the bargain. An externality in the original situation (the noise of their quarrel) provides the basis for the desired (or undesired) entry of other parties.

The United States clearly held a strong interest in Egypt's and Israel's settling their differences. Thus, it is hardly surprising that the United States interjected itself into the Middle East negotiations along with substantial offers of economic and military assistance. If some existing parties — such as the Soviet Union, in the comprehensive plan envisioned in the Geneva accords — are perceived as having an interest in no settlement, they may be frozen out of the negotiation for analogous reasons.

It is not necessary for an added party to have a tangible interest in the substance of a settlement; there may be an institutional reason, as was the case with the World Bank in the Indian-Pakistani negotiations over the Indus River. The Bank had financial resources and technical expertise available to facilitate a settlement.[35]

Case 2. Adding parties may spread or eliminate risks from the bargain of the original participants. An earlier section considered the possible advantages of adding issues to exploit risk dependencies. Separate negotiations on rain umbrella and suntan oil concessions could be combined; the resulting "diversified" issue in a single negotiation would be worth more to all parties than when the questions were separate. Now, consider the reverse situation in which the issues (which involve inherent uncertainty) are held constant while parties are added to spread or eliminate original risks.

Two countries may be negotiating over the construction of a risky project, say an experimental energy technology system with an agreed chance of success estimated at one-half. For expositional purposes, assume that each country's risk attitudes toward such a project can be described simply: each would be willing to risk losing $250 million for a possible $500 million gain, but an even chance of losing $375 million against a $750 million gain is too much risk for either to bear. Say that the project's costs are known to be $750 million, and its benefits (if successful) would be $1.5 billion over cost. Under such circumstances the two-country bargaining would be inconclusive, while the addition of a third similar party could spread the risk in a way that would be beneficial to all. Each project sponsor would be happy with a $250 million cost balanced by a $500 million share of potential benefits. Thus, addition of the third party would allow mutually beneficial agreement.[36]

Negotiation of the financial terms of mineral agreements in developing countries is often rendered very difficult by the price uncertainty of the mine's ultimate product. In a market slump, large losses could result; a boom may send profits to extreme levels. The mining taxation system can significantly affect the risk. Trying to decide in advance the proper mixture and level of relatively fixed charges (which shift price risk to the company) or contingent charges (such as profit shares, which shift price risk to the country) may be an extraordinarily difficult task if both parties are risk-averse. One solution to this problem could be to sell bonds to relatively less risk-averse third parties in specially created markets. These bonds could be denominated in the price of the commodity. The (certain) proceeds of the sale could then be the subject of bargaining. Each side, of course, might elect to hold some proportion of the bonds. By indirectly involving others, such bonds could mitigate the price risk inherent in the agreement, opening or widening a zone of agreement.[37]

Case 3. Addition or subtraction of parties in a negotiation over collective or other special goods may alter the zone of agreement for the original participants. Special characteristics of the negotiating issue in question may lead to inclusion or exclusion of parties. Three examples are particularly noteworthy.

The inclusion of additional parties may ease negotiations over the establishment or maintenance of a collective good. A collective good has the property that it is difficult to exclude nonpurchasers of the good from its benefits, but that the benefits can be extended to additional parties at relatively low marginal cost. Negotiators trying to set up or share the costs of a defense alliance, for example, are confronted with such a situation. Alliance benefits — defense against an attack — may readily be extended to like-minded countries. Barring cases of special added geographic vulnerability, new members should lower the costs to other members. A larger alliance may also reduce the probability of attack. Thus, the addition of as many parties as possible may enhance a zone of agreement in such a situation by lowering costs and increasing benefits.[38]

Several states or nations in a region may be negotiating to build a regional power-generating plant. Economies of scale tend to be considerable in power generation. Thus, in order to enjoy the lowest average costs, the group may seek to add members in the early stages. Their presence may facilitate attainment of an original agreement.

Finally, consider an ongoing, tacit negotiation in a collusive oligopoly. What the participants might dub the "collective good"—the higher price and profits from restricted production—has benefits in fixed supply. This is a situation in which the participants would like to have as few members as possible and perhaps would seek to drive smaller rivals out of the ongoing bargain and erect barriers to subsequent entry.[39]

Two observations about cases 2 and 3 are worth making. First, the "added" parties could be new active participants or they could be passively involved, possibly through some outside connection to one of the original negotiators. Second, the rationale offered for adding parties could equally well serve as reason for expanding the coalition if the original negotiation were defined to include potential participants. One necessary condition for the success of a coalition is usually taken to be that it can do better ("create more value") than its members can individually or in competing coalitions. The economic factors of cases 2 and 3 may create potential for the addition of parties that, for some reason, were not regarded as part of the original game. The phrase "for some reason"—which may refer to psychological, institutional, political, historical, or other factors—is the main difference between this analysis and traditional analyses of coalition formation in a game initially defined to include these potential participants. Whether this phenomenon is regarded as adding parties or as aligning members in coalitions, the same underlying factors are at work.

6.2.3 Indirect Addition of Parties Can Affect the Strategic Complexion of a Negotiation by Improving or Worsening the Consequences of No Agreement

Raising an opponent's cost of no agreement can positively influence one's bargaining position. This may be accomplished by indirect addition of a party that one's opponent finds antithetical. Shortly before World War II, the Soviets bargained openly with the British and

French for a mutual-assistance pact against German aggression while they secretly negotiated a nonaggression treaty with the Germans. The open Anglo-French discussions significantly enhanced the Soviet position in these latter talks.[40] The 1971 Maltese-British negotiations over renewed base rights also provide an instructive example. To obtain radically improved terms, the Maltese made highly visible overtures to the Soviets about locating one of their bases in Malta, as well as overtures to Libya and other Arab states for large assistance payments in return for Malta's neutrality. Not only did this put pressure directly on Britain, but NATO anxiety, which the Maltese carefully cultivated, served indirectly to increase the pressure. In addition, other NATO members ultimately agreed to provide supplemental aid to Malta well beyond the terms of the British settlement.[41] In these cases, the costs of failing to reach a favorable settlement were sharply increased for the opponent by the indirect inclusion of other parties.

When envisioning future negotiations, one side may indirectly use additional parties to change the expected nature of this encounter and make future undesirable action by the opponent much more costly. In the early 1960s a negotiation about the expropriation of Kennecott Copper's major Chilean mine, El Teniente, seemed increasingly likely. Kennecott sought early on to involve a variety of other parties to change the nature of the upcoming bargain from a one-time, bilateral encounter to a potentially long-term, multilateral one.

> [Kennecott] offered to sell a 51 percent interest in El Teniente and turned to the Export-Import bank and the proceeds of the sale of equity to finance expansion [of the mine]. The loan was guaranteed by the Chilean government and made subject to New York law. It insured as much as possible of its assets under a U.S. guarantee against expropriation. The output was to be sold under long-term contracts with Asian and European customers, and the collection rights were sold to a consortium of European banks and a consortium of Japanese institutions. The result was that customers, governments, and creditors shared Kennecott's concern about future changes in Chile. When Chile acted to expropriate the operation, Kennecott was able to call these parties in on its side.[42]

Not only was there a risk-spreading aspect to these moves, but the involved parties could possibly take actions to affect the Chilean choices. Moreover, Chile was likely to have future dealings with these entities. Although the additional parties' initial role was passive, their involvement was deliberately sought and their influence was significant. Similar attempts to involve a variety of outside parties in what otherwise might be strictly bilateral exchanges are embodied in the terms of many modern mineral agreements.[43]

This analysis again comes very close to that of mainstream game theory, wherein the outcome of bargaining among one set of players depends on the other potential agreements by other (potential) competing or overlapping coalitions. Instead of calling Malta's overtures to Eastern bloc and Arab countries "adding parties" to the British-Maltese negotiation, one could just as accurately refer to this case as "exploiting potential coalition formation." The conventional interpretation, however, would require one to analyze the nonaggression negotiations in the first instance as the "Anglo-French-German-Russian negotiation"; the Kennecott-Chile dealings would likewise have to be specified initially as involving the whole range of subsequent parties. The two formulations differ significantly in analytically designating the original situation as bilateral or multilateral. The context will often indicate which of these approaches is more suitable. Sometimes the range of actual and potential parties is obvious at the outset, and the conventional approach readily applies. Especially in protracted negotiations, however, the perceived possibilities of issue or party alteration normally change over time with new information, interpretations, or competitive moves. In such cases, an approach like the one in this chapter may be more insightful. In either interpretation, however, the strategic implication is similar: the first side's cultivation of third parties can change the nature of the original bargaining by lessening the attractiveness of no agreement for the second side or, sometimes, by enhancing its own alternatives to a negotiated agreement.

6.3 Summary and Conclusions

That the parties and issues initially taken to constitute a negotiation are themselves often subject to strategic manipulation is the first contention of this chapter. Therefore, the standard analysis of negotiations should be concerned with whether adding or subtracting issues or parties is desirable or appropriate. A simple graphic approach may assist the analysis. The list below summarizes the main propositions investigated in this chapter.

A. Adding issues can yield one-sided gains to the exercise of power. (Section 6.1.2)
    Case 1. Unrelated, unexploited power
    Case 2. Intrinsic power from commitments

B. Adding issues can yield joint gains that create or enhance a zone of possible agreement. (Section 6.1.3)
   Case 1. Differentially valued, unrelated issues
   Case 2. Overcoming distributional impediments
   Case 3. Issues with positive dependencies
C. Adding issues can reduce or destroy a zone of possible agreement. (Section 6.1.4)
   Case 1. Issues that themselves have no zone of agreement
   Case 2. Issues that themselves do have zones of agreement
D. Adding or subtracting issues may solidify coalitions, strengthen commitments, or alter the parties to a negotiation. (Section 6.1.5)
E. Adding or subtracting parties can alter the zone of possible agreement among the original parties. (Section 6.2.2)
   Case 1. Parties who themselves have an interest in settlement (or in no settlement)
   Case 2. Elimination or spreading of risks from the original bargain
   Case 3. In negotiations over collective goods or those subject to scale economies
F. Indirect addition or subtraction of parties can improve or worsen the consequences of no agreement. (Section 6.2.3)

The first section in this chapter showed how adding issues can yield one-sided gains to the exercise of power. Such power can derive from an unrelated area, or it can come from successful commitment tactics within the negotiation. This "linkage through leverage" is a traditional theme in the study of international relations. The same sort of power may be used to keep an item off the negotiating agenda.

In a more positive vein, issue addition can yield joint gains that enhance or create a zone of possible agreement. Separation of issues may preclude any chance of individual settlement, while combining the same issues may make advantageous agreement possible. This chapter explored three ways for this result to come about: adding differentially valued, unrelated issues; bringing in items as side payments to overcome distributional obstacles; and putting together issues with positive interdependence (such as complementarities, interactions, or risk-reduction characteristics). The mechanisms underlying these features of issue addition explain some of the attractions of package deals and single negotiating texts. Analysis of issue addition also suggests that bottom lines for negotiations should be drawn with all the issues in mind and helps to explain why sequential resolution of items in negotiation can preclude some beneficial settlements.

Unfortunately, combining issues may also reduce or destroy a zone of possible agreement. Adding a very divisive issue to a negotiation and requiring joint settlement may prevent resolution of otherwise tractable issues. In some cases, the combination of individually resolvable issues may wreck the chances of settling any of them. A variety of other reasons — negative interactions, adding issues of interest only to a subset of the negotiators, or stimulating the formation of opposing coalitions — may militate against linkage. Diverse other reasons for adding issues include solidifying coalitions, adding desirable parties, or strengthening commitments to positions, bottom lines, or negotiated settlements. Subtraction or separation can have opposite effects.

Factors that complicate the manipulation of issues may, of course, be present. Unintended complexity or unforeseen interrelationships, as well as organizational and informational requirements, may accompany an expanded agenda. Particularly if there is an element of coercion, the negotiating atmosphere may be poisoned. (On some occasions, of course, one or another side may desire these results.) Small, tractable bargains may repeatedly escalate into large, intractable ones as a trading ethos takes hold. Needless to say, long-term relationships may suffer in the process. The many examples of mutually profitable issue addition cited, however, make the obvious point that these undesirable consequences are not necessary outcomes.

Just as the issues may be manipulated, so may the parties. Parties are commonly added that have influence on or interest in the substance of the negotiation, that may strengthen a coalition directly or by leverage from other areas, that can enable commitments to be made, or that may lend legitimacy to a bargain or aid in its implementation. The zone of possible agreement may be altered by outside entities that value or dislike a settlement among the original parties. Essentially passive addition of parties may spread or eliminate risk, exploit economies, or lower the cost of a collective good. All these actions may facilitate advantageous agreement. Subtraction of parties has symmetrical functions.

The indirect addition of outside parties can significantly affect the original negotiations. If agreement with a third party suddenly becomes the alternative to agreement with the original bargaining partner, one's position in the first negotiation may improve. Since settlements in one group depend on potential agreements in other (potential) groups, it is not surprising to see cultivation of these other groups in order to give the alternative the appearance of greater likelihood. Finally, if one side expects possible future negotiations with the other side, it may try to involve other parties indirectly. The added parties may serve to raise the costs of subsequent action by opponents and thus may position the first side more advantageously.

Across these varied cases there are similarities. Analysis should not take the parties and issues in a negotiation as given. A variety of means, ends, and outcomes are possible from their manipulation, many of which can be analytically related by simple devices. Formally, of course, if the original definition of the negotiations were expansive enough, the resulting "supergame" would be amenable to conventional analysis and the notions of adding parties and issues would be superfluous. But this would be to define a real phenomenon out of existence. As Kenneth Oye noted, "Tactical issue linkage is exceedingly difficult to predict." "Linkees" have failed to anticipate the OPEC embargo, the Third World link between Special Drawing Rights and development assistance, the Eisenhower link between the Suez affair and monetary policy, and so forth. Analysis surely does not wholly negate Oye's observation that "no clear criteria have emerged for predicting patterns of issue linkage."[44] Taken together, however, the foregoing propositions offer an approach to expanding stylized negotiation analysis a good part of the way toward the game of all possible players and subjects.

Notes

1. Background: Of Nodules, Navies, and Negotiation

1. Evan Luard, *The Control of the Seabed: An Updated Report* (New York: Taplinger Publishing Co., 1977), pp. 15–16; see also United Nations Ocean Economics and Technology Office, *Manganese Nodules: Dimensions and Perspectives* (Dordrecht, Holland: D. Reidel, 1979).

2. "Johnson Asks Joint Exploitation of Sea Resources," *New York Times*, July 14, 1966, p. 10.

3. United Nations General Assembly, 22 U.N. GAOR, C.1 (1515th Mtg.), I, U.N. Doc.A/C.1/p.v. 1525 (1967).

4. United Nations General Assembly Resolution 2749, 25 U.N. GAOR, Supp. (no. 280), 24 U.N. Doc. A/8028 (1970).

5. *New York Times,* July 22, 1979, p. E20.

6. Third United Nations Conference on the Law of the Sea, "Report of the Chairman of Negotiating Group 2," New York, April 1980.

7. "Calling it a happy day, the chief American delegate, Elliot L. Richardson, said it was 'all but certain' that the text would be ready for signing in 1981. 'Historians looking back on this session of the conference,' he added, 'are likely to see it as the most significant development of the rule of law since the founding of the United Nations itself.'" *New York Times,* August 30, 1980, p. 1.

8. "President Vows U.S. Won't Sign Sea-Law Treaty," *New York Times,* July 10, 1982, p. 1; Bernard H. Oxman, "Summary of the Law of the Sea Convention," in *Law of the Sea,* ed. Bernard Oxman, David Caron, and Charles Buderi (San Francisco: ICS Press, 1983), p. 147.

9. See, for example, U.S. Department of State, "Approaches to Major Problems in Part XI of the Draft Convention on the Law of the Sea," February 24, 1982.

10. Foreign Policy Association, "World Law of the Oceans: Narrowing

Options for the U.S.," in *Great Decisions '79* (New York: Foreign Policy Association, 1979), pp. 64–73. For a much expanded discussion of the history and rationale for the conference, see Hollick, *U.S. Foreign Policy and the Law of the Sea* (Princeton, N.J.: Princeton University Press, 1981).

11. John Temple Swing, "Who Will Own the Oceans?" *Foreign Affairs*, 54 (April 1976):531.

12. These fears were part of the rationale for the earlier seabed arms control negotiations. See Bennet Ramberg, "Tactical Advantages of Opening Positioning Strategies: Lessons from the Seabed Arms Control Talks 1967–1970," in *The Negotiation Process: Theories and Applications*, ed. I. William Zartman (Beverly Hills: Sage Publications, 1978), pp. 133–174.

13. See, for example, Hollick, pp. 160–240.

14. John R. Stevenson and Bernard H. Oxman, "Preparations for the Law of the Sea Conference," *American Journal of International Law*, 68 (January 1974):1.

15. See, for example, Luard, *Control of the Seabed*, pp. 29–168; or Foreign Policy Association, *Great Decisions*, pp. 65–66.

16. John R. Stevenson and Bernard H. Oxman, "The Third UN Conference on the Law of the Sea: The 1974 Caracas Session," *American Journal of International Law*, 69 (January 1975):3.

17. Ibid., p. 4.

18. Edward Miles, "The Structure and Effects of the Decision Process in the Seabed Committee and the Third United Nations Conference on the Law of the Sea," *International Organization*, 31 (Spring 1977):184.

19. Bernard H. Oxman, "The Third UN Conference on the Law of the Sea: The Seventh Session (1978)," *American Journal of International Law*, 73 (1979):4–5.

20. Stevenson and Oxman, "Third UN Conference," pp. 6–12.

21. Richard G. Darman, "The Law of the Sea: Rethinking U.S. Interests," *Foreign Affairs*, 56 (January 1978): 373–375.

22. See Wolfgang Hauser, "An International Fiscal Regime for Deep Seabed Mining: Comparisons to Land-Based Mining," *Harvard International Law Journal*, 19 (1978):761–770.

23. Oxman, "The Seventh Session," pp. 9–24.

24. James C. Burrows, "The Net Value of Manganese Nodules to United States Interests With Special Reference to Market Effects and National Security," in *Deepsea Mining*, ed. Judith T. Kildow (Cambridge: MIT Press, 1979), p. 125.

25. Lance Antrim, Patricia Spencer, and William Woodhead, *Cobalt, Copper, Nickel and Manganese: Future Supply and Demand and Implications for Deep Seabed Mining* (Washington, D.C.: U.S. Department of Commerce, Office of Ocean, Resource and Scientific Policy Coordination, 1979), pp. 17–50.

26. Burrows, p. 139.

27. United Nations General Assembly, "Declaration on the Establishment of a New International Economic Order," G. A. Res. 3201, 29 GAOR (6th Sp. Sess.), Supp. (no. 2), U.N. Doc. A/9555 (1974).

28. United Nations General Assembly, "Permanent Sovereignty over Natural Resources," G.A. Res. 3171, 28 U.N. GAOR, Supp. (no. 300), U.N. Doc. A/9030 (1974).

29. Bernard H. Oxman, "The Third United Nations Conference on the Law of the Sea: The 1976 New York Sessions," *American Journal of International Law,* 71 (1977):253.

30. Ronald S. Katz, "Financial Arrangements for Seabed Mining Companies: An NIEO Case Study," *Journal of World Trade Law,* 13 (1977):212.

31. United Nations, Third United Nations Conference on the Law of the Sea, "Economic Implications of Seabed Mineral Development in the International Area, Report to the Secretary General," 29 U.N. GAOR, U.N. Doc.; A Conf. 62/25 (1974):30; J. D. Nyhart, L. Antrim, A. Capstaff, A. Kohler, and D. Leshaw, *A Cost Model of Ocean Mining and Associated Regulatory Issues* (Cambridge: MIT Sea Grant Report MITSG 78-14, 1978), pp. 1–30; and F. Diederich, W. Miller, and W. Schneider, *Analysis of the MIT Study on Ocean Mining* (Frankfurt: Battelle-Institut, 1979), p. 10.

32. See S. K. B. Asante, "Restructuring Transnational Mineral Agreements," *American Journal of International Law,* 73 (1979):335–371; M. Fritzsche and A. Stockmayer, "Mining Agreements in Developing Countries," *Natural Resources Forum,* 2 (1978):215–227; M. Gillis et al., *Taxation and Mining* (Cambridge, Mass.: Ballinger, 1978); Hauser, "International Fiscal Regime"; R. F. Mikesell, "Trends in Foreign Investment: Agreements in the Resource Industry," *Resources Policy* (September 1978):194–199; D. Smith and L. Wells, *Negotiating Third World Mineral Agreements* (Cambridge, Mass.: Ballinger, 1975); and S. Zorn, "New Developments in Financing Third World Mineral Agreements," *Natural Resources Forum,* 1 (1977):239–250.

33. M. Gillis, M. Bucovetsky, and L. Wells, "Comparative Mineral Tax Systems," in *Taxation and Mining,* ed. M. Gillis (Cambridge, Mass.: Ballinger, 1978), p. 122.

34. R. F. Mikesell, "Financial Considerations in Negotiating Mine Development Agreements," *Mining Magazine,* April 1974, p. 258.

35. Mikesell, "Trends," p. 194.

36. Henry Kissinger, speech at UNCTAD IV in Nairobi, Kenya, reproduced in U.S. Department of State, Bureau of Public Affairs, Office of Media Services (PR 224.6), Washington, D.C., May 1976.

37. For an extended analysis of this situation and a proposal to deal with it institutionally, see David Lax and James K. Sebenius, "Insecure Contacts and Resource Development," *Public Policy,* 29 (1981):417–436.

2. Course of the Financial Negotiations

1. Third United Nations Conference on the Law of the Sea, "Revised Single Negotiating Text," A/Conf. 62/WP.8/Rev. 1/pt. I (May 6, 1976), pp. 71–76.

2. Third United Nations Conference on the Law of the Sea, "Informal

Composite Negotiating Text," U.N. Doc. A/Conf. 62/WP.10 (1977), pp. 160–164.

3. For example, see Rebecca L. Wright, *Ocean Mining: An Economic Evaluation* (Washington, D.C.: U.S. Department of the Interior, Ocean Mining Administration, May 1976).

4. Nyhart et al., *A Cost Model.* A short description of the model is contained in Appendix 2 at the end of this chapter.

5. Third United Nations Conference on the Law of the Sea, "Reports of the Committees and Negotiating Groups on Negotiations at the Seventh Session Contained in a Single Document Both for the Purposes of Record and for the Convenience of Delegations," Geneva (May 19, 1978), p. 97.

6. United States Department of State, "Delegation Report for the Seventh Session of the Third United Nations Conference on the Law of the Sea," Washington, D.C. (1978), p. 18.

7. Third United Nations Conference on the Law of the Sea, "Report by the Chairman of Negotiating Group 2 to the First Committee," NG2/10, New York (September 13, 1978), p. 4.

8. Cited in Oxman, "The Seventh Session," p. 41.

9. Diederich, Miller, and Schneider, *Analysis of the MIT Study.*

10. Third United Nations Conference on the Law of the Sea, "Report to the First Committee by the Chairman of Negotiating Group 2, Ambassador T. T. B. Koh (Singapore)," NG2/12, Geneva (April 8, 1979), pp. 4–5.

11. Ibid.

12. Ibid., p. 7.

13. Third United Nations Conference on the Law of the Sea, "Report on Negotiations Held by the Chairman of the Working Group of 21," A/Conf. 62/C.1/L. 26, New York (August 21, 1979), p. 8.

14. Portions of this appendix are taken verbatim from the executive summary of the report. See Nyhart, pp. ES1–ES13.

3. Elements of Agreement

1. See James K. Sebenius and Mati L. Pal, "Evolving Terms of Mineral Agreements: Risk, Reward, and Participation in Deep Seabed Mining," *Columbia Journal of World Business*, 15 (1980):75–83.

2. For a comparison of the role of the MIT model with that of three other analytic models in political negotiations, see James K. Sebenius, "The Computer as Mediator: Law of the Sea and Beyond," *Journal of Policy Analysis and Management*, 1 (1981):77–95.

3. The IROR, of course, may be a technically flawed measure in some cases. A good discussion of this can be found, for example, in Jack Hirshleifer, "On the Theory of Optimal Investment Decision," reprinted in *Modern Developments in Financial Management*, ed. S. Myers (Hinsdale, Ill.: Dryden Press, 1976), pp. 282–305. It is used here because financial arrangements delegates quickly began to refer to the IROR over the several net present values or the simple "payback period" that were also routinely provided by the model. The

particular cash flows underlying Figure 3.1 are such that the NPV and IROR yield identical decisions. It is interesting to note that some company representatives at the workshops prior to the model's publication were unhappy even with the reporting range of NPV results, arguing that this unjustly specified the firm's "allowable profit." In Figure 3.1, the effect on the rate of return is measured as the natural logarithm of the absolute drop in the rate of return of an integrated mining project. The magnitude of the drop is calculated with respect to the MIT baseline case assumptions for an equity-financed project. See J. Sebenius et al., "Revenue Sharing from Deep Ocean Mining," Review Draft no. 2, Massachusetts Institute of Technology, August 1979, p. 11.

4. Roger Fisher and William Ury, *Getting to Yes* (Boston: Houghton Mifflin, 1981), pp. 42–43.

5. This is similar to the discussion in Howard Raiffa, *Decision Analysis: Introductory Lectures on Choices under Uncertainty* (Reading, Mass.: Addison-Wesley, 1968), pp. 190–196.

6. K. J. Arrow and R. C. Lind, "Uncertainty and the Evaluation of Public Investment Decisions," *American Economic Review*, 60 (1970):363–378.

7. Ronald Katz, "Financial Arrangements for Seabed Mining Companies: An NIEO Case Study," *Journal of World Trade Law*, 13 (May/June 1979):218.

8. There is some discussion of issue linkage in the international relations literature. For the most part, however, it concerns linkages that are forced by unexploited power in another area, such as OPEC forcing discussions on other North-South issues. See, for example, Branislav Gosavic and John Gerard Ruggie, "On the Creation of a New International Economic Order: Issue Linkage and the Seventh Special Session of the UN General Assembly," *International Organization*, 30 (Spring 1976):309–345. An exception to the recurrent theme of forced linkage is given by Robert Tollison and Thomas Willett, "An Economic Theory of Mutually Advantageous Issue Linkage in Negotiation," *International Organization*, 33 (Autumn 1979):309–345, wherein they give a complicated example of negotiations over a collective good whose production is subject to scale economies. (Chapter 6 generalizes these observations.)

4. Disagreement in the Large

1. A fine account of the bureaucratic politics within the U.S. government is given in Ann L. Hollick, *U.S. Foreign Policy and the Law of the Sea* (Princeton, N.J.: Princeton University Press, 1981).

2. This framework evolved through close collaboration with David Lax. A more extensive version is contained in David Lax and James K. Sebenius, "Negotiation and Management: Some Analytic Themes," Harvard Business School Working Paper 82–83, June 1983.

3. This abstracts from questions of other possible "side effects" of negotiation. For an exposition, see Fred Charles Iklé, *How Nations Negotiate* (New York: Harper and Row, 1964).

4. For varied discussions of the extent and implications of creeping juris-

diction, see, for example, Robert E. Osgood, "U.S. Security Interests in Ocean Law," *Ocean Development and International Law,* 2 (1974):1–36, or Elliot L. Richardson, "Power, Mobility, and the Law of the Sea," *Foreign Affairs,* 58 (1980):902–919.

5. An elaboration is contained in Hollick, pp. 188–189.

6. Ibid., p. 387.

7. See, for example, Osgood, pp. 1–2; Richard G. Darman, "The Law of the Sea: Rethinking U.S. Interests," *Foreign Affairs,* 56 (1978):373–395; Finn Laursen, "Security versus Access to Resources: Explaining a Decade of U.S. Ocean Policy," *World Politics,* 35 (1982):197–205; or Hollick, pp. 234–235.

8. See Hollick, pp. 174–175, 234–235.

9. See John R. Stevenson, in *Department of State Bulletin* 62 (1970):341; or Hollick, p. 235.

10. See the U.S./UN Press Release 83 (69), December 2, 1969.

11. Edward C. Wenk, *The Politics of the Ocean* (Seattle: University of Washington Press, 1972), pp. 283–284.

12. The chain of reasoning is suggested and discussed more fully in Hollick, pp. 196–239.

13. United Nations General Assembly Resolution 2750C(XXV), December 17, 1970.

14. U.S. Department of State, *Department of State Bulletin* 62 (1970):737–738.

15. National Petroleum Council, *Petroleum Resources under the Ocean Floor* (Washington, D.C., 1969), pp. 69–70.

16. A detailed account of this is contained in Hollick, pp. 208–232.

17. Laursen, pp. 215–217.

18. See Hollick, p. 314; Laursen, pp. 218–222; and William C. Brewer, Jr., "Deep Seabed Mining: Can an Acceptable Regime Ever Be Found?" *Ocean Development and International Law,* 11 (1982):38–39.

19. See United Nations Convention on the Law of the Sea, UN Doc. A/Conf. 62/122 (1982), or Bernard Oxman, "Summary of the Law of the Sea Convention," in *Law of the Sea,* ed. Bernard Oxman, David Caron, and Charles Buderi (San Francisco: ICS Press, 1983), pp. 147–161.

20. Henry Kissinger in *Department of State Bulletin* 75 (1976):398.

21. Henry Kissinger, "International Law, World Order, and Human Progress," address before the American Bar Association Annual Convention, Montreal, August 11, 1975. Reprinted in U.S. Department of State Press Release no. 408, August 11, 1975, p. 9.

22. Richardson, "Power, Mobility," p. 911.

23. See Laursen, p. 209, and Darman, pp. 379–380.

24. Brewer, p. 40.

25. Richard M. Nixon, "Report to the Congress," *U.S. Foreign Policy for the 1970s,* February 18, 1970.

26. See Darman, p. 375, and Laursen, p. 203.

27. Darman, p. 386.

28. Ibid., p. 388.

29. "President Vows U.S. Won't Sign Sea-Law Treaty," *New York Times,* July 10, 1982, p. 1.

30. See, for example, Darman, pp. 376–380, or Osgood, pp. 1–36.

31. Leigh Ratiner, "The Law of the Sea: Crossroads for U.S. Policy," *Foreign Affairs,* 60 (1982):1011.

32. *New York Times,* July 10, 1982, p. 1.

33. Darman, p. 388.

34. Ratiner, p. 1012.

35. See, for example, David Caron, "Reconciling Domestic Principles and International Cooperation," in Oxman, Caron, and Buderi, eds., *Law of the Sea,* pp. 6–8.

36. Kissinger, "International Law," p. 4.

37. "Deep Seabed Hard Mineral Resources Act of 1980," Public Law no. 96-283; see also Lewis I. Cohen, "International Cooperation on Seabed Mining," in Oxman, Caron, and Buderi, eds., *Law of the Sea,* pp. 101–109.

38. "Act of Interim Regulation of Deep Seabed Mining," *Bundesgesetzblatt,* part I, 9080 (August 22, 1980).

39. Discussion of the mini-treaty option can be found, for example, in Darman, pp. 393–394, or Ratiner, pp. 1010–1011, 1017–1019.

40. See, for example, Thomas A. Clingan, Jr., "Freedom of Navigation in a Post-UNCLOS III Environment," presentation at the Duke University Law of the Sea Symposium, October 29, 1982; Ratiner, p. 1011; or Richardson, p. 918.

41. An account of this event is in Theodore H. White, "Weinberger on the Ramparts," *New York Times Magazine,* February 6, 1983, p. 22. Reference to the Carter policy is contained in Richardson, p. 902.

42. John Lehman, "The Navy and the Law of the Sea," letter to the editor, *Washington Post,* July 30, 1982. See also Mary McGrory, "Sailing the Sea Treaty Shoals without the Lighthouse of Facts," *Washington Post,* July 22, 1982. The related contention that a widely accepted LOS treaty, though helpful, could not guarantee a halt to claims and restrictions had been advanced earlier, notably in a 1977 National Intelligence Estimate. See Hollick, p. 362.

43. See, for example, the discussion and references in W. Michael Reisman, "The Regime of Straits and National Security: An Appraisal of International Lawmaking," *American Journal of International Law,* 74 (1980):48–53; and John Norton Moore, "The Regime of Straits and the Third United Nations Conference on the Law of the Sea," *American Journal of International Law,* 74 (1980):77–85.

44. See John R. Stevenson, Testimony before the Subcommittee on International Organizations and Movements, House Committee on Foreign Affairs, 92nd Cong., 2d sess., April 10, 1973, p. 12.

45. For discussions of these rights, see, for example, Osgood, pp. 10–11, 24–26; or Richardson, pp. 903–910.

46. Quoted in Edward F. Oliver, "Malacca: Dire Straits," *U.S. Naval Institute Proceedings* (June 1973):29.

47. Ibid, pp. 27–33.

48. Clarence A. Hill, Jr., "U.S. Law of the Sea Position and Its Effect on the Operating Navy: A Naval Officer's View," *Ocean Development and International Law*, 3 (1976):347.

49. Osgood, p. 27.

50. James A. Doyle, Jr., "National Security and the Law of the Sea," address before the Carnegie Endowment for International Peace, Washington, D.C., June 22, 1981, pp. 6–7.

51. W. Howard Wriggens, "Up for Auction: Malta Bargains with Great Britain, 1971," in I. William Zartman, *The 50% Solution* (New York: Anchor-Doubleday, 1976), pp. 208–234.

52. Hollick, p. 273.

53. "Madrid Bans Refueling for F-15s in Visit to Saudis," *New York Times*, January 13, 1979, p. 3.

54. Richardson, p. 909.

55. Ibid.

56. Darman, p. 378.

57. See, along with its references, Joseph S. Nye, "Ocean Rulemaking from a World Politics Perspective," *Ocean Development and International Law*, 3 (1975):29–52. See also Joseph S. Nye, "Political Lessons of the New Sea Regime," in Oxman, Caron, and Buderi, eds., *Law of the Sea*, pp. 119–125.

58. Ibid, pp. 44–45.

59. Moore, p. 82.

60. Clingan, "Freedom of Navigation."

61. United Nations, Third United Nations Conference on the Law of the Sea, "Closing Statement by the President on the Law of the Sea," Press Release, SEA/MB/14, December 10, 1982, p. 2.

62. See, for example, the testimony of Horace B. Robertson, Jr., before the House Committee on Merchant Marine and Fisheries, July 27, 1982; or the Report of the Committee on the Law of the Sea, American Branch of the International Law Association, June 1982; see also Ratiner, p. 1019.

63. See, for example, Darman, p. 380.

64. "Statement by Mr. Satya N. Nandan, Chairman of the Fiji Delegation to the Formal Signing Session," Third United Nations Conference on the Law of the Sea (mimeo), December 1982, p. 2.

65. United Nations, "Closing Statement," p. 2.

66. "Statement by the President," the White House, Office of the Press Secretary, December 30, 1982, p. 1.

67. Richardson, p. 918.

68. For a summary, see Lance Antrim and James K. Sebenius, "Incentives for Ocean Mining under the Convention," in *Law of the Sea: U.S. Policy Dilemma*, ed. Bernard Oxman et al. (San Francisco: ICS Press, 1983), p. 84.

69. See, for example, Arthur D. Little, Inc., "Technological and Economic Assessment of Manganese Nodule Mining and Processing," prepared for the Department of the Interior, Stock no. 024-000-00842-B (Washington, D.C.: Government Printing Office, 1977), recently summarized and updated

in H. Enzer, "Economic Assessment of Ocean Mining," presented at the joint meeting of the Institute for Mining and Metallurgy, the Society of Mining Engineers of AIME, and the Metallurgical Society of the AIME, London, May 1980. See also Charles River Associates, Inc., "Analysis of Major Policy Issues Raised by the Commercial Development of Ocean Manganese Nodules," CRA Report no. 383 (Cambridge, Mass.: National Science Foundation, 1981).

70. "Cartel of the Sea," *Wall Street Journal*, April 20, 1982, p. 30.
71. See Antrim and Sebenius, p. 89.
72. Ibid., p. 90.
73. Science Applications, Inc., "Alternatives for Technology Transfer to the Enterprise," SAI Report no. Sa1-460-80-401LJ (La Jolla, Calif.: Science Applications, 1978), p. 61.
74. "Koh: Mining Issues May Go to World Court," *The Interdependent*, 8 (1982):1.
75. Darman, p. 388.
76. For a sampling of precedential arguments against the treaty, see John Breaux, "The Diminishing Prospects for an Acceptable Law of the Sea Treaty," *Virginia Journal of International Law*, 19 (1979):257–261; Robert A. Goldwin, "Locke and the Law of the Sea," *Commentary* (June 1981):46–50; Walter Berns, "Mining the Seas for a Brave New World," *Regulation* (November–December 1981):15–18; or Darman, "Law of the Sea."
77. Breaux, pp. 260–262.
78. Darman, pp. 386–388; Berns, pp. 15–16.

5. Differences and Joint Gains

1. As suggested by the first paragraph in this chapter, nonconvexities in preferences or production, however, can lead identical individuals to gains from trade. For example, two risk lovers may gain from agreeing to a mutual lottery. Technology that displays increasing returns to scale may stimulate joint arrangements among identical agents with equal access to it. In this chapter, however, attention is mainly restricted to the "usual economic world" where both preferences and technologies are convex.

2. The axioms include symmetry, independence, continuity, boundedness, and additivity. For a discussion and proof, see Robert Axelrod, "Conflict of Interest: An Axiomatic Approach," *Journal of Conflict Resolution*, 11 (January 1967):87–99.

3. The contrast between "distributive" and "integrative" bargaining was made in R. E. Walton and R. B. McKersie, *A Behavioral Theory of Labor Negotiations* (New York: McGraw-Hill, 1965) and has been picked up and elaborated by other authors. For example, see Howard Raiffa, *The Art and Science of Negotiation* (Cambridge, Mass.: Harvard University Press, 1982).

4. Michael W. K. Malouf and Alvin E. Roth, "Disagreement in Bargaining: An Experimental Approach," *Journal of Conflict Resolution*, 25 (1981):329–348.

5. Robert Axelrod, *Conflict of Interest* (Chicago: Aldine, 1970), pp. 67–77.

6. Dean G. Pruitt and Steven A. Lewis, "The Psychology of Integrative Bargaining," in *Negotiations: Social Psychological Perspectives,* ed. Daniel Druckman (Beverly Hills: Sage, 1977); Dean G. Pruitt, "Integrative Agreements: Nature and Antecedents," paper presented at the Conference on Bargaining inside Organizations, Boston University, October 15, 1982.

7. Further, we are not concerned here with many of the other possible reasons for negotiation, such as spreading propaganda, gathering intelligence, influencing third parties, diverting an opponent from the use of force, maintaining contact, or communicating on other matters entirely. See Fred Charles Iklé, *How Nations Negotiate* (New York: Harper and Row, 1964).

8. George C. Homans, cited in I. William Zartman, *The 50% Solution* (Garden City, New York: Anchor-Doubleday, 1976), p. 10.

9. John Harsanyi, "Games of Incomplete Information Played by Bayesian Players," parts I–III, *Management Science,* 14 (1967–1968):159–982; 320–334; 486–502.

10. Robert J. Aumann, "Agreeing to Disagree," *Annuals of Statistics,* 4 (1976):1236–39.

11. Use of such "objective" or agreed-probability randomization to enlarge the set of possible agreements or strategies is discussed in Howard Raiffa, *Decision Analysis: Introductory Lectures on Choices under Uncertainty* (Reading, Mass.: Addison-Wesley, 1968), pp. 133–138. There are many other uses of randomization that are not explicitly considered in this chapter. As Thomas Schelling noted in *The Strategy of Conflict* (Cambridge, Mass.: Harvard University Press, 1960), "It may be no exaggeration to say that the potentialities of randomized behavior account for most of the interest in game theory during the past one and one-half decades" (p. 175). Randomization may be used for purposes of secrecy or to ensure "security levels" in certain games. There may also be other reasons for randomization; see H. Chernoff, "Rational Selection of Decision Functions," *Econometrica,* 22 (1954):422–443.

12. K. J. Arrow and R. C. Lind, "Uncertainty and the Evaluation of Public Investment Decisions," *American Economic Review,* 60 (1970):363–378.

13. A discussion and formal definition of "common knowledge" are contained in Section 5.2.6 and in Aumann, "Agreeing to Disagree."

14. Stephen A. Ross, "On the Economic Theory of Agency and the Principle of Similarity," in *Essays on Economic Behavior under Uncertainty,* ed. M. Balch, D. McFadden, and S. Wu (Amsterdam: North-Holland, 1974), pp. 215–242.

15. Raiffa, *Decision Analysis,* p. 215.

16. Technically speaking, assume that there exist probability spaces (Ω, S, μ_i), $i = 1,2$, with elements $x \in \Omega$, with S as the σ-algebra of all subsets of the sample space Ω, and with the probability measures μ_1 and μ_2 absolutely continuous with respect to each other. This means that there is no element $A \in S$ for which $\mu_1(A) = 0$ and $\mu_2(A) \neq 0$, or $\mu_1(A) \neq 0$ and $\mu_2(A) = 0$. Let μ_i be a probability measure that is absolutely continuous with respect to λ. Then the $f_i(\xi)$, generalized probability density functions or Radon-Nikodym derivatives $f_i(\xi) = d\mu_i/d\lambda$, are unique up to sets of measure zero (in λ), for $i = 1,2$.

NOTES TO PAGES 150-172

17. See, for example, Hayne E. Leland, "Optimal Risk Sharing and the Leasing of Natural Resources with Application to Oil and Gas Leasing on the OCS," *Quarterly Journal of Economics,* 29 (1978):414–437; or Robert Wilson, "The Theory of Syndicates," *Econometrica,* 36 (1968):119–132.

18. This result can also be extracted from Wilson's analysis of the syndicate problem, pp. 123–126.

19. Conditions similar to (5.6) were derived by Karl Borch, "The Safety Reloading of Reinsurance Premiums," *Skandinavisk Aktuariehdskrift* (1960): 163–184.

20. S. Kullback and R. A. Liebler, "On Information and Sufficiency," *Annals of Mathematical Statistics,* 22 (1951):79–80.

21. A. Renyi, "On Measures of Entropy and Information," in *Proceedings of the Fourth Berkeley Symposium in Mathematical Statistics,* ed. Jerzey Neymann (Berkeley: University of California Press, 1961), pp. 547–561.

22. It is easy to see this by considering a discrete random variable x_i, $i = 1, \ldots, n$, and choosing to announce the g_i to maximize expected value of the reward function $\sum_i (a \ln(g_i) + b) f_i$, where $\sum_i g_i = 1$ and f_i is the *true* probability mass function of x_i. It is immediate that $g_i = f_i$, for all i, is the solution. Lying does not pay in this case.

23. The following argument is inspired by G. H. Hardy, J. E. Littlewood, and G. Polya, *Inequalities* (Cambridge: Cambridge University Press, 1934), p. 151.

24. See Ralph Keeney and Howard Raiffa, *Decisions with Multiple Objectives* (New York: John Wiley, 1976), p. 162.

25. See Leland, "Optimal Risk Sharing," pp. 418–419.

26. R. Garnaut and A. C. Ross, "A New Tax for Natural Resource Projects," in *Mineral Leasing as an Instrument of Public Policy,* ed. M. Crommelin and A. R. Thompson (Vancouver: University of British Columbia Press, 1977), p. 81.

27. Leland, "Optimal Risk Sharing," p. 433.

28. D. K. Reece, "An Analysis of Alternative Bidding Systems for Leasing Offshore Oil," *Bell Journal of Economics,* 10 (1979):688.

29. Steven Cheung, "Transaction Costs, Risk Aversion, and the Choice of Contractual Arrangements," *Journal of Law and Economics,* 12 (1969):26.

30. K. J. Arrow and R. K. Lind, "Uncertainty and the Evaluation of Public Investments," *American Economic Review,* 60 (1970):364–378.

31. Michael Rothschild and J. E. Stiglitz, "Increasing Risk: I. A Definition," *Journal of Economic Theory,* 2 (1970):225–243.

32. Wilson, pp. 119–132.

33. Sanford J. Grossman and Joseph E. Stiglitz, "Information and Competitive Price Systems," *American Economic Review,* 46 (1979):246–253.

34. Robert J. Aumann, "Agreeing to Disagree," *Annals of Statistics,* 4 (1976):1236–39; John Geanakoplos and Heraklis Polemarchakis, "We Can't Disagree Forever," *Journal of Economic Theory,* 26 (1982):192–200.

35. Paul Milgrom, "An Axiomatic Characterization of Common Knowledge," *Econometrica,* 49 (1981):219–222.

36. Paul Milgrom and Nancy Stokey, "Information, Trade, and Common Knowledge," *Journal of Economic Theory,* 26 (1982):17–27.

37. Martin Feldstein, "The Social Time Preference Rate in Cost-Benefit Analysis," *Economic Journal,* 74 (1964):360–379.

6. Negotiation Arithmetic

1. William Wallace, "Atlantic Relations: Policy Coordination and Conflict," *International Affairs,* 52 (April 1976):164.

2. Roger Fisher, "Fractionating Conflict," in *International Conflict and Behavioral Science: The Craigville Papers,* ed. Roger Fisher (New York: Basic Books, 1964), p. 98.

3. Robert Tollison and Thomas Willett, "An Economic Theory of Mutually Advantageous Issue Linkages in International Negotiations," *International Organization,* 33 (Autumn 1979):448.

4. Kenneth A. Oye, "The Domain of Choice: International Constraints and Carter Administration Foreign Policy," in *Eagle Entangled: U.S. Foreign Policy in a Complex World,* ed. Kenneth A. Oye, Donald Rothchild, and Robert J. Lieber (New York: Longman, 1979), p. 18.

5. François de Callières, *On the Manner of Negotiating with Princes,* trans. A. F. Whyte (Boston: Houghton Mifflin, 1919; originally published, Paris: Michel Brunet, 1716), pp. 109–110.

6. Notice that this graphic analysis can readily handle both continuous and discrete issues. Tollison and Willett, pp. 441–443, suggest "discontinuous" policy options as "possible extensions" of their analysis. Arthur Stein in a recent article, "The Politics of Linkage," *World Politics,* 32 (1980):62–81, limits his analysis to discrete issues by the exclusive use of 2 × 2 game matrices, which he says are "widely considered to be the most appropriate" models for such analysis. The choice restricts consideration to two parties each with two discrete choices.

7. Roger Fisher and William Ury, *Getting to Yes* (Boston: Houghton Mifflin, 1981), pp. 41–43.

8. Oye, pp. 15–16.

9. J. J. Tedeschi, B. R. Schlenker, and T. V. Bonoma, *Conflict, Power and Games* (Hawthorne, N.Y.: Aldine, 1978).

10. M. Deutsch and R. M. Krauss, "Studies of Interpersonal Bargaining," *Journal of Conflict Resolution,* 6 (1962):52–76; Jeff Rubin and Bert Brown, *The Social Psychology of Bargaining and Negotiation* (New York: Academic Press, 1975).

11. For an extended discussion, see S. B. Bacharach and E. Lawler, *Bargaining* (San Francisco: Jossey-Bass, 1981), pp. 104–130.

12. The usual caveats about unitary, rational actor models in bargaining

analyses apply. They are intelligently considered in Tollison and Willett, pp. 441–442, and Stein, pp. 79–81.

13. See Howard Raiffa, *The Art and Science of Negotiation* (Cambridge, Mass.: Harvard University Press, 1982), pp. 210–217.

14. Of course, a key aspect of negotiating judgment lies in the subjective decisions by, say, a delegation head that package 1 is preferable to proposed package 2, that conceding on this issue in return for movement on that one is worthwhile, or that the other side will value one set of concessions more than another. Trying to make these decisions over several issues is an implicit application of the ideas of multi-attribute value theory. It is perhaps worth noting that "value" need not be denominated in monetary terms. The technology for handling multiple-objective problems has been extensively developed in recent years; for example, see Ralph Keeney and Howard Raiffa, *Decision with Multiple Objectives: Preferences and Value Tradeoffs* (New York: John Wiley, 1976), or Scott Barclay and Cameron Peterson, "Multi-Attribute Models for Negotiations," Technical Report 76-1, Decisions and Designs, Inc. (McLean, Va., 1976). Actual applications have included the Panama Canal negotiations and negotiations over Philippine base rights; see Raiffa, pp. 166–186. Tanker safety standard negotiations are discussed in Jacob W. Ulvila and Warren G. Snider, "Negotiation of Oil Tanker Standards: An Application of Multi-Attribute Value Theory," *Operations Research*, 28 (January–February 1980):81–96. Middle Eastern oil negotiations are the subject of Rex Brown and Cameron Peterson, "An Analysis of Alternative Middle Eastern Oil Agreements," Technical Report, Decisions and Designs, Inc. (McLean, Va., 1975).

15. A related situation is described in Branislav Gosavic and John Gerard Ruggie, "On the Creation of a New International Economic Order: Issue Linkage and the Seventh Special Session of the UN General Assembly," *International Organization,* 30 (Spring 1976):309–345.

16. This is a straightforward application of the analysis in Thomas Schelling, *The Strategy of Conflict* (Cambridge, Mass.: Harvard University Press, 1960), pp. 21–52.

17. Fred Charles Iklé, *How Nations Negotiate* (New York: Harper and Row, 1964), pp. 222–235.

18. Once one enters the world of decisions under uncertainty, more analytic machinery is required than was needed for the value theory–based analysis. Utility theory is an appropriate approach and is admirably treated in Keeney and Raiffa.

19. See Peter Bachrach and Morton S. Baratz, "Two Faces of Power," *American Political Science Review,* 56 (December 1962):947–952.

20. For more detail see Chapters 1–3.

21. Tollison and Willett, pp. 430–437.

22. Rubin and Brown, pp. 275–277.

23. Iklé, p. 99.

24. Evan Luard, *The Control of the Seabed: An Updated Report* (New York: Taplinger, 1977), pp. 152–153.

25. Robert Tollison and Thomas Willett, "Institutional Mechanisms for Dealing with International Externalities: A Public Choice Perspective," in *The Law of the Sea: U.S. Interests and Alternatives*, ed. Ryan C. Amacher and Richard J. Sweeney (Washington, D.C.: American Enterprise Institute, 1976), p. 98.

26. Iklé, p. 224.

27. Fisher, p. 93.

28. Ernst Haas, "Why Collaborate? Issue Linkage and International Regimes," *World Politics*, 32 (April 1980):373.

29. Roger Fisher and William Ury, "Principled Negotiation: A Working Guide," draft, Harvard Negotiation Project, Harvard Law School, 1979, p. 106.

30. Wallace, p. 179.

31. de Callières, p. 125.

32. Iklé, p. 119.

33. Douglas Bennett and Kenneth Sharpe, "Agenda Setting and Bargaining Power: The Mexican States versus Transnational Automobile Corporations," *World Politics*, 32 (October 1979):81. Of course, adding a party in this case may be interpreted as the *means* of adding an issue, as in case 1 of Section 6.1.2.

34. A. H. Raskin, "The Newspaper Strike: A Step by Step Account," in *The 50% Solution*, ed. I. William Zartman (Garden City, N.Y.: Anchor-Doubleday, 1976), pp. 453–454.

35. Fisher and Ury, "Principled Negotiation," p. 90.

36. One could observe technically that the sum of the parties' risk premiums may decline as the number of parties increases. Assume that the owner of a business has a negative exponential utility function with risk-aversion parameter γ_s. The uncertain end-of-period net value of his business is normally distributed with mean μ and variance σ^2. He is negotiating with a possible buyer for the business who also has a negative exponential utility function with risk-aversion parameter γ_b, where the buyer is more risk-averse than the seller ($\gamma_b > \gamma_s$). The seller's certainty equivalent (CE_s) is $\mu - (\gamma_s/2)\sigma^2$, while the buyer's certainty equivalent (CE_b) is $\mu - (\gamma_b/2)\sigma^2$. There is no possible zone of agreement since the seller wants more than the buyer will offer ($CE_s > CE_b$). But if the buyer brings in $(n-1)$ identical partners who will split up the proceeds evenly, their collective certainty equivalent (CE_n) will be $n(\mu/n - (\gamma_b/2n^2))\sigma^2)$ or $\mu - (\gamma_b/2n)\sigma^2$. As n increases, $CE \rightarrow \mu$ and a positive bargaining range for the sale price opens up of size $(CE_n - CE_s) = (\gamma_s - \gamma_b/n)(\sigma^2/2)$, which approaches the risk premium of the seller, $(\gamma_s/2)\sigma^2$, as n becomes large. Observation that the cost of risk bearing declines as the number of participants increases has been made in a public-finance context by K. J. Arrow and R. K. Lind, "Uncertainty and the Evaluation of Public Investment Decisions," *American Economic Review*, 60 (1970): 364–378; and in a capital-markets setting by J. Lintner, "The Market Price of Risk, Size of Market, and Investor's Risk Aversion," *Review of Economics and Statistics*, 52 (February 1970):98.

37. The idea advanced by Donald Lessard in a Harvard Business School

Finance Seminar that developing countries might turn to financial markets to shed risk in addition to diversifying their real economies or trying to manipulate markets suggested this bargaining application.

38. See Mancur Olson and Richard Zeckhauser, "An Economic Theory of Alliances," *Review of Economics and Statistics,* 48 (August 1966):266–279.

39. See Mancur Olson, *The Logic of Collective Action* (Cambridge, Mass.: Harvard University Press, 1965), pp. 37–41.

40. Iklé, p. 55.

41. W. Howard Wriggens, "Up for Auction: Malta Bargains with Great Britain, 1971," in *The 50% Solution,* ed. I. William Zartman (Garden City, New York: Anchor-Doubleday, 1976), pp. 208–233.

42. David Smith and Louis Wells, *Negotiating Third World Mineral Agreements* (Cambridge, Mass.: Ballinger, 1975), p. 143.

43. For an extremely complicated Indonesian example, see William Fruhan, *Financial Strategy* (Homewood, Ill.: Richard D. Irwin, 1979), pp. 129–148. The analytic basis for such moves is elaborated in David A. Lax and James K. Sebenius, "Insecure Contracts and Resource Development," *Public Policy,* 29 (1981):417–436.

44. Oye, p. 18.

Bibliography

Allen, Michael H. "The 1974 Jamaican Bauxite Negotiations as a Case Study in Bargaining." M.S. diss. (Government), University of the West Indies, 1977.

Antrim, Lance, Patricia Spencer, and William Woodhead. *Cobalt, Copper, Nickel and Manganese: Future Supply and Demand and Implications for Deep Seabed Mining.* Washington, D.C.: U.S. Department of Commerce, Office of Ocean, Resource and Scientific Policy Coordination, 1979.

Arrow, K. J., and R. C. Lind. "Uncertainty and the Evaluation of Public Investment Decisions." *American Economic Review,* 60 (1970):364–378.

Asante, Samuel K. B. "Restructuring Transnational Mineral Agreements." *American Journal of International Law,* 73 (1979):335–371.

Aumann, Robert J. "Agreeing to Disagree." *Annals of Statistics,* 4 (1976):1236–39.

Axelrod, Robert. "Conflict of Interest: An Axiomatic Approach." *Journal of Conflict Resolution,* 11 (January 1967):87–99.

——— *Conflict of Interest: A Theory of Divergent Goals with Applications to Politics.* Chicago: Markham, 1970.

Bacharach, S. B., and E. Lawler. *Bargaining.* San Francisco: Jossey-Bass, 1981.

Bachrach, Peter, and Morton S. Baratz. "Two Faces of Power." *American Political Science Review,* 56 (1962):947–952.

Barclay, Scott, and Cameron Peterson. "Multi-Attribute Models for Negotiations." Technical Report 76-1. McLean, Va.: Decisions and Designs, Inc., 1976.

Bennett, D. C., and K. E. Sharpe. "Agenda Setting and Bargaining Power: The Mexican State Versus Transnational Automobile Corporations." *World Politics,* 32 (October 1979):57–89.

Berns, Walter. "Mining the Seas for a Brave New World." *Regulation* (November–December 1981):15–18.

BIBLIOGRAPHY

Bishop, Robert L. "Game Theoretic Analyses of Bargaining." *Quarterly Journal of Economics,* 77 (1967):559–602.
Borch, Karl. "The Safety Reloading of Reinsurance Premiums." *Skandinavisk Aktuariehdskrift* (1960): 163–184.
Breaux, John. "The Diminishing Prospects for an Acceptable Law of the Sea Treaty." *Virginia Journal of International Law,* 19 (1979): 257–261.
Brewer, William C., Jr. "Deep Seabed Mining: Can an Acceptable Regime Ever Be Found?" *Ocean Development and International Law,* 11 (1982): 38–39.
Brown, Rex, and Cameron Peterson. "An Analysis of Alternative Middle Eastern Oil Agreements." Technical Report. McLean, Va.: Decisions and Designs, Inc., 1975.
Burrows, James C. "The Net Value of Manganese Nodules to U.S. Interests, with Special Reference to Market Effects and National Security." In *Deepsea Mining,* ed. Judith T. Kildow, pp. 124–139. Cambridge, Mass.: MIT Press, 1979.
Callières, François de. *On the Manner of Negotiating with Princes,* trans. A. F. Whyte. Boston: Houghton Mifflin, 1919; originally published, Paris: Michel Brunet, 1716.
Caron, David D. "Reconciling Domestic Principles and International Cooperation." In *Law of the Sea: U.S. Policy Dilemma,* ed. Bernard Oxman et al., pp. 3–12. San Francisco: ICS Press, 1983.
Charles River Associates, Inc. "Analysis of the Major Policy Issues Raised by the Commercial Development of Ocean Manganese Nodules." CRA Report no. 383. Cambridge, Mass.: National Science Foundation, 1981.
Chernoff, H. "Rational Selection of Decision Functions." *Econometrica,* 22 (1954):422–443.
Cheung, Steven. "Transaction Costs, Risk Aversion, and the Choice of Contractual Arrangements." *Journal of Law and Economics,* 12 (1969):23–42.
Clingan, Thomas A., Jr. "Freedom of Navigation in a Post-UNCLOS III Environment." Presentation at Duke University Law of the Sea Symposium, October 29, 1982.
Cohen, Lewis I. "International Cooperation on Seabed Mining." In *Law of the Sea: U.S. Policy Dilemma,* ed. Bernard Oxman et al., pp. 101–110. San Francisco: ICS Press, 1983.
Darman, Richard G. "The Law of the Sea: Rethinking U.S. Interests." *Foreign Affairs,* 56 (January 1978):373–395.
——— "U.S. Deepsea Mining Policy: The Pattern and the Prospects." In *Deepsea Mining,* ed. Judith T. Kildow, pp. 159–192. Cambridge, Mass.: MIT Press, 1980.
Deutch, Morton, and R. M. Krauss. "Studies of Interpersonal Bargaining." *Journal of Conflict Resolution,* 6 (1962):52–76.
Diederich, F. J., W. Mueller, and W. Schneider. *Analysis of the MIT Study on Ocean Mining.* Frankfurt: Battelle-Institut, 1979.
Doyle, James A., Jr. "National Security and the Law of the Sea." Address

before the Carnegie Endowment for International Peace, Washington, D.C., June 22, 1981.

Enzer, Herman. "Economic Assessment of Ocean Mining." Presented at the joint meeting of the Institute for Mining and Metallurgy, the Society of Mining Engineers of AIME, and the Metallurgical Society of the AIME, London, May 1980.

Faber, Mike, and Roland Brown. "Changing the Rules of the Game: Political Risk, Instability and Fairplay in Mineral Concession Contracts." *Third World Quarterly,* 2 (1980):100–120.

Federal Republic of Germany. "Act of Interim Regulation of Deep Seabed Mining." *Bundesgesetzblatt,* part I, 9080, August 22, 1980.

Feldstein, Martin. "The Social Time Preference Rate in Cost-Benefit Analysis." *Economic Journal,* 74 (1964):360–379.

Fisher, Roger. "Fractionating Conflict." In *International Conflict and Behavioral Science: The Craigville Papers,* ed. Roger Fisher, pp. 91–109. New York: Basic Books, 1964.

Fisher, Roger, and William Ury. "Principled Negotiation: A Working Guide." Unpublished manuscript, Harvard Law School, 1979.

——— *Getting to Yes.* Boston: Houghton Mifflin, 1981.

Foreign Policy Association. "World Law of the Oceans: Narrowing Options for the U.S." In *Great Decisions '79,* pp. 64–73. New York: Foreign Policy Association, 1979.

Friedheim, Robert L., and William J. Durch. "The International Seabed Resources Agency and the New International Economic Order." *International Organization,* 31 (Spring 1977):343–384.

Fritzsche, Michael, and Albrecht Stockmayer. "Mining Agreements in Developing Countries." *Natural Resources Forum,* 2 (1978):215–227.

Fruhan, William. *Financial Strategy: Studies in the Creation, Transfer, and Destruction of Shareholder Value.* Homewood, Ill.: Richard D. Irwin, 1979.

Garnaut, Ross, and Anthony Ross. "A New Tax for Natural Resource Projects." In *Mineral Leasing as an Instrument of Public Policy,* ed. M. Crommelin and A. R. Thompson. Vancouver: University of British Columbia Press, 1977.

Geanakoplos, John, and Heraklis Polemarchakis. "We Can't Disagree Forever." *Journal of Economic Theory,* 26 (1982):192–200.

Gillis, Malcolm, et al. *Taxation and Mining.* Cambridge, Mass.: Ballinger, 1978.

Goldwin, Robert A. "Locke and the Law of the Sea." *Commentary* (June 1981):46–50.

Gosovic, Branislav, and John Gerard Ruggie. "On the Creation of a New International Economic Order: Issue Linkage and the Seventh Special Session of the UN General Assembly." *International Organization,* 30 (Spring 1976):309–345.

Grossman, Sanford J., and J. E. Stiglitz. "Information and Competitive Price Systems." *American Economic Review,* 46 (1979):246–253.

Haas, Ernst B. "Why Collaborate? Issue Linkage and International Regimes." *World Politics,* 32 (April 1980):357–405.

BIBLIOGRAPHY

Hardy, G. H., J. E. Littlewood, G. Polya. *Inequalities.* Cambridge: Cambridge University Press, 1934.

Harsanyi, John. "Games of Incomplete Information Played by Bayesian Players," parts I-III. *Management Science,* 14 (1967-1968):159-182; 320-324; 486-502.

Hauser, Wolfgang. "An International Fiscal Regime for Deep Seabed Mining: Comparisons to Land-Based Mining." *Harvard International Law Journal,* 19 (Fall 1978):759-812.

Hill, Clarence A., Jr. "U.S. Law of the Sea Position and Its Effect on the Operating Navy: A Naval Officer's View." *Ocean Development and International Law,* 3 (1976):347.

Hirshleifer, Jack. "On the Theory of Optimal Investment Decision." Reprinted in *Modern Developments in Financial Management,* ed. S. Myers, pp. 282-305. Hinsdale, Ill.: Dryden Press, 1976.

Hollick, Ann L. *U.S. Foreign Policy and the Law of the Sea.* Princeton, N.J.: Princeton University Press, 1981.

International Law Association, American Branch. "Report of the Committee on The Law of the Sea." Washington, D.C., June 1982.

Iklé, Fred Charles. *How Nations Negotiate.* New York: Harper and Row, 1964.

International Encyclopedia of the Social Sciences, s.v. "Negotiation." (By Fred Charles Iklé.)

Katz, Ronald. "Financial Arrangements for Seabed Mining Companies: An NIEO Case Study." *Journal of World Trade Law,* 13 (May/June 1979):209-222.

Keeney, Ralph, and Howard Raiffa. *Decisions with Multiple Objectives: Preferences and Value Tradeoffs.* New York: John Wiley, 1976.

Keohane, Robert O., and Joseph S. Nye. *Power and Interdependence: World Politics in Transition.* Boston: Little, Brown, 1977.

Kissinger, Henry. Speech in Nairobi, Kenya, May 1976. Reprinted in U.S. Department of State, Bureau of Public Information, Office of Media Services, PR 224.6. Washington, D.C., May 1976.

Koh, T. "Mining Issues May Go to World Court." *The Interdependent,* 8 (1982):1.

Kullback, Solomon. *Information Theory and Statistics.* New York: John Wiley, 1959.

Kullback, Solomon, and R. A. Liebler. "On Information and Sufficiency." *Annals of Mathematical Statistics,* 22 (1951):79-86.

Lall, Arthur. *Modern International Negotiation: Principles and Practice.* New York: Columbia University Press, 1966.

Laursen, Finn. "Security versus Access to Resources: Explaining a Decade of U.S. Ocean Policy." *World Politics,* 35 (1982):197-229.

Lax, David, and James K. Sebenius. "Insecure Contracts and Resource Development." *Public Policy,* 29 (1981):417-436.

―――. "Negotiation and Management: Some Analytic Themes." Harvard Business School Working Paper 82-83, June 1983.

Lehman, John. "The Navy and the Law of the Sea." Letter to the editor, *Washington Post*, July 30, 1982.

Leland, Hayne E. "Optimal Risk Sharing and the Leasing of Natural Resources, with Application to Oil and Gas Leasing on the OCS." *Quarterly Journal of Economics*, 92 (August 1978):414–437.

Little, Arthur D., Inc. "Technological and Economic Assessment of Manganese Nodule Mining and Processing." Prepared for the Department of the Interior, Stock no. 024-000-00842-B. Washington, D.C.: Government Printing Office, 1977.

Lintner, John. "The Market Price of Risk, Size of Market, and Investor's Risk Aversion." *Review of Economics and Statistics*, 52 (February 1970):87–99.

Luard, Evan. *The Control of the Seabed: An Updated Report.* New York: Taplinger, 1977.

Malouf, Michal W. K., and Alvin E. Roth. "Disagreement in Bargaining: An Experimental Approach." *Journal of Conflict Resolution*, 25 (1981):329–348.

McGrory, Mary. "Sailing the Sea Treaty Shoals without the Lighthouse of Facts." *Washington Post*, July 22, 1982.

Mikesell, R. F. "Financial Considerations in Negotiating Mine Development Agreements." *Mining Magazine*, April 1974, pp. 257–269.

——— "Trends in Foreign Investment: Agreements in the Resource Industry." *Resources Policy*, September 1978, pp. 194–199.

Miles, Edward. "The Structure and Effects of the Decision Process in the Seabed Committee and the Third United Nations Conference on the Law of the Sea." *International Organization*, 31 (Spring 1977):159–234.

Milgrom, Paul. "An Axiomatic Characterization of Common Knowledge." *Econometrica*, 49 (1981):219–222.

Milgrom, Paul, and Nancy Stokey. "Information, Trade, and Common Knowledge." *Journal of Economic Theory*, 26 (1982):17–27.

Moore, John Norton. "The Regime of Straits and the Third United Nations Conference on the Law of the Sea." *American Journal of International Law*, 74 (1980):77–85.

Nandan, Satya N. "Statement by Mr. Satya N. Nandan, Chairman of the Fiji Delegation to the Formal Signing Session," Third United Nations Conference on the Law of the Sea (mimeo). Kingston, Jamaica, December 1982.

National Petroleum Council. *Petroleum Resources under the Ocean Floor.* Washington, D.C., 1969.

New York Times. "Johnson Asks Joint Exploitation of Sea Resources." July 14, 1966, p. 10.

——— January 13, 1979, p. 3.

——— July 22, 1979, p. E20.

——— August 30, 1980, p. 1.

——— "President Vows U.S. Won't Sign Sea-Law Treaty." July 10, 1982, p. 1.

Nicolson, Harold. *The Evolution of Diplomatic Method.* London: Constable, 1954.

BIBLIOGRAPHY

Nixon, Richard M. "Report to the Congress, U.S. Foreign Policy for the 1970s," February 18, 1970.

Nye, Joseph E. "Ocean Rulemaking from a World Politics Perspective." *Ocean Development and International Law,* 3 (1975):29–52.

——— "Political Lessons of the New Sea Regime." In *Law of the Sea: U.S. Policy Dilemma,* ed. Bernard Oxman et al., pp. 113–126. San Francisco: ICS Press, 1983.

Nyhart, J. D., et al. *A Cost Model of Deep Ocean Mining and Associated Regulatory Issues.* Cambridge, Mass.: MIT Sea Grant Report MITSG 78-4, 1978.

Oliver, Edward F. "Malacca: Dire Straits." *U.S. Naval Institute Proceedings,* June 1973, p. 29.

Olson, Mancur, Jr. *The Logic of Collective Action.* Cambridge, Mass.: Harvard University Press, 1965.

Olson, Mancur, Jr., and Richard Zeckhauser. "An Economic Theory of Alliances." *Review of Economics and Statistics,* 48 (August 1966):266–279.

Osgood, Robert E. "U.S. Security Interests in Ocean Law." *Ocean Development and International Law,* 2 (1974):1–36.

Oxman, Bernard H. "The Third United Nations Conference on the Law of the Sea: The 1976 New York Sessions." *American Journal of International Law,* 71 (April 1977):247–269.

——— "The Third United Nations Conference on the Law of the Sea: The Seventh Session (1978)." *American Journal of International Law,* 73 (January 1979):1–41.

——— "Summary of the Law of the Sea Convention." In *Law of the Sea: U.S. Policy Dilemma,* ed. Bernard Oxman et al., pp. 147–164. San Francisco: ICS Press, 1983.

Oxman, Bernard, David Caron, and Charles Buderi, eds. *Law of the Sea: U.S. Policy Dilemma.* San Francisco: ICS Press, 1983.

Oye, Kenneth A. "The Domain of Choice: International Constraints and Carter Administration Foreign Policy." In *Eagle Entangled: U.S. Foreign Policy in a Complex World,* ed. Kenneth A. Oye, Donald Rothchild, and Robert J. Lieber. New York: Longman, 1979.

Pecquet, Antoine. *Discours sur l'art de négocier.* Paris: Nyon Fils, 1737.

Pruitt, Dean G. "Integrative Agreements: Nature and Antecedents." Paper presented at the Conference on Bargaining inside Organizations, Boston University, October 15, 1982.

Pruitt, Dean G., and Steven A. Lewis. "The Psychology of Integrative Bargaining." In *Negotiations: Social Psychological Perspectives,* ed. Daniel Druckman. Beverly Hills: Sage, 1977.

Raiffa, Howard. *Decision Analysis: Introductory Lectures on Choices under Uncertainty.* Reading, Mass.: Addison-Wesley, 1968.

——— *The Art and Science of Negotiation.* Cambridge, Mass.: Harvard University Press, 1982.

Ramberg, Bennett. "Tactical Advantages of Opening Positioning Strategies: Lessons from the Seabed Arms Control Talks, 1967–1970." In *The*

Negotiation Process: Theories and Applications, ed. William I. Zartman, pp. 133–174. Beverly Hills: Sage, 1978.

Rao, C. R. *Linear Statistical Inference and Its Applications,* 2nd ed. New York: John Wiley, 1973.

Ratiner, Leigh. "The Law of the Sea: Cross-roads for U.S. Policy." *Foreign Affairs,* 60 (1982):1011.

Reagan, Ronald. "Statement by the President." The White House, Office of the Press Secretary, December 30, 1982.

Reece, D. K. "An Analysis of Alternative Bidding Systems for Leasing Offshore Oil." *Bell Journal of Economics,* 10 (1979):659–669.

Reisman, W. Michael. "The Regime of Straits and National Security: An Appraisal of International Lawmaking." *American Journal of International Law,* 74 (1980):48–53.

Renyi, A. "On Measures of Entropy and Information." In *Proceedings of The Fourth Berkeley Symposium in Mathematical Statistics,* ed. Jerzy Neymann, pp. 547–561. Berkeley: University of California Press, 1961.

Richardson, Elliot L. "Comments on Financing" (mimeo). U.S. Department of State, March 10, 1977.

——— "Statement on Financing" (mimeo). Delivered to Committee I Chairman's Working Group of the Whole, New York, June 2, 1977.

——— "National Security and the Law of the Sea." Speech delivered on July 14, 1979, in Bath, Maine, reprinted in "Current Policy no. 80." Washington, D.C.: Department of State, Bureau of Public Affairs, August 1979.

——— "Power, Mobility and the Law of the Sea." *Foreign Affairs,* 58 (1980):902–919.

Robertson, Horace B., Jr. "Testimony before the House Committee on Merchant Marine and Fisheries" (mimeo), July 27, 1982.

Ross, Stephen A. "The Economic Theory of Agency: The Principal's Problem." *American Economic Review,* 53 (May 1973):134–139.

——— "On the Economic Theory of Agency and the Principle of Similarity." In *Essays on Economic Behavior under Uncertainty,* ed. M. Balch, D. McFadden, and S. Wu, pp. 215–240. Amsterdam: North-Holland, 1974.

Rothschild, Michael, and J. E. Stiglitz. "Increasing Risk, I: A Definition." *Journal of Economic Theory,* 2 (1970):225–243.

Rothstein, Robert L. *Global Bargaining: UNCTAD and the Quest for a New International Economic Order.* Princeton, N.J.: Princeton University Press, 1979.

Rubin, Jeff, and Bert Brown. *The Social Psychology of Bargaining and Negotiation.* New York: Academic Press, 1975.

Sawyer, Jack, and Harold Guetzkow. "Bargaining and Negotiations in International Relations." In *International Behavior: A Social-Psychological Analysis,* ed. Herbert C. Kelman, pp. 466–520. New York: Holt, Rinehart and Winston, 1965.

Schelling, Thomas C. *The Strategy of Conflict.* Cambridge, Mass.: Harvard University Press, 1960.

Science Applications, Inc. "Alternatives for Technology Transfer to the En-

terprise." SAI Report no. SAI-460-80-401LJ. La Jolla, Calif.: Science Applications, 1978.
Sebenius, James K. "The Computer as Mediator: Law of the Sea and Beyond." *Journal of Policy Analysis and Management,* 1 (1981):77–95.
Sebenius, James K., J. D. Nyhart, and Douglas McLeod. "Revenue Sharing from Deep Ocean Mining." Review Draft no. 2, Sloan School of Management and Department of Ocean Engineering, Massachusetts Institute of Technology, August 1979.
Sebenius, James K., and Mati L. Pal. "Emerging Trends in Mineral Agreements: Risk, Reward, and Participation in Deep Seabed Mining." *Columbia Journal of World Business,* 15 (1980):75–83.
Smith, D., and L. Wells. *Negotiating Third World Mineral Agreements.* Cambridge, Mass.: Ballinger, 1975.
Stein, Arthur. "The Politics of Linkage." *World Politics,* 32 (1980):62–81.
Stevenson, John R. Testimony before the Subcommittee on International Organizations and Movements. House Committee on Foreign Affairs, 92nd Cong., 2d Sess., April 10, 1973.
Stevenson, John R., and Bernard H. Oxman. "The Preparations for the Law of the Sea Conference." *American Journal of International Law,* 68 (January 1974):1–32.
——— "The Third United Nations Conference on the Law of the Sea: The 1974 Caracas Session." *American Journal of International Law,* 69 (January 1975):1–30.
Swing, John Temple. "Who Will Own the Oceans?" *Foreign Affairs,* 54 (April 1976):527–546.
Tedeschi, J. J., B. R. Schlenker, and T. V. Bonoma. *Conflict, Power and Games.* Hawthorne, N.Y.: Aldine, 1978.
Tollison, Robert D., and Thomas A. Willett. "Institutional Mechanisms for Dealing with International Externalities: A Public Choice Perspective." In *Law of the Sea: U.S. Interests and Alternatives,* ed. Ryan C. Amacher and Richard J. Sweeney, pp. 77–101. Washington, D.C.: American Enterprise Institute for Public Policy Research, 1976.
——— "An Economic Theory of Mutually Advantageous Issue Linkages in International Negotiations." *International Organization,* 33 (Autumn 1979):425–449.
Ulvila, Jacob W., and Warner M. Snider. "Negotiation of Tanker Standards: An Application of Multi-attribute Value Theory." *Operations Research,* 28 (January–February 1980):81–95.
United Nations General Assembly. 22 U.N. GAOR, C.1 (1515th mtg.). I, U.N. Doc. A/c.1/p.v. 1515, 1967.
——— Res. 2749. 25 U.N. GAOR, Supp. 1 (no. 28). 24 U.N. Doc. A/2028, 1970.
——— Res. 2750C. 25 U.N., December 7, 1970.
——— "Permanent Sovereignty over Natural Resources." G.A. Res. 3171. 28 U.N. GAOR, Supp. (no. 30). U.N. Doc. A/9030, 1974.
——— "Declaration on the Establishment of a New International Economic

Order." G.A. Res. 3201. 29 U.N. GAOR (6th Spec. Sess.), Suppl. (no. 1). U.N. Doc. A/9555, 1974.

United Nations Ocean Economics and Technology Branch. *Manganese Nodules: Dimensions and Perspectives.* Dordrecht, Holland: D. Reidel, 1979.

United Nations. Third United Nations Conference on the Law of the Sea. "Economic Implications of Seabed Mineral Development in the International Area, Report to the Secretary General." 29 U.N. GAOR. U.N. Doc. A/CONF. 62/25, 1974.

────── Third United Nations Conference on the Law of the Sea. "Revised Single Negotiating Text." A/CONF.62/WP.8/REV.1/Part I, May 6, 1976.

────── "Explanatory Memorandum of the President." 32 U.N. GAOR. U.N. Doc. A/CONF.62/WP.10/Add.I, 1977.

────── "Informal Composite Negotiating Text." U.N. Doc. A/CONF.62/WP.10, 1977.

────── "Reports of the Committees and Negotiating Groups on Negotiations at the Seventh Session Contained in a Single Document Both for the Purposes of Record and for the Convenience of Delegations." Geneva, May 19, 1978.

────── "Report by the Chairman of Negotiating Group 2 to the First Committee." NG2/10. New York, September 13, 1978.

────── "Report to the First Committee by the Chairman of Negotiating Group 2, Ambassador T.T.B. Koh (Singapore)." NG2/12. Geneva, April 8, 1979.

────── "Second Report to the First Committee by the Chairman of Negotiating Group 2, Ambassador T.T.B. Koh (Singapore)." A/CONF.62/C.1/L.22. Geneva, April 25, 1979.

────── "Report on Negotiations Held by the Chairman and the Coordinators of the Working Group of 21." A/CONF.62/C.1/L.26. New York, August 21, 1979.

────── "Report of the Chairman of Negotiating Group 2." New York, April 1980.

────── U.N. Doc. A/CONF. 62/122, 1982.

────── Third United Nations Conference on the Law of the Sea, "Closing Statement by the President of Conference on the Law of the Sea." Press Release, SEA/MB/14, December 10, 1982.

United States. Laws of the United States. "Deep Seabed Hard Mineral Resources Act of 1980." Public Law no. 96-283.

United States Department of State. *Department of State Bulletin,* 62 (1970):737–738.

────── Press Release no. 408, August 11, 1975.

────── Department of State Bulletin, 75(1976).

────── "Delegation Report for the Seventh Session of the Third United Nations Conference on the Law of the Sea." Washington, D.C., 1978.

────── "Approaches to Major Problems in Part XI of the Draft Convention on the Law of the Sea." Washington, D.C.: February 24, 1982.

United States Department of the Interior, Bureau of Mines. *Minerals and Materials.* Washington, D.C.: Government Printing Office, 1978.

United States Mission to the United Nations. Press Release 83, December 2, 1969.

Wall Street Journal. "Cartel of the Sea." April 20, 1982, p. 30.

Wallace, William. "Issue Linkages among Atlantic Governments." *International Affairs,* 52 (April 1976):163–179.

Walton, R. E., and R. B. McKersie. *A Behavioral Theory of Labor Negotiations.* New York: McGraw-Hill, 1965.

Wenk, Edward C. *The Politics of the Ocean.* Seattle: University of Washington Press, 1972.

White, Theodore H. "Weinberger on the Ramparts." *New York Times Magazine,* February 6, 1983.

Wilson, Robert. "The Theory of Syndicates." *Econometrica,* 36 (1968):119–132.

Wright, Rebecca L. *Ocean Mining: An Economic Evaluation.* Washington, D.C.: U.S. Department of the Interior, Ocean Mining Administration, May 1976.

Zartman, I. William. "Negotiations: Theory and Reality." *Journal of International Affairs,* 29 (Spring 1975):69–77.

——— *The 50% Solution.* Garden City, N.Y.: Anchor-Doubleday, 1976.

———, ed. *The Negotiation Process: Theories and Applications.* Beverly Hills: Sage, 1978.

Zorn, Stephen. "New Developments in Third World Mining Agreements." *Natural Resources Forum,* 1 (1977):239–250.

Index

Adding and subtracting issues and parties, 182–217. *See also* Linkage
Ad valorem, see Royalties
Africa, 9
Agenda setting, 10, 73, 182
Agents, 143–144, 207–208
Agreements, 106–107
Alaska, 202
Alliances, 113
Alternatives: to a negotiated agreement, 72–73, 106–107; to the Law of the Sea, 82–84
Ambiguity in a treaty, 125, 128
ANP, *see* Attributable net proceeds
Antarctica, 9
Antecedents to the Law of the Sea, 11–12
Application fee, 25, 39, 40, 41–45, 96
Aqaba, Gulf of, 85
Arab States, 213–214
Arbitration, 28–29, 128, 207–208
Archipelagic states, 74, 81, 85, 107
Argentina, 28, 187
Asia, 9
Asymmetric information, 3, 136–139, 171–177
Atlantic Ocean, 74
Attributable net proceeds, 26, 29, 30, 33, 36–40, 41–45, 54, 55, 62
Australia, 9, 102, 103
Authority, *see* International Seabed Authority
Axelrod, Robert, 114, 116

Bab el Mandeb, Straits of, 74
Bangladesh, 87
BATNA, *see* Alternatives
Battelle-Institut, 35
Bengal, Bay of, 87
Berlin, 202
Betting, 3, 56, 129, 132, 138, 139, 146–163, 171–177
Bilateral relations, 86–88, 108
Binding/nonbinding nature of a contract, 141. *See also* Renegotiation
Bottom line, 10, 66, 68–69, 182, 198, 215
Brazil, 11, 74, 87
Bundling issues, *see* Linkage

Cameroon, 33
Camp David, 67, 188
Canada, 9, 11, 19, 74, 102, 103, 209
Carter, Jimmy, 81, 82, 84, 88, 90, 94, 105, 107
Certainty, 72. *See also* Uncertainty
Challenger, H.M.S., 7
Chile, 213–214
China, 9, 38
Chronological review of the Law of the Sea negotiations, 24–28
Claiming value, 194. *See also* Creating value
Claims registry, *see* International Seabed Authority
Coalitions, 19, 72, 203

245

INDEX

Coastal states, 11–12, 75–76, 81, 85–94, 107
Cobalt, see Mineral resources
Cold War, 202
Commerce Department, U.S., 45, 66
Commercial transport, 75. See also Territorial seas
Commitment to positions, 28, 52, 187, 191, 204, 208
Committee I, 12–13, 24–25
Committee II, 12–13
Committee III, 13
Common heritage, 2, 8, 9, 12, 14, 23, 30, 53, 69, 78, 79, 107, 193
Common Market, 192
Configuration, 107. See also Reconfiguration
Conflict of interest, 114–116
Constant sum bargains, see Distributive bargains
Consumers of minerals, see Producer/Consumer
Continental shelves, see Navigation; Territorial seas
Contingent agreements, 56–57, 61, 119–120, 121, 122, 123, 135, 137, 139–141, 145–149, 164, 171–177
Copper, see Mineral resources
Cost Model of Ocean Mining and Associated Regulatory Issues, see Massachusetts Institute of Technology model
Countries endorsing the Law of the Sea, 9
Countries opposed to the Law of the Sea, 9
Creating value, 106–107, 114, 192–200, 212. See also Joint gains
Cuban missile crisis, 203
Customary law, 75, 91–94. See also International law

Darman, Richard, 82–83, 89, 104
de Callières, François, 183, 184, 206
Deep Seabed Hard Mineral Resources Act of 1980, 102
Defense Department, U.S., 66, 75, 76–77, 78, 88, 106
Dependencies, 196, 198, 203
Depreciation, 41–45
Destroying value, 200–203
Developed countries, see North/South

Developing countries, see North/South
Differences, 3, 10, 50, 55–61, 70, 73, 113–181, 198
Dispute resolution, 13, 109, 124, 128
Distributive bargains, 73
Doyle, James, 87

Eastern bloc countries, see East/West
East/West, 14, 16, 17, 26, 30, 39, 127
Economic zone, see Territorial seas
Ecuador, 89
Egypt, 55–56, 64, 67, 85, 186, 210
Eisenhower, Dwight, 217
El Teniente, 213–214
Endowments, differences in, 116, 117–118, 130
Energy production, 8, 11
Engo, Paul, 33
Enterprise, U.S. carrier, 87
Enterprise, 2, 14–15, 17, 18, 20, 23, 24, 26, 29, 30, 36–40, 41–45, 48, 50, 54, 55, 56, 61–70, 78–79, 82, 95–106, 127, 128
Environmental protection, 86
Europe, 9
European Base Case, 31, 32
European Coal and Steel Committee, 206
European Economic Community (EEC), 38, 39, 41, 43, 45, 51, 53–55, 62–63
European Economic Community proposal to settle the financial arrangements, 29, 41, 53–54, 62–63
Evensen, Jens, 29, 32, 34, 38, 49, 51, 52–54, 55, 69–70
Ex post considerations, 139–141

Falkland Islands, 187
Fees, 8, 29, 193. See also Application fee; Financial arrangements
Fiji, 74, 92
Final-offer arbitration, 28. See also Arbitration
Financial arrangements, 8, 9–10, 12, 13–23, 24–48, 49–70, 71, 78, 80–84, 91, 95–106, 107, 193. See also Application fee; Profit shares; Royalties
First United Nations Conference on the Law of the Sea (Geneva), 74–85
Fisher, Roger, 55, 183, 186, 205–206
Fishing rights, 2, 8, 11, 12, 74, 75, 77,

INDEX

Fishing rights (*Continued*)
 78, 80, 83, 85, 89, 107, 199. *See also*
 Territorial sea
Fixed charges, 25, 29, 35, 41–45, 131, 134
Flexible/rigid, 37, 64–66
Forcible challenge to mobility restrictions, 88–91, 108
Ford, Gerald, 78, 81, 94, 107
Fragmented linkage, 204. *See also* Linkage
France, 9, 35, 102, 103, 127, 192, 213–214
Freedom of the high seas, *see* Territorial seas
Free Rider alternative to the Law of the Sea, 91–94, 108

G-77, *see* Group of 77
General Assembly, 8, 17, 22. *See also* United Nations
Geneva negotiating session (1978), 26–30, 41–42, 53–54, 62–63
Geneva negotiating session (1979), 34–37, 43, 54, 61, 62–63
Germany, 18, 35, 83, 127, 192, 213–214
Gibraltar, Straits of, 74
Great Britain, 87, 89, 127, 187, 209, 212–213
Grotius, Hugo, 12
Group of 77, 16–17, 24–25, 30–31, 36, 38, 49, 56, 60, 61–62, 204. *See also* North/South

Haas, Ernst, 204
HARA utilities, 153, 162–163
Hard-core issues, 15, 193
Hardening/softening of positions, 37–38
Hormuz, Straits of, 74, 87
House Ways and Means Committee, 205
Hyperbolic absolute risk aversion, *see* HARA utilities

Iceland, 11, 74, 89
Iklé, Fred, 192, 198, 202
India, 25, 29, 32, 39, 41–42, 53–54, 62–63, 102–103, 210. *See also* North/South
Indian Ocean, 74
Indian proposal 1 to settle the financial arrangements, 25–26, 29, 41, 53–54, 62–63
Indian proposal 2 to settle the financial arrangements, 29, 42, 53–54, 62–63
Indonesia, 74, 85, 87
Indus River, 210
Information, 116, 152, 171–177
Integrative bargains, 73, 115, 116
Interests in a negotiation, 11, 16–18, 66, 72, 73, 82–83, 106–107
Interior Department, 76–77, 99
International Atomic Energy Agency, 80
International Court of Justice, 91
International law, 11, 13, 31, 75, 84, 86, 91–94
International Law Commission, 13
International Marine Consultative Organization, 188
International Monetary Fund, 104
International Resources Bank, 22
International Seabed Authority, 14–15, 19, 20, 31, 35, 37, 39, 48, 51, 60, 61, 78, 79, 82, 95–106, 193, 204
International Whaling Commission, 188
Iran, 87, 88
Israel, 9, 55–56, 64, 67, 85, 186, 210
Issues, 3, 10, 61–70, 72; adding and subtracting, 182–207, 214–217. *See also* Linkage

Jagota, S., 32
Japan, 9, 29, 30, 41, 43, 53–55, 62–63, 77–78, 102, 103, 127, 208
Japanese proposal to settle the financial arrangements, 29, 41, 53–54, 62–63
Jerusalem, 200–201
Johnson, Lyndon, 7
Joint gains, 106, 107, 113–181; in the Law of the Sea negotiations, 70, 73, 81, 84
Jurisdictional issues, *see* Territorial seas

Kennecott Copper, 213–214
Khrushchev, Nikita, 202
Kissinger, Henry, 8, 22, 78, 79, 80, 83
Koh, T. T. B., 1, 9, 15, 26–40, 41–44, 49–50, 51, 53–55, 62–63, 69–70, 91, 93, 102

INDEX

Koh proposal 0 to settle the financial arrangements, 30, 42
Koh proposal 1 to settle the financial arrangements, 32–33, 42, 54, 62–63
Koh proposal 2A to settle the financial arrangements, 37, 43, 54, 62–63
Koh proposal 2B to settle the finanical arrangements, 37, 43, 54, 62–63
Koh proposal 3A to settle the financial arrangements, 38–39, 43–44, 54–55, 62–63

Land-based mineral producers, 79, 98, 143, 209
Landlocked states, 13, 80, 199
Latin American countries, 9, 76
Law, international, see International law
Law of the Sea, description of the final treaty, 78–80
Legal and Technical Commission, 100
Legitimacy of outcomes, 140
Lehman, John, 84, 86
Less developed countries, see North/South
Libya, 87, 88, 90, 213–214
Linked issues, 8, 10, 14, 36, 55–56, 66–69, 70, 72, 73, 76, 80–84, 89, 92, 105, 106, 182–207, 214–217
Lotteries, 35, 58–59
Luard, Evan, 199
Lump-sum taxes, 163–171

Malacca Strait, 74, 87
Malaysia, 85, 87
Malta, 7, 75, 87, 213–214
Manganese nodules, see Mineral resources
Marine mammals, 12
Maritime law, see International law
Maritime states, see Coastal states
Massachusetts Institute of Technology model, 1, 2, 10, 18, 27, 30–33, 35–36, 45–48, 50–55, 56, 57, 59, 70, 95
Mauritius, 38
Mediation, 10, 34, 49, 55, 69, 129, 144–149, 155, 158, 207–208
Mediterranean Sea, 74
Merchant Marine Committee, 205
Methodist, see Quaker-Methodist Seminar

Mexico, 208
Middle East, 88, 93, 200, 210
Mineral agreements, trends in, 19–23
Mineral resources, 2, 7, 9, 11, 12–13, 14, 15, 16, 23, 26, 45–48, 75–76, 78, 80–84, 102, 107, 163, 190, 211
Mining, see Mineral resources; Seabed mining
Mini-treaty, 83–84, 94, 102, 103, 108–109, 190
MIT model, see Massachusetts Institute of Technology model
Monnet, Jean, 206
Moore, John Norton, 90
Morocco, 85

Nandan, Satya, 92
Nash equilibrium, 159, 160
National Oceanic and Atmospheric Administration, 1, 45
National security, see Security
Navigation, 2, 14, 74–77, 80–94, 105–109, 190. See also Territorial seas
Navy, U.S., 11, 74, 75, 84, 86, 87, 89, 90
Negative exponential utilities, 152–153
Negotiating Group 2, 1, 3, 15, 18, 26–27, 30, 33, 34–39, 49–50, 53, 56, 64, 69–70, 71
Negotiation analysis, 2, 3, 71, 73
Negotiations, Trends in mineral agreement, 19–23
"Neptune" (newspaper), 31
Netherlands, 9
New International Economic Order (NIEO), 17, 104, 105, 143, 204. See also North/South
Newspaper Guild, 208
New York Negotiating Session (1977), 24–26, 41, 53–54, 62–63
New York Negotiating Session (1978), 30–34, 42, 54, 62–63
New York Negotiating Session (1979), 37–40, 43–44, 54–55, 62–63
NG 2, see Negotiating Group 2
Nickel, see Mineral resources
Nixon, Richard M., 81, 94, 107, 206
No agreement, see Alternatives to a negotiated agreement
Nodules, see Mineral resources

INDEX

North Atlantic Treaty Organization
(NATO), 87, 88, 89, 188, 196,
213-214
North Korea, 74, 89
North/South, 7, 9, 13-14, 15, 16-17,
18-20, 22-23, 24-25, 28, 29,
30-31, 36-38, 55, 56, 57, 62, 64-70,
76, 78, 79, 80, 81, 83, 89, 98, 104,
105, 106, 107, 127, 143, 163, 189,
193-194, 199, 204, 217
Norway, 18, 29, 42, 53-54, 55, 62-63
Norway proposal 1A to settle the
financial arrangements, 29, 42, 53-54,
55, 62-63
Norway proposal 1B to settle the
financial arrangements, 29, 42, 53-54,
62-63
Norway proposal 2 to settle the financial
arrangements, 32, 42, 54, 62-63
Norway proposal 3 to settle the financial
arrangements, 38, 43, 54-55, 62-63
Nyhart, J. D., 27, 45, 48

Oceans, significance of, 7-10
Oil, 11, 77, 80, 101, 106, 164, 167, 217.
See also Mineral resources
Order of settling issues, 10, 66-67, 70,
198. See also Issues
Organization and procedures of the Law
of the Sea, 12-13
Organization for Economic Cooperation
and Development (OECD), 188, 196
Organization of Petroleum Exporting
Countries (OPEC), see Oil
Overflight, 74, 85, 89. See also Navigation; Territorial seas
Oxman, Bernard, 17
Oye, Kenneth, 183, 217

Packages of issues, 80-81. See also
Linkage
Pakistan, 38, 210
Parallel system, see Financial arrangements
Pardo, Arvid, 7-8, 107
Pareto frontier or Pareto optimal,
148-150, 153, 154, 161, 178, 184,
198, 200
Parties in a negotiation, 3, 16-18;
adding and subtracting, 73, 182-184,
207-217

Passage, see Territorial seas
Persian Gulf, 74, 87
Peru, 89
Petroleum industry, see Oil
Philippines, 74
Pioneer investment, 100, 102
Pollution, 2, 11, 12, 13, 74
Portugal, 88
Power, 66
Precedents set by seabed regime, 103,
109, 143
Preemptive action, 187
Preferences, differences in, 116,
117-118
Principal-agent relationship, 143-144.
See also Agents
Principled negotiations, 27, 52-53
Probability, 132, 134; differences in,
56-57, 114, 116, 119-130, 144-149.
See also Differences
Producers of minerals, see Producer/consumer
Producer/consumer, 16, 17, 19
Production opportunities, differences in,
142. See also Differences
Profitability of seabed mining, 28, 30,
57. See also Enterprise; Seabed mining
Profit shares, 8, 25, 35, 39-40, 41-45,
59-60, 61, 131, 134, 163-171, 193.
See also Financial arrangements
Profits taxes, 21
Publishers' Association, 208
Pueblo, 89

Quaker-Methodist Seminar, 18, 31,
37-38, 51

Randomization, 3, 119, 120-130, 135,
139, 144-149, 165
Reagan, Ronald, 10, 71, 72, 81-84, 86,
90, 93, 94, 96, 104, 107, 109
Reconfiguration, 73, 107
Red Sea, 74
Renegotiation, 20-23, 69
Resolution on Permanent Sovereignty
over Natural Resources, 17, 22
Resolution on Pioneer Investment, 102
Resource rent tax, 164
Resource zone, see Territorial sea
Richardson, Elliot L., 1, 8, 49, 71, 80, 82

INDEX

Rigid financial arrangements, *see* Flexible/rigid
Risk, 3, 10, 20–23, 35–36, 50, 55, 57–60, 61, 73, 114, 116, 129, 130–132, 134, 135, 142, 153–171, 197, 210–211. *See also* Differences
Royalties, 8, 20–21, 25, 29, 35, 37–40, 41–45, 56, 60, 97, 131, 134, 163–171, 193. *See also* Financial arrangements; International Seabed Authority

Safeguard clause, 33, 37
Saudi Arabia, 88
Scientific research, 8, 12, 13, 74, 80, 190
Seabed Authority, *see* International Seabed Authority
Seabed mining, 8, 9–10, 12, 13–23, 24, 28, 30, 33, 56, 57, 59–60, 95, 98, 134, 143, 188, 193, 203. *See also* Financial arrangements; Massachusetts Institute of Technology model
Seabed mining engineering-cost model, *see* Massachusetts Institute of Technology model
Seabed regime, *see* Financial arrangements; Fees; Profit shares; Royalties
Sea Grant Program, 27, 45
Security, 8, 11–12, 14, 16, 74, 76, 83, 85, 87, 107, 196–197
Sensitivity analysis, 27, 48
Sequential negotiations, 66–67, 70, 198. *See also* Order of settling issues
Siberia, 202
Side payments, 194–196
Sidra, Gulf of, 84
Signatories to the Law of the Sea Convention, 9
Sinai, 55–56, 67, 186
Singapore, 9, 15, 26, 74, 102
Single negotiating text, 10, 13, 28–29, 49, 55, 67, 68, 198
Softening of positions, *see* Hardening/softening of positions
Soviet proposal to settle the financial arrangements, 29, 42, 62–63
Soviet Union, 9, 11, 29, 42, 62–63, 75, 77–78, 87, 88, 92, 102, 103, 105, 107, 202, 209, 210, 212–214
Spain, 85, 88
Special Drawing Rights, 217
Specificity of the financial terms of the Law of the Sea, 18–19, 22
State Department, U.S., 45, 66, 78, 83
Straits states, 85, 107
Submarines, 74, 83, 85–94. *See also* Navigation; Territorial seas
Subtracting issues and parties, *see* Adding and subtracting issues and parties
Suez Canal, 74, 217
Sustainability of an agreement, 141
Swing, John Temple, 11

Technology of seabed mining, 13, 14, 99
Territorial seas, 2, 11–12, 13, 74–78, 79–80, 80–84, 190. *See also* Navigation
Third parties, 208, 216. *See also* Parties
Third World, *see* North/South
Threats, 187
Time, 3, 50, 60, 61, 73, 114, 116, 132–133, 134, 135, 142, 177–181. *See also* Differences
Tollison, Robert, 183, 189, 195, 200
Trading issues, 81, 205. *See also* Issues
Transit rights, 8, 25. *See also* Navigation; Territorial seas
Treasury Department, U.S., 45
Truman, Harry, 85
Turkey, 9

Uncertainty of seabed economics, 23, 27, 33, 35, 48, 51–52, 69
United Nations, 7, 12, 15, 26, 31, 35, 74, 76, 102, 127
United Nations Conference on Trade and Development, 35
United Nations Seabed Committee, 75
United States, 202, 209, 210; alternatives to the Law of the Sea, 85–109; Law of the Sea policy, 2, 3–4, 9, 11, 14, 16, 25–26, 29, 30, 38, 40, 41–44, 51, 53–55, 62–63, 72, 73, 74–78, 81–84, 85–89, 105, 127; rejection of the Law of the Sea Treaty, 2, 3, 8–9, 10–11, 71, 81–106
United States proposal 1A to settle the financial arrangements, 25–26, 29, 41, 53–54, 62–63

INDEX

United States proposal 1B to settle the financial arrangements, 25, 41, 53–54, 62–63
United States proposal 2 to settle the financial arrangements, 29, 42, 53–54, 62–63
Ury, William, 55, 186, 205–206
US/EEC/Japan proposal to settle the financial arrangements, 38, 43, 54–55, 62–63
USSR, *see* Soviet Union
Utility, *see* von Neuman-Morgenstern utility

Valuation, differences in, 114, 117–118
Variable sum bargains, 73, 115. *See also* Integrative bargains
Venezuela, 9

von Neuman-Morgenstern utility, 72, 144–171, 179–181
Vote on the Law of the Sea, 9

Wallace, William, 182–183, 189, 206
Western nations, *see* East/West
WG 21, *see* Working Group of 21
Willett, Thomas, 183, 189, 195, 200
Working Group of 21, 38
World Bank, 104, 210
World War II, 212–214

Zero sum, 55, 186
Zone of possible agreement, 3, 10, 34, 54, 62, 68, 73, 119, 120, 122, 125, 196, 197, 198, 200–203, 206, 209, 211, 215

3 1144 00208054 6